FROM DUSK
TO DAWN

FROM DUSK TO DAWN

Autobiography
of a Pakistan Cricket Legend

FAZAL MAHMOOD

with Asif Sohail

Edited and with a Foreword by
MUEEN AFZAL

OXFORD
UNIVERSITY PRESS

OXFORD

UNIVERSITY PRESS

Great Clarendon Street, Oxford OX2 6DP

Oxford University Press is a department of the University of Oxford.
It furthers the University's objective of excellence in research, scholarship,
and education by publishing worldwide in

Oxford New York

Auckland Bangkok Buenos Aires Cape Town Chennai
Dar es Salaam Delhi Hong Kong Istanbul Karachi Kolkata
Kuala Lumpur Madrid Melbourne Mexico City Mumbai Nairobi
São Paulo Shanghai Taipei Tokyo Toronto

Oxford is a registered trade mark of Oxford University Press
in the UK and in certain other countries

ISBN 0 19 579779 5

Typeset in Palatino
Printed in Pakistan by
Mehran Printers, Karachi.
Published by
Ameena Saiyid, Oxford University Press
Plot No. 38, Sector 15, Korangi Industrial Area,
Karachi-74900, Pakistan.

CONTENTS

FOREWORD

Fazal Mahmood bowled Pakistan to official Test status with his great bowling at Karachi in 1951–52. He took 7 wickets for 123 runs against Nigel Howard's MCC team and this gave Pakistan the match as well as the rubber. Pakistan's first Test series after getting official Test status was in India in 1952–53. Pakistan lost the opening Test in Delhi but went on to Lucknow to win the second Test. This was Pakistan's first Test victory. Bowling on jute mat, Fazal took 5 for 52 in the first innings (India's total being 106) and 7 for 42 in the second innings.

In 1954, Pakistan went on its first tour to England where it was to play four Test matches. It was a very wet summer. By the time the final Test started at the Oval in August, Pakistan was 1–0 down, having lost at Trent Bridge. England was then the best team in cricket. At the Oval, Pakistan's first innings folded up for 133. Undaunted, the Pakistani bowlers struck back and got a key psychological advantage by dismissing England for 130—thereby gaining a first innings lead. Fazal, having taken 6 for 53, was in his element. When England went in to bat in the second innings on the fourth day, they needed 168 runs to win. They started very well and were 109–2, and with Denis Compton and Peter May in, 59 runs were needed. Fazal came in to bowl and got both May and Compton. When Godfrey Evans was out, also to Fazal, the match was once again wide open. It went into the final day and Pakistan ultimately won by 24 runs. England's last 8 wickets fell for 34 runs and Fazal finished with 6 for 46, giving him match figures of 12 for 99.

Pakistan played its first official series with the West Indies in the Caribbean in 1958. They went into the final Test at Port-of-Spain 3–0 down. Pakistan won this match by an innings and one run. Fazal was a key architect of the victory with 6 for 83 in the first innings. This was the only match in the series in which the Pakistani bowlers were able to use a sharper seam-sewn cricket ball. Pakistan played its first one-off Test match against Australia at Karachi in September 1956. They were bowled out for 80 in the first innings, Fazal taking 6 for 34. In the second innings, the Australians fared a little better, as did Fazal, who took 7 for 80 to finish with match figures of 13 for 114. Pakistan won by 9 wickets.

Fazal Mahmood probably played the most prominent role in putting Pakistan on the international cricket map. He, however, generously argues in this book that Nazar Muhammad and Imtiaz Ahmad played the major role. Mahmood Hussain and Khan Muhammad, the two great fast bowlers, also played their part. As did A.H. Kardar, who handled the team with poise and acumen as captain. Then there was Hanif Muhammad whose intense concentration as a batsman made him an instant legend. However, Fazal's contribution to Pakistan's early triumphs was unmatched.

As a bowler, Fazal was quite outstanding by the standards of any generation. In Test cricket, his lineage can be traced through the Australian 'demon' bowler Spofforth, the great S.F. Barnes of England, Tiger O'Reilly of Australia, and Alec Bedser of England. In February 1974, when I was in Melbourne, Lindsay Hasset invited me to a grade cricket final for which he was doing the radio commentary. When the match was over, he took me down to the pavilion for drinks. Frank Tyson and Ian Johnson were there. We started discussing Pakistani cricket and Fazal's name came up. Hasset had never seen Fazal bowl. 'What was he like?' he asked. 'Like Bedser, only better,' was the reply. Frank Tyson had played his first Test match at the Oval in 1954 while Ian Johnson had captained the Australians at Karachi in 1956.

Spofforth, Barnes, O'Reilly, Bedser, and Fazal all specialized in the ball which would land on the leg stump and break away viciously towards the off stump. They bowled leg breaks or leg spin at above medium pace and managed to come faster off the wicket than other bowlers. Each of them had a repertory of different bowling styles in his armoury, but it was a particular delivery which made each one distinctive and successful. Bill O'Reilly was the only one of the five who also bowled the googly. That was a ball unknown in Spofforth's time. When Barnes was asked if he could bowl a googly, he said that he did not and, after a pause, added that he did not need it. Bedser and Fazal, as regular new ball bowlers, never considered bowling the 'bosie'.

The careers of the five show that, with experience and time, they relied increasingly on the ball which came in to the right hander from leg stump. Spofforth originally relied on sheer pace but he soon began to rely on accuracy. It was his variation of pace and the break-back that gained him immortality in the 'Ashes' Test at the Oval in 1882. England needed 85 to win and were at one stage 51 for 2. Spofforth changed ends, and in his last eleven overs took 5 wickets for 12 runs. His match figures of 14 for 90 gave Australia its first win on English soil by 7 runs.

S.F. Barnes has often been regarded as the greatest bowler in cricket history. He had a menacing presence and preferred league cricket to county cricket. He specialized in what came to be known as the 'Barnes ball'. This would pitch between leg and middle and then go on towards the off stump. Barnes was plucked from the Lancashire league by Maclaren and taken on the Australian tour of 1901–2. He took 5 for 65 on his first appearance in a Test and England won by an innings and 124 runs. In the second Test match, he bowled well to get 6 for 42 in the first innings and 7 for 121 in the second. He then broke down and could not play. England lost 4–1. On the 1911 tour, Barnes gained immortality with his great spell in Australia's first innings when he helped to reduce them to 38 for 6 on a perfect wicket. He took 5 wickets for 6 runs in eleven overs.

Sir Donald Bradman and a few others have regarded O'Reilly as the most difficult bowler of his type. O'Reilly took his first 100 Test wickets on pitches which were far easier than those in earlier days—pitches which were meant to last five days rather than 3 or 4 days. In 1934, at Old Trafford, he took 7 for 189 in an England total of 627 for 9 declared. At one stage in that high scoring game, he dismissed Walters, Wyatt, and Hammond in a single over. Whatever the circumstances, O'Reilly never lost his tenacity or accuracy. While his topspinners and googlies could be lethal, R.S. Whittington talks of his 'medium-paced leg breaks' which 'winged like blowflies from the blind spot for the off bail'. These were delivered from his great height with a start of twelve paces. His balls came at you 'as if delivered by some old-time crusader given five minutes to stone down Jerusalem', says Whittington in his *Time of the Tiger*.

Alec Bedser started as a conventional fast-medium bowler who brought the ball in and very effectively used the in-swinger with the new ball. He got Bradman out on a few occasions with this delivery. However, as his Test career developed, he began to experiment with and bowl the 'Barnes ball'. Neville Cardus notes that this ball was bowled with the seam held horizontally (similar to the grip used by O'Reilly), and would pitch between leg and middle and would 'turn to the off and move in dangerously near the stumps'. Bedser was to take five wickets or more in a Test innings fifteen times. He was one of the major factors in England's as well as Surrey's ascendancy in the 1950s. The Test figures of these five bowlers are shown below:

	Tests	Wickets	Average	Wkts per match
F.R Spofforth	18	94	18.41	5.22
S.F. Barnes	27	189	16.43	7.00
W.I. O'Reilly	27	144	22.59	5.41
A.V. Bedser	51	236	24.89	4.62
Fazal Mahmood	34	139	24.70	4.08

For different reasons, all five bowlers played less Test cricket than they would have if they had played today. In comparing Fazal's performance with those of the other great bowlers, some qualifications need to be made. When Fazal played, Pakistan was nearly always (except against New Zealand in 1955–6) the weaker side. Second, Pakistan's catching and fielding in those days was rather poor. Fazal writes in his book about Imtiaz Ahmad's great wicket-keeping abilities. But, during the period in question, he did not always keep wicket. Third, Fazal played—except when in England—in conditions which favoured batsmen. (A caveat is in order. Fazal did bowl on matting wickets in Pakistan, India, and the West Indies. But, it required a bowler of his special abilities to exploit the mat. S.F. Barnes did so on the South African tour of 1913–14, where his bowling was described as being 'unplayable'.) Finally, one must take note of the outstanding batsmen Fazal bowled against. These included the three W's, Sobers, Butcher, Kanhai, and Collie Smith of the West Indies, Len Hutton, Denis Compton, David Sheppard, Peter May, Ted Dexter, Tom Graveney, and Colin Cowdrey of England, Vinoo Mankad, Manjrekar, and Lala Amarnath of India, Bert Sutcliffe of New Zealand, and Neil Harvey, Norman O'Neill, and Keith Miller of Australia.

For bowlers who bowl at medium or fast pace, it is always difficult to bowl the fast leg break or spinner with accuracy. This is a ball which is bowled with the wrist and the body rather than with the seam. This is why it has been a rare phenomenon in Test cricket. When bowled at medium to fast pace, the ball (the old 'Barnes ball') has very often been described as a 'leg-cutter'. Sir Donald Bradman, in *The Art of Cricket*, describes an in-swinging leg-cutter which he received from Bedser at Adelaide in 1947 in the following words, 'This particular ball dipped in from the off side and I had to go with it to defend my leg stump only to see it whip back and take the off.'

Fazal describes in this book the various types of balls he bowled. His description of the technique used for each type of delivery is instructive. His cutter, combined with variations in the movement of the ball through the air, made him a devastating proposition on a green, drying, or matting wicket. He was a dangerous bowler anyway, even in good batting conditions. I recall the opening day's play in the Lahore Test against the West Indies in March 1959. That was the last Test match played at the beautiful Bagh-i-Jinnah cricket ground. Fazal clean bowled Bynoe for one and got Alexander lbw for 21, to make the West Indies 38 for 2 on a perfect wicket. Sobers

came in to join Kanhai and was dropped at slip by Maqsood off
Fazal. The two went on to add 162 runs in a total of 469. Fazal's
bowling before lunch that day showed his complete mastery
over the art of swing bowling and the use of the cutter.

In this book the reader will discover many memorable stories
related first hand by Fazal Mahmood. These are a part of the
folklore of Pakistani cricket. They bring to life not only some of
the great heroes of Pakistani cricket but also some of the greatest
cricketers of the world of the 1940s and 1950s. The stories range
from Test cricket to the Ranji Trophy to the leagues in northern
England. Behind the narrative there is the extraordinary
personality of one of Pakistan's greatest cricketers. He is candid
about his distaste for the materialism that has crept into the
game of late. It is not a case of envy but one of bias—bias in
favour of what was a less complicated way of playing cricket
for the glory of the game itself; of days when batsmen would
'walk' and when great adversaries on the field cultivated close
friendships off the field.

There is so much cricket today that it is often impossible to
keep track of what happened only three months ago. Fazal has
written about an era of Pakistani cricket when during a period
of ten years (1952–62) he could only play thirty-four Test
matches. That is about three Tests a year. In those days,
followers of the game could not only recall the details of all Test
cricket played but enshrine in their memories some of the
game's most unforgettable moments. For me, one such moment
relates to the Dacca (now Dhaka) Test of early March 1959,
against the West Indies. Pakistan batted first and were all out
for 145 runs with only Wallis Mathias going beyond 50. Then
West Indies opened with Kanhai and Jack Holt, but lost both for
19. Sobers and Alexander shared a 37-run stand for the third
wicket. Then more wickets fell, and it was 68 for 5. I was at the
Aitchison College Founder's Day sports and, in between the
school announcements, Mr Goldstein (the headmaster) would
announce the cricket scores as they were received over the
wireless from Dhaka. Within minutes it was all over: 68 for 5
became 76 all out. The last six West Indian batsmen (including

Collie Smith and Solomon) had failed to score and Fazal had taken 6 for 34. Pakistan went on to win the Test match by 41 runs and Fazal Mahmood finished with 12 wickets for 100 runs.

This book captures such vivid reminiscences from a man who achieved much for Pakistan cricket. It also contains intriguing viewpoints on bowling techniques as well as on contemporary cricketing issues. These will make this book interesting reading for keen followers of the game.

Mueen Afzal
37, Gulberg V, Lahore

PREFACE

The best form of public service is to serve humanity. It was about four years ago that Asif Sohail, a sports journalist of Lahore, approached me with the idea of writing a book on twelve to fourteen Test match cricketers with whom I had played and enjoyed cricket. In the beginning, I was reluctant for it was a daunting task to recall and write down the memories of the good old days. Moreover, to select cricketers without any bias was a cumbersome exercise.

Nevertheless, after much persuasion, I agreed. I decided to dedicate the book to the concept of fair play—which is what 'cricket' meant to most of us in those days. Asif Sohail did the necessary research work by collecting and arranging the records and details of the feats of these cricketers. He also helped in collecting and arranging the photographs. A very warm letter from my dear friend Keith Miller motivated me to go ahead with the idea.

I have tried to portray Test cricketers who were extraordinary. I might have left out some great contemporaries but only because I lacked information about them. The cricketers I have chosen were personally known to me. They were legends in their times, were dedicated to cricket, and were of the highest calibre. They achieved great heights through their hard work and sense of responsibility. They all had a sense of fair play, were oblivious to material interests and were always ready to promote human welfare on and off the field.

These cricketers lived up to the expectations of their people. They helped, advocated, and practised cricket. They never bragged about their unique performances. 'Do good and forget' was their motto. They were immortal and their names, and the glory and respect attained by them, shall live as long as cricket is played.

As I worked to recount my encounters with some great cricketing contemporaries, I began to feel that I should also write at length about my own association with cricket—from childhood at the Kinnaird High School in Lahore to the Lord's cricket ground in London. I have accordingly tried to recall the memories of a period in which I played first-class and Test cricket from 1944 to 1962. There may be some errors in this book but these are not intentional.

I would specially like to mention two friends whose passion and love for the game of cricket is exceptional. In fact, it was their assistance and support that enabled me to complete this book. Syed Iftikhar Ali Bokhari, a former Cambridge University and first-class cricketer, extended all his help in compiling this book, and suggested that the complete career records of these great cricketers be included with their profiles. Iftikhar Bokhari was a member of the upper house of parliament in Pakistan, the Senate, from 1988–91. During this period, he also served as the minister of state for finance and economic affairs.

Mr Mueen Afzal, secretary general, finance and economic affairs, government of Pakistan, a diehard cricket lover and member of the MCC, did a tremendous job. He read the manuscript of the book and suggested certain amendments. He also suggested that I write the technical section on my brand of bowling, which I hope will be of use to those wanting to excel in the art of fast swing bowling and the cutter. The chapter 'The Changing Face of Cricket' was also his suggestion. It was he who contacted and negotiated with the publishers and ensured the publication of this book. I am very grateful to both these gentlemen.

It would be unfair if I did not mention the name of Ashraf Ali Khan Lodhi for the photographs included in the book. I would also like to thank Shahid Saadullah, sports editor of *The News/Jang* London, for going through the transcript and offering valuable suggestions.

My special thanks to Najum Latif, a former cricketer and a collector of books, music, antiques and films, for providing some of the photographs for this book.

I would like to emphasize that the thoughts and recollections contained in this book are entirely my own. I hope that these will bring back some nostalgic memories of the early period of cricket in the subcontinent.

I believe that the reader would certainly like to know how I spend my time these days. Perhaps some may be surprised to learn that I still work for my living. I celebrated my 75th birthday on 18 February 2002.

After the historic win at the Oval the government of Pakistan gave 25 acres of land to every member of the team. I was allotted land in village 331-EB in tehsil Bureawala, a remote town about 290 kilometer from Lahore. Adjacent to this land, I was able to buy some more land from my East Lancashire league cricket earnings where I played as a professional in the late 1950s. The whole land was given on *mastarji*. Mastarji means a contract between the landlord and the tenant under which the former cultivates the land and owns the crop. In return he gives a fixed amount to the landlord annually.

A few years after my retirement from the police service in February 1987, I decided to do farming myself and shifted to the village. I found the job demanding and challenging, fortunately, cricket had taught me endurance and determination. I took farming as a challenge and never hesitated to working along with the farmers. I ploughed my land with a tractor and during chilly winter nights I got up from my warm bed to avail my turn of canal water for my land. In a very short time I learned the art of farming. I must admit that my friend—a Cambridge Blue and former first-class cricketer—Syed Iftikhar Ali Bokhari helped me throughout my new adventure.

My stay in the village revealed to me the miserable plight of the local people. There was ignorance all around. There was no high school in my area. Though there were primary schools in some areas but there was no school for girls. During the fifty-five-year history of Pakistan all the governments made policies to provide education to the people but very little attention was given to providing education facilities to villagers. We cannot progress in the comity of nations unless there is an increase in the literacy rate of our country.

It is believed that if you want to progress, you must educate your women. In a feudal society, the education of women is mostly neglected. So I decided to open a school for girls in the village which would be upgraded to a women's university in the next ten to twelve years. Land was earmarked for the project. A percentage of my total proceeds from farming was allocated for the project. The work started and we built rooms to start primary classes. It was difficult in the beginning but the response of the local people was tremendous. Then my friends in Lahore extended their valuable help in terms of a monthly donation which helped in running the day-to-day affairs of the school and paid the salaries of the staff, and utility bills. At present a middle school is functioning and about fifty-five girls are enrolled.

Fazal Mahmood
95-B, Fazal Street,
Ghari Shahu, Lahore

From Childhood to Retirement

Part I

1

School Days and Early Memories

I was born in Lahore on 18 February 1927. My forefathers had migrated from Kahkshan, in Central Asia and settled in Gujrat. In the early 1920s, my father, Professor Ghulam Hussain, settled in Lahore. From the age of six, the game of cricket fascinated me. Actually, I was inspired by my father who had raised the first cricket team at Islamia College, Railway Road, Lahore. He had great love for the game. He would take me with him to the college nets where I became familiar with the college players. Government College and Islamia College, Railway Road were arch rivals in cricket. Their teams would play every final of the Punjab University cricket championship. My father took me to these finals as a 'good luck mascot', exhorting me to become a bowler and one day beat Government College. I, therefore, developed a strong passion for the game. My father bought me a tiny bat and a tennis ball. He would place a tumbler on a small table at about stump height and ask me to hit the glass with the ball. He taught me to bowl the leg-cutter.

My father was a great source of strength for me. He was in middle school when my grandfather died. It was a difficult time for him as he had to look after his widowed mother and younger brother, Mehboob, but he faced these difficulties with great courage. From middle to post-graduation, he stood first in every examination. He was selected for the Indian Civil Service (ICS) but declined a British government job. He took part in the Reshami Roomal movement, and during the Khilafat Movement, migrated to Afghanistan with Ubaidullah Sindhi. He also served time in prison for his involvement in the movement. After his release from jail, he brought out his own newspaper, *Inqilab*, but soon had to close it down as the British government confiscated his press. He was arrested again and got news of my birth while in jail. After his release this time, he joined Islamia College, Railway Road, and eventually retired as its principal.

I obtained my primary education at the Kinnaird High School, which is near the Lahore Railway Station. I studied there for five years. We would play cricket in the school ground with a small plant in the garden used as the stumps. From Kinnaird, I shifted to Iqbal High School and stayed there till Class VII. When I was about twelve years old, I joined Islamia High School, Saddar Bazaar, Lahore Cantt. By then I had started playing with the Punjab Cricket Club. This club had its nets in a ground near Bibian Pak Daman. I would go an hour before the net schedule, help the groundsman fix the matting, and then bowl in the nets alone till the other players arrived. At that age, my arms were not strong and I could not bowl fast, but with continuous practice, I had improved my length.

An interesting event not only boosted my confidence but also encouraged me to take decisions independently. A day before a local holiday, one of our school teachers directed the class to attend school the next day as he was behind in covering the syllabus. My club was to play a match that day against the King Edward Medical College cricket team. During breakfast that day, I decided to go ahead and play. My performance was very good, and I took 6 wickets for only 8 runs and led my team to victory. The next day, my photograph was published in the *Civil & Military Gazette*, a local newspaper, with the headline 'School boy does wonders'. I took the newspaper to school and entered the class with a smile. But, soon enough, the smile vanished when the teacher asked those boys who had not attended the special class the day before to stand up. A few boys, including myself, stood up. The teacher started caning the boys. When it was my turn, I thrust out my hand and showed him the photograph in the paper. The teacher took the paper and left the classroom. After a few minutes, the school bell rang and all the boys were asked to assemble in the ground. After a short time, the headmaster and other teachers arrived in the ground.

I was frightened as I thought that now the headmaster would punish me in front of everyone. Suddenly, the voice of the headmaster speaking to the boys struck my ears. It was a depressing experience as I was too young to understand what might happen. Only when I heard the clapping of the boys did I realize that the headmaster was telling them about my great achievement. I was called to stand up on a table so that all the boys could see me. All this was unbelievable. The school was closed for the remainder of the day. The boys lifted me on their shoulders and took out a procession chanting slogans praising me.

Even during my school days, I was conscious about physical fitness. My daily routine was a ten-mile jog and 500 jumps with a skipping rope early in the morning. Every session was equivalent to a ten to fifteen mile workload, and included bowling, fielding, and other practice. In summer, I used to swim seventy to eighty lengths at a stretch in the swimming pool of the King Edward Medical College. The swimming exercise was a great boon to my health as throughout my cricketing career, I never felt the slightest pain in my groin, the tenderest muscle in the body.

At the age of ten or eleven, I was lucky enough to be coached by Saleh Muhammad. He was a fine left-arm bowler and could bowl untiringly in long spells while maintaining his line and length. He made a great debut in the Bombay Quadrangular in 1913 and took 3 wickets for 36 runs and 3 wickets for 11 runs in the match. He also represented Northern Punjab against MCC at Lahore in November 1925. Saleh Muhammad taught me how to bowl the off-break. He played for the Muslims in the Bombay Pentangular as did his son Inayat Khan in 1943 and 1944. Inayat also played first-class cricket in Pakistan.

After matriculation, I was admitted to the Islamia College, Lahore in 1940. This was the time when the All-India Muslim League had passed the 'Lahore Resolution' and begun its struggle for a separate homeland for the Muslims of the subcontinent. Islamia College played a vanguard role in that struggle. I took part in rallies and processions along with my college fellows Mian Salahuddin, affectionately known as Mian Salli, Nazar Muhammad, Imtiaz Ahmad, and Malik Mubarik. Often we were baton-charged and tear-gassed. One day, Anwar Hussain, the captain of our college cricket team and later on, during the Indian tour of 1952, the vice-captain of the Pakistan team, came to my residence and together we went to Mochi Gate garden where Mr Muhammad Ali Jinnah was to address a public meeting.

At that time, the Islamia College cricket team was one of the best teams of united Punjab. My selection to the college team came in my second year. Players like Gul Muhammad, Nazar Muhammad, Hafeez Kardar, Maqsood Ahmad, Imtiaz Ahmad, Shujauddin, and Zulfiqar Ahmad were also in the team. Subsequently, they all played Test cricket for Pakistan. Hassan Abbas, Khawaja Nazir, and Malik Mubarik were also in the college team with us. Mubarik was a very fine batsman. He had created a new Punjab University record by scoring 225 runs against Government College, Lahore.

I was selected for the College First XI in 1941. The same year, in the inter-collegiate final against Government College, I got 5 wickets for 13 runs. I had concentrated too much on cricket and did not secure good grades in the intermediate examination. Next year, I was selected in the Punjab University team. In a match against Lucknow University, I took 4 wickets for 20 runs. I also captained the college team in 1945. My team included two Hindus, Gayan Sagar and Navel Kishore. It was unbelievable that two Hindu players were playing in the Islamia College team. They were both residents of Taxali Gate, inside the walled city of old Lahore. Kishore was the son of Seth Tulli. When the Pakistan team visited India in 1952, Gayan Sagar received us in Amritsar.

I remember an incident which reflects the discipline practised in our days. There was a film at Lahore's Ritz cinema which I wanted to watch. The college net practice started at 1 p.m. I obtained permission from the team captain, Hassan Abbas, and seniors Nazar Muhammad and Gul Muhammad, to leave for the movie at 3.25 p.m. I went to the cinema on my bicycle and purchased the ticket for one anna. It was a concessional ticket for students. During the interval, I saw Professor Colonel Aslam coming into the hall and looking for me. He soon spotted me and asked me to come out of the hall. I took my cycle and reached the college nets. Colonel Aslam did not scold me but instead advised me 'films will come and go but missing a day's practice could ultimately affect your performance for life.' I was ashamed of myself and in a low tone said, 'Sir, I had spent one anna on the film.' Back came his reply with a coin equivalent to four annas: 'You can have it but do not miss your daily practice again.' After graduation, I wanted to join the Government College, Lahore. Colonel Aslam got to know about it. He cycled down to my house, took me to the college, and made sure that I stayed on at Islamia College. Gone are the days when paternal relationships between a student and the teacher could be so deep and strong.

Islamia College and Government College were arch rivals in college cricket in those days. They would be pitched against each other in almost all the finals of the Punjab University cricket championships. The hotly contested matches remind me of present day matches between Pakistan and India or between England and Australia. There would be a festival-like atmosphere during the matches. The spectators, who came from the old city, were supporters of either one or the other college. It was a test of our nerves playing amid the constant shouting of the crowd. This helped us to develop endurance and, in our test careers, we never succumbed to crowd pressure anywhere we played. In 1944, our college team beat Government College in the final of the Punjab University cricket championship. I took eleven wickets in the match. During those days, the Punjab University also played a match against Benaras University on the university ground (now Old Campus ground), Lahore. I took 6 wickets for only 14 runs and created a new record in inter-varsity cricket championships. The same year I was declared the best bowler of the Punjab University.

Those good old days are still fresh in my mind. I cannot forget the Arab Hotel which was close to my college. We would have lunch there and it cost us only a few paisas in those days. One day I overate at the hotel and fell seriously ill. My father consulted Dr Yar Muhammad, Dr Yousaf, and Dr Mumtaz. They were all renowned doctors. They suggested complete rest for me. In summer, our family used to visit Simla (now Shimla). However, in 1941 the venue was changed and we started to go to Kashmir. My father owned about two kanals of land there. I was told to go to Kashmir to rest. Professor Mirza Abdul Hameed Baig of my college was the president of the Punjab Hiking and Mountaineering Club. He gave me books on health and sex and advised me to follow a regime of natural cure. I still follow it to this day. I reached Srinagar and stayed there for two months. Early in the morning, I would climb up the Chashma Shahi height and drink its calcium-rich water and bring a good quantity of it back with me. I would swim in the famous Dal Lake and eat fresh red apples from the trees. My daily diet comprised of fresh vegetables, milk, fruits, and honey. I would attend daily practice in the nets of SP College.

It was exhilarating to climb up those beautiful mountains and hike untrodden paths! (I was also the captain of the Punjab Hiking & Mountaineering Club during my college days and got my colours in swimming). The change of climate did me good and I recovered fully after a couple of weeks. During my convalescence, I followed a healthy diet of fresh fruits and vegetables, and I have kept this up throughout my life.

Nisar, a resident of Amritsar, was a good wicket keeper. On one occasion, he came to Lahore and told us that the Nawab of Manavadar was to raise a cricket team. Manavadar was a state near Junagarh in India. In those days, the nawabs of Indian states patronized upcoming cricketers. Mushtaq Ali, Lala Amarnath, Gul Mohammad, Amir Elahi, and many others played for different cricket teams sponsored by nawabs. Nisar was affectionately known as Nisar 'pora' (Pora is a typical Punjabi word which means one who spreads concocted stories). We never took him seriously. Mir Muhammad Hussain, former secretary of the BCCP (now PCB), was a member of the Manavadar state hockey team. Through him, we learnt that

Nisar Pora was in fact telling us the truth this time. When the offer was made to us, the state cricket team was touring Ajmer. I joined the team there along with Kardar, Zafar Ahmad, Aslam Khokhar, and Maqsood. We had to face a fully-fledged United Provinces (UP) team. Bashir Ahmad, another former secretary of BCCP, also played for the UP. However, the UP team was bowled out for 18 runs.

We insisted that the Nawab should visit Kashmir with the Manavadar cricket team. Nisar Pora and I were sent to Kashmir to arrange house boats, one for the team and the other with a *shikara* for the Nawab. All the arrangements were made, but at the last moment the tour was cancelled due to a whim of the Nawab.

The Indian states had a very positive effect on the promotion of cricket in those days. It was the closest we came to present-day professionalism in those early days in the subcontinent. However, the interest of the nawabs and maharajahs was unpredictable. The pattern of patronage of the game had been set by His Highness Sir Ranjitsinhji Vibhaji of Nawanagar, and the achievements of his nephew, Duleepsinhji, as well as those of Nawab Iftikhar Ali Khan Pataudi, left an indelible imprint on the development of cricket in the subcontinent.

Joining the Lahore Gymkhana cricket club was not possible during my college days, but I became a member of the club after Partition. I would often visit the Gymkhana cricket ground and only be included in the team when they ran short of players. During my college days, the Lahore Gymkhana cricket ground was the most prestigious in the province. Every cricketer dreamt of playing there. Sir George Abel, ICS, secretary to the governor of the Punjab and later to the viceroy, was the captain of the Gymkhana side. He also led the NICA in the Ranji Trophy and was a fine opening batsman. When he went back to England, he was appointed a director in the Bank of England.

When Javed Burki took the team to England in 1962, the Pakistan team was invited to a function in London. Sir George Abel was also a guest. Burki paid some left-handed compliments to the British in the vernacular. To Burki's surprise, Abel returned the compliments in typical Punjabi. After the function, journalists asked him what had transpired between him and Burki. 'Burki paid his compliments to me and I returned them very effectively,' Sir George replied with a straight face. I had a meeting with George Abel in 1962 when I was sent in as a makeshift arrangement. I called him and, although he was a very busy man, he invited me to have breakfast with him. He was then a public service commissioner in England.

I remember that in one match against the Lahore Gymkhana, I clean bowled the then captain, C.J. Wilson, round his legs. He was totally baffled and said, 'spun late!' C.J. was an army officer posted in Lahore who later rose to the ranks of Lt. Gen. He visited Pakistan in the late 1970s and we had a pleasant lunch together. He had become the head of a tobacco company. During our conversation, I said: 'C.J., I believe you are taking a lot of interest in football'. 'How do you know?', he asked. I replied that it was a small world, and one kept track of one's friends. 'Are you interested?', he asked. On my request, he finally sanctioned £20,000 for the promotion of football in Pakistan. According to our plan, two teams were to be raised with one to tour England and the other Europe. Twelve coaches were to be picked from Pakistan for training and coaching courses in England. It is most unfortunate that the entire scheme was dropped due to domestic politics in Pakistan.

2

First-Class Cricket and Playing for Pakistan

The turning point in my cricketing career came in 1944. On 4 March 1944, I played my maiden first-class match representing the Northern India Cricket Association against Southern Punjab in the Ranji Trophy. Dr Jahangir Khan, an All-India Test cricketer, was our captain. My performance in the match was very satisfying as I got the wicket of Lala Amarnath, the great Indian Test all-rounder. Incidentally, that was also my first wicket in first-class cricket. After Amarnath's wicket, the captain took me off bowling, saying, 'Fazal, you have done your job'. I also scored 38 not out, batting at number 11.

In the next match, which was a semi-final against Western India at Rajkot, I got 6 for 65 and 2 for 59. Kardar, my teammate, scored an impressive 143 runs in the second innings. However, we lost the match. Amir Elahi and Gul Muhammad could not play in this match as they were playing professional cricket with the Maharaja of Baroda. They represented the NICA in the first match but the Maharaja refused to release them for this very important match. As a result, we were left with only eleven players, including the manager of the team.

When I started playing first-class cricket, the most important and well-contested tournament in India was the Bombay Pentangular. Four teams comprising the Muslims, the Hindus, the Britishers, and the Parsis participated in it. Hindus vs. Muslims was similar to the India vs. Pakistan matches of today. Players were invited from all over India to represent either of the two teams. This gave a communal complexion to the matches. The Indian cricket board later substituted the Pentangular with a zonal tournament. India was divided into four zones—North, South, West and East. Each team was to play two matches in Bombay (now Mumbai). North Zone included Karachi, NWFP, and the Northern India Cricket Association. South Zone included Amritsar, Jalandhar, Ludhiana, and Patiala. However, the most popular tournament in India then, as now, was the Ranji Trophy named after the great Ranji.

I represented North Zone in the zonal tournament. The first match that I played against the East Zone in Bombay had Nawab Iftikhar Ali Khan Pataudi as our captain. I took 4 wickets, including that of Syed Mushtaq Ali, in my opening over. However, in the second innings I received a good hammering from him, and he scored a century. From our side, Kardar scored 99 runs while Inayat Khan scored 70. We won this match but lost the next. Kardar again was unlucky to miss his century by just one run. This tournament was considered to be a trial match for selecting the All-India team to tour England. My performance in these two matches was satisfactory and I was almost sure that I would tour England with the team. Nawab Iftikhar Ali Khan Pataudi wanted me in the Indian team as, having played in England, he knew the conditions there and he felt that I would be successful on those wickets. He pressed the selectors to include me in the team, but they felt that I was too young. Kardar, however, was selected for the tour.

In December 1946, Nazar and I were selected to play for The Rest of India against All-India in the England XI. The match was played at the Feroze Shah Kotla ground, Delhi. C.K. Nayudu was our captain. I took 7 wickets in that match. After the match, Vijay Merchant, the captain of All-India team, publicly admitted that my absence was one of the major causes for their failure in England. The Hindu newspaper *Partab* printed the story under the headline '*Fazal ki jai*' (victory for Fazal). A few days after the match, Mr Muhammad Ali Jinnah visited the Islamia College and I was introduced to him by the principal with the words,

'Sir, this boy is doing wonders'. Mr Jinnah, a follower of cricket, hugged me and said, 'Keep it up young man. Keep it up.'

I must mention here the conversation of two great cricketers, narrated to me by my friend and senior sports journalist, the late Sultan F. Hussain. Nawab Iftikhar Ali Khan Pataudi ('Pat' to close friends) and Prince Duleepsinhji had watched the match between The Rest and All-India in England XI at the Feroze Shah Kotla ground. Sultan listened in on the conversation between them during the course of play. According to Sultan, Pat said to the Prince: 'I want to watch this young bowler from Lahore. His name is Fazal Mahmood. I think he could be a match winner in the future.' Sultan went on to tell me that the two great cricketers had watched me bowling a few overs in the match in which I had played havoc with the top half of the All-India in England XI. 'Well, Prince, what do you think of this young bowler?' Pat asked. The Prince shook his wise and seasoned head and said, after a significant pause, 'He is good. He should romp home. I wish I could be in Sydney to watch him bowl on that track. He could be lethal.'

The next match with the All-India in England XI was in Calcutta (now Kolkata) after a gap of almost one month, so I came back to Lahore where I had to lead the Punjab University team against Benaras University. We won that match.

I reached Calcutta on 26 December 1946, and the match was to be played on 31 December. I had intended to further improve my performance in that match, but everything went wrong because of my carelessness. I was staying at the Broadway hotel. It was the Christmas season, and people were busy merry making. I too joined them in the company of some friends, and lost myself in the festive life of Calcutta. I hardly slept during those four or five days and neglected the daily practice. On the day of the match, I was tired. Our captain lost the toss and gave me the new ball to bowl against Syed Mushtaq Ali, who hammered me ruthlessly. I got only one wicket for more than a hundred runs. That night I could not sleep as I realized that my recreation was at the expense of my performance. I offered my morning prayers and promised myself that from then on I would not indulge in any kind of merriment before the start of a match. We lost the match badly.

The Indian cricket board cancelled the remaining trial matches and declared that the matches played in the zonal tournament would be considered trial matches. I laid out a busy schedule for myself in preparation for these matches. After one month's practice, I reached Bombay to play for the North Zone in the zonal tournament match against the South Zone. The turf was a batsman's paradise. South Zone included the great test off-spinner Ghulam Ahmad while Kishenchand, the former Indian Test cricketer, and I were batting for the North Zone. I batted well against every bowler, particularly Shinde, who later became an Indian Test player. Kishenchand asked me not to be too harsh on Shinde otherwise he would be replaced by a better bowler. This was a typical tactic in those days to attempt to keep a mediocre bowler on to score runs more easily. This tactic was sometimes used against international sides as well. Besides taking 6 wickets, I scored my maiden first-class century (100 not out) in that match. We lost the second match against the West Zone. I took 5 wickets in that match. The last trial match was played at Delhi. In this match I again took 5 wickets. All these matches were of 8-ball overs.

My performance against the All-India in England XI and in the Zonal tournament was good enough for the selectors to take me seriously for the All-India team tour to Australia. I was confident that I would be selected. At the end of the last trial match at Delhi in March 1947, the selectors announced the team. Vijay Merchant was to lead the team. As I heard my name being called out, I rushed to the telegraph office to send a telegram to my parents in Lahore. At nineteen, I was the 'babe of the Indian side'. The players were asked to report to the training camp at Poona (now Pune) by 15 August. From Delhi, I reached Lahore. There was a curfew in the city because of riots and it was not possible to conduct net practice. The Partition took place on 14 August, and three days later I reached Karachi. From there, I left for Bombay by air. In Bombay, I learnt that Merchant had pulled out of the team because of fitness problems and Lala Amarnath was the new captain. I reached Poona. The players were accommodated in the bungalow belonging to the Indian actress Shanta Apte. The practice sessions had to be curtailed because of persistent monsoon rains. We spent most of the time in the company of Shanta who sang for us. We spent two weeks in the camp without any practice. Finally, the cricket board abandoned the camp and the players were asked to report to Calcutta on 9 October from where they were to fly to Australia.

By this time, the partition of India had taken place. After the camp, I had to reach Lahore. This was difficult amid the bloodshed and carnage in some parts of the subcontinent. From Poona, I travelled by train to Bombay. C.K. Nayudu was also travelling with me. I was spotted in the train by a couple of extremists who wanted to harm me but C.K. Nayudu very effectively saved me from them. He pulled out his bat and told them to keep away from me. From Bombay, I luckily got a seat which had become available at the last minute due to cancellation by a Hindu passenger. I reached Karachi and straight away went to a cricket ground and found some known persons there. I was relieved that I was now safe. It took me three days to reach Lahore from Karachi.

The plight of the refugees in Karachi and Lahore was woeful. I had grown up in pre-Partition India and had seen communal clashes. But the ferocity, savagery, and bloodshed that was committed during partition jolted me. I did not have the faintest idea that there existed such deep rooted hatred among the people who had been living together for decades. I decided not to go on the Australian tour. Lala Amarnath contacted me as he was keen that I should go with the team. I sent a telegram to Lala informing him of my decision. Then I was contacted by the West Punjab chief minister, Iftikhar Hussain Mamdot. I had a very friendly relationship with him as his younger cousin, Munnawar Ali Khan (Manney Khan to close friends), was my friend. I called Mamdot *barrey bhai* (big brother). Mamdot told me that the Indian Punjab chief minister had contacted him to persuade (Fazal) to join the All-India team which was about to start the Australian tour. I asked him, '*Barrey bhai*, do you want me to bring laurels for India?' After hearing this, he made no further attempts to persuade me.

With this decision, I wasted five good years of cricket. I was then a very promising youth and playing against Bradman would have given me great exposure in the world of cricket. However, I had taken my decision in the best interests of my new country, and I have no regrets even today. However, sometimes I do wish that I had played against Sir Donald Bradman.

I was invited to join service in Pakistan and was offered positions in the Pakistan Army and the police department. The IG Police, Qurban Ali Khan, impressed me with his personality. I opted for service with the police and joined the department on 21 September 1947. I was sent straight to Birdwood Barracks in Lahore for training. After that, I went to the Police Training School in Hungo, a small town about 25 kilometres from Kohat. Cricket was unknown in that part of the world. It disappointed me and lowered my morale. However, I developed a plan to carry on my bowling practice. I selected the lawn in my residence and measured the length of the wicket from its back wall. I would bowl almost thirty-five overs a day against the wall. The drill instructor of the school was amazed with my daily routine and asked me about the game. After listening to a one-hour lecture, he remarked, 'I know the game well—*ha'ki'*, by which he meant hockey.

3

Tour of Ceylon and the MCC in Pakistan

In September 1948, when the West Indies cricket team was playing against an Indian XI in Amritsar, Aslam Khokhar, Muhammad Amin, and I were sitting in the Nedou's Hotel in Lahore, now the Avari Hotel, discussing the tour. We all wished that the West Indies team would come to Pakistan so that we could play against them. We went to Mamdot Villa, the residence of the chief minister of West Punjab, Nawab Iftikhar Hussain Mamdot, who was also the president of the BCCP, and requested him to invite the West Indies team for a test match in Lahore. The invitation was conveyed through the Board of Control for Cricket in India. The West Indies accepted our invitation and agreed to play one Test in Lahore in November 1948. The Pakistani board had to arrange for the team's accommodation, food, and the daily allowances of the players during their stay in Pakistan. They needed foreign exchange for the purpose. It was a big amount for this newly-formed cricket board with no funds at its disposal. However, the late Liaquat Ali Khan, the then prime minister of Pakistan, graciously sanctioned the required foreign exchange. We organized the match at the Bagh-i-Jinnah ground. The West Punjab government contributed Rs 5000 ($88) towards the cost of entertaining the West Indies team. An ardent club cricketer of Lahore, Zahoor alias 'Joora', provided us with *shahmiyanas*, *kannats*, and crockery free of cost. The Lahore match gave BCCP a net profit of Rs 18,000 ($316).

The West Indies had defeated the MCC in England in the winter of 1947–48. Amid the suffering that followed Partition, there was no cricket in Pakistan. Most of our boys were not able to get any practice. However, we were determined to play against the West Indies. The Lahore Test was a hotly-contested one. Our opening batsmen, Nazar Muhammad and Imtiaz Ahmad, made a great debut in international cricket by raking up a century partnership in the first innings. They made 148 runs for the first wicket, providing a solid start to the team. We were all out for a modest score of 241. When the West Indies started their innings, they soon struggled for runs. Munawar Ali Khan created a sensation in his first over. He bowled out the opening batsman, Carew, first ball. On his second delivery, West Indies' captain Goddard's middle stump flew into the air, broken in two pieces. Clyde Walcott arrived at the crease to save the hat-trick. Munawar bowled with extreme pace and accuracy. Walcott played and edged the ball in the gully, but was dropped. Had Nazar held that catch, the hat-trick would have been a rare world record. Munawar was at his best in the match. His rhythm was excellent. Imtiaz and skipper Mian Saeed scored centuries in the second innings.

The Lahore match was a unique experience for our team, and particularly for me. George Headley was known as the 'Black Bradman' in international cricket. I met this great cricketer during the match. He was thirty-nine then. Pakistan won the toss and had scored 190 plus at the end of the first day's play along with losing a couple of wickets. It was a bright, sunny morning. The wicket was placid and conditions were ideally suited for batting. The West Indies bowled defensively. After the day's play was over, I asked George why they did not go flat out to get the batsmen out. The answer was very educative, 'We will go flat out tomorrow when there will be moisture in the air and it will be a little foggy.' It happened exactly as he had forecast. Next morning, the West Indies bowlers dominated the proceedings, and the Pakistan team was all out for 241.

During the match, George Headley strained a back muscle and was hospitalized. The West Indies were in a tight corner in the first innings and were struggling for runs. They had lost 8 wickets for 201 runs. George was summoned from the hospital and, in spite of the fact that he was bandaged round his waist, he padded up, came in with a runner, and played a cavalier innings. His hook shots and square drives left everyone bewildered, and he scored an unbeaten 57. The West Indies took a 67 run lead. His innings taught the youngsters the finer points of batting. It was the first time in my career I heard the words 'Cool, man, cool', meaning 'be patient'. He would address these remarks to his fellow batsman who wanted to take a cheeky single.

A few months after the West Indies tour, the BCCP got an invitation from the Ceylon (now Sri Lanka) cricket board to play a two-Test match series. Although hampered by lack of funds, the BCCP accepted the invitation because it did not want to pass the opportunity of providing our best players with the experience of playing under foreign conditions against teams of merit. Accordingly, an appeal for donations was made and it met with an instant and encouraging response. Fayyaz Hussain, president of the Pakistan motion pictures association, took great interest in collecting funds. His association contributed Rs 6500 ($ 127). The Muslim mercantile community living in Colombo contributed Rs 13,000 ($236) at the request of Abdul Salim Khan, our trade commissioner in Colombo. The total donation received from Ceylon was more than Rs 26,000 ($472). The West Punjab government donated Rs 2500 ($45). The Karachi Race Club gave Rs 8000 ($164), and the government of the former East Pakistan also contributed Rs 1000 ($18). In spite of all these contributions, the tour resulted in a net loss of about Rs 10,000 ($181) to the BCCP. The air travelling expenses and the cost of equipping the side were very high. However, from a cricketing point of view, the Ceylon tour was highly successful.

The standard of cricket was very high in Ceylon, but we won the two-Test match series 2–0. In the first innings, Ceylon could score only 112 runs while we made 399. Mian Saeed, Maqsood, and Alimuddin contributed 93, 85, and 66 respectively. In the second innings, Ceylon was all out for 95 runs and Pakistan won its first ever Test on foreign soil by an innings and 192 runs. In the second Test, Ceylon made 311 in its first innings. Pakistan responded positively. Both Nazar Muhammad and Murrawat Hussain scored centuries, getting 170 and 164. I also contributed 65 useful runs without losing my wicket. In the second innings, Ceylon was all out for a modest total of 210. Nazar and Imtiaz scored the required 47 runs, and we won the match by 10 wickets. These two victories against Ceylon boosted our confidence.

My performance against the West Indies in 1948 had not been satisfactory. I had not taken any wickets in the match. The people thought that 'Fazal is now finished'. I was once an All-India cricketer, so I practised hard to gain my old form and was selected for the Ceylon tour. I got 12 wickets and scored 36 and 65 not out in the two Tests. That was enough to prove to the critics that I was not finished. When the Ceylon team reciprocated the tour in March 1950, I took 16 wickets in two Tests.

In March 1952, Queen Elizabeth II was to visit Ceylon. The Ceylon Cricket Board had arranged a match with the MCC team to mark the Queen's visit. They invited players from Pakistan, India, and Australia to form a Commonwealth team. Imtiaz and I were invited from Pakistan, while Vinoo Mankad and Polly Umrigar came from India, and Keith Miller, Neil Harvey, and Greane Hole represented Australia. The remaining four players were selected from Ceylon. I had the great experience of sharing the new ball with the greatest all-rounder of his time, Keith Miller, and keenly watched his bowling from my end.

After Partition in 1947, there was no cricket board in Pakistan. The provincial teams, or NICA and KCCA, affiliated with the BCCI before Partition, were in disarray. There was no active cricket in Pakistan. Amid the turmoil and upheaval of Partition, the formation of a cricket board in the new country was an extremely difficult task. Nevertheless, it was the effort of some ardent cricket followers in Pakistan that led to the formation of the Board of Control for Cricket in Pakistan in November 1947. The chief minister of West Punjab, Khan Iftikhar Hussain Khan of Mamdot, was elected its first president, while Yousuf A. Haroon from Karachi was elected as the vice-president. Muhammad Ali Jinnah, the governor-general of Pakistan, very graciously became its first patron. The areas which constituted Pakistan after Partition had a lot of talent so it was not difficult for the BCCP to form a reasonably well balanced team to field in international cricket.

There was no infrastructure available in the new country. Pakistani cricket had to start almost from scratch. The financial position of the BCCP was zero. It offered life membership to wealthy people, who could donate a few thousand rupees to run the affairs of cricket in the country. People like the late Mian Salahuddin and Nawab Aslam Khan Mamdot donated five thousand rupees each and became life members of the BCCP.

There were neither rajas nor maharajas nor banks nor other institutions to look after the financial requirements of the players. We were given five rupees as daily allowance during the matches, not as match fee but for expenses to reach the ground in time in a tonga. When we became Test cricketers, we were given one pound sterling daily. I must say with pride that the players of those days did not crave for money. We were proud to be wearing the green Pakistani blazers. We had determination, strong will, sincerity of purpose, an honest approach, and no vested interests. We had one desire and that was to build a strong Pakistan team. The team progressed by leaps and bounds. It performed well against the West Indies, won all four Tests against Ceylon in series at home and abroad, and, finally, defeated the strong MCC team in Karachi.

India proposed our name for full membership in the ICC meeting held in London in 1952, and the West Indies seconded it. We were given a full Test status. Apart from the BCCP officials, the players deserved credit for this because it was they who toiled and worked for the promotion of cricket in Pakistan. No one can forget the services rendered by Mian Muhammad Saeed, Nazar Muhammad, Imtiaz Ahmad, Khan Muhammad, Munawar Ali Khan, Murrawat Hussain, and Maqsood Ahmad.

In fact, it was the performance of these great cricketers that helped Pakistan get the ICC membership.

After the Ceylon tour to Pakistan, I was transferred to Rawalpindi. There was limited cricket in that city, and this upset me. Often, I thought of giving up cricket because there seemed no future for the game in Pakistan. However, when the BCCP announced the schedule of matches with the MCC team that was to arrive in Pakistan in November 1950, I forgot my previous despondency and took one month's leave from duty to participate in the matches. After reaching Lahore, I went straight to Minto Park for a good practice session with my old friends.

The MCC team under Nigel Howard arrived and played the first match of the tour in Sialkot. This match was a test of my abilities as there was a general impression in the BCCP that I was not good enough for international matches. I had to prove them wrong. I took five wickets in the match and scored 42 runs. My performance forced the selectors to include me in the first unofficial Test at Lahore. The BCCP announced that Abdul Hafeez Kardar would lead the Pakistan team in Test matches against the MCC. During the match, I pulled a thigh muscle and could not get any wicket. The match was drawn.

The team reached Karachi to play the second Test match. A day before the match, while I was in my hotel room, I switched on the radio and found that I had not been selected in the team. I could not believe that I had been dropped and was crestfallen. But, late at night, I received a telephone call from the late Dr Dilawar Hussain, one of the selectors, who asked me to come to the ground in the morning in proper kit. 'You are in the team,' he told me. I was overjoyed.

The next morning, my performance was excellent as in the pre-lunch session I battered the MCC batting line-up. They lost some 7 or 8 wickets for only 100 plus runs. When I was going to the pavilion for lunch, I heard a loud voice: *'Tehr ja jawana'* (Halt, young man). I saw Dr Dilawar standing near the sidescreen calling out to me. When I went up to him, he said, 'The way I have spent the past night is known only to me.

Puttera thoon manu phansi dhe pandha thoun la liya aye' (Son, you have saved me from the gallows), he said in typical Punjabi. I was beginning to wonder what he meant when he told me that he had included me in the team by lying to the other selectors that Justice A.R. Cornelius had directed him to include Fazal in the team. To me, it was tragic that I needed *sifarish* to get into the national team. Anyhow, Pakistan easily beat the MCC at Karachi and, when I played the winning stroke, about 20,000 spectators raised slogans of 'Pakistan Zindabad.'

At the end of the match, Prime Minister Khawaja Nazimuddin, who was also watching the match, called Kardar and me over. The prime minister was jubilant. He held our hands and said, 'Pakistan Zindabad.' The crowd also joined in. The prime minister then invited the team to dinner in Karachi, which was to take place ten days later. I left for Rawalpindi by the Frontier Mail the same evening as I had to resume my job. I applied to the SP for a week's leave to attend the prime minister's dinner in Karachi. 'It is a mere dinner. Forget about that and take care of your duty,' he said, and refused to grant me leave. In the evening, a friend of mine who had joined the army called upon me. I was dejected. He asked me what the matter was and I told him the whole story. He consoled me and left saying, 'You will get the leave within one hour.' After one hour, a DSP came and told me that my leave request had been accepted. Later, I learnt that my friend talked to his officer who was friendly with the military secretary of Prime Minister Khawaja Nazimuddin. The officer used his connections and the orders for my leave came through from the Prime Minister's House. I attended the dinner in Karachi. When Khawaja Nazimuddin saw me, he commented: 'So you got the permission.' Then, during that grand dinner, he made an historic announcement that 'the players who serve Pakistan would be considered on duty during all national and international competitions.' That solved my problem. Now I could play cricket without any hindrance.

4

The Pakistan Eaglets

Justice A.R. Cornelius formed the Pakistan Eaglets Society soon after independence. The purpose was to provide upcoming cricketers with opportunities to play cricket in an environment of international standard. Justice Cornelius used his wide range of contacts for the promotion of cricket in Pakistan. He raised a team and arranged its first tour to England in 1951. Khan Muhammad, Imtiaz Ahmad, Maqsood Ahmad, Zulfiqar Ahmad, Mahmood Hussain, and M.E.Z. Ghazali were some of the members of the team, and former Ranji Trophy player, Mian Muhammad Saeed, was its captain. The finances of the touring cricketers were so arranged that those who could foot their bills did so, and the Society bore the expenses of the others. The services of former England fast bowler Alf Gover were acquired for a month and every player received extensive coaching in his famous coaching school. The players were able to get a good insight into English wickets and climatic conditions. These were to prove valuable in 1954. They played matches against teams of good county standard. When the team returned home, there was a visible change in the quality and outlook of the players. Imtiaz Ahmad and Mahmood Hussain benefited most from the England tour and the subsequent coaching at Alf Gover's school. Imtiaz was an improved batsman. Mahmood Hussain, who used to bowl with a round arm action, came back with a perfect overhead action. Imtiaz Ahmad exhibited his new found talent by scoring 300 runs against the Commonwealth XI at Bombay.

In mid-1953, Justice A.R. Cornelius informed me, in Montgomery, that I was to lead the second Pakistan Eaglets team to England. I was to train at Alf Gover's school and would be able to watch the English and Australian players in action when they played for the Ashes. My department sanctioned one thousand rupees for my expenses in England. Aslam Khokhar, Yousuf Jaffar, Alimuddin, Ghazali, Khalid Ibadullah, Anwar Rasheed, Ismail Gul, and Ikram Elahi were members of the team. After twenty-eight days of training at the coaching school, the team played against several clubs consisting of professionals and county players.

The Pakistan Eaglets team's tour of England in 1953 was very successful. As the tour progressed, we introduced ourselves as well as Pakistan to different parts of England. The people there realized that Pakistani cricketers were different from what they had been led to believe. We were defeated by the Royal Air Force team at Kingston-on-Thames, but my performance in both batting and bowling was reasonable. Besides taking two wickets for 30 runs, I scored 21 not out in the first innings and 47 in the second.

We went to Ebbw Vale in Wales to play against the West Indies. The West Indies team consisted of Worrell, Weekes, Martin Dale, Valentine, and Roy Marshall. We were worried about playing against what was virtually a full-strength West Indies team. The night before the start of the match, I held a meeting with the players and we decided to give it our all. The next morning, Justice A.R. Cornelius was present at the ground. I was informed by the manager of the team that the Pakistan Eaglets were going to get about £15 against £300 to be received by the West Indies. I did not like the idea and approached the secretary of the club to tell him that it was an unfair deal. After some protracted discussion, he went in to speak to the club committee and came back with an offer of £30. This too was not a fair offer and, after further negotiations, it was decided that we would receive £90.

The main feature of the match was that, batting at the number three position, I scored 104 not out. Aslam Khokhar scored 55 runs. The strong West Indies side could only get the wickets of Ghazali, Alimuddin (29), and Khalid Ibadullah (34). Our score was 238 for 3. There was a stir in the ground because of what had happened to the West Indies bowlers, but greater laurels and encouragement were in store for us. The West Indies were 137 for 5 when stumps were drawn early on their request. They had to travel a long distance for their next match. I bowled throughout the West Indies innings and took four wickets including those of Worrell (43), Marshal (28), and Weekes (24). The match ended in a very honourable draw for Pakistan. Our players were very happy and jubilant—not only had they played out a draw but had done so with aplomb. They got their share of the £90, and everyone bought new suits with the money.

The tour was very successful. We not only gained much knowledge about English conditions but made friends as well. On the tour, I played in eighteen matches, captured 93 wickets and scored 713 runs. Credit for the concept and its implementation must go to Justice A.R. Cornelius. This was one of his many contributions to the development of cricket in Pakistan.

5

India: 1952–53

After becoming a member of the ICC, we received an invitation from the Indian cricket board to play a five-Test match series. The BCCP agreed. We were joyful and excited at the prospect of facing the Indians in cricket. India was not new for us. Many of us had already played against each other. Some of us had played together in the same team in the Ranji Trophy and zonal tournaments. However, there were some apprehensions that the timing of the tour was perhaps improper. The wounds of large-scale carnage on both sides of the Wagah border that followed soon after the announcement of the partition plan, had not yet healed. The political relations between the two countries were not normal. Amid these fears, we crossed the Wagah border on Wednesday, 8 October, and were warmly received on the Indian side by a large number of cricket fans.

Our tour began with a match against the North Zone in Amritsar. It was a drawn match, but our players got good practice ahead of the first Test at Delhi. Hanif scored centuries in both innings. From Amritsar, we reached Delhi by train, and were received at the Delhi railway station by the Indian captain Lala Amarnath and officials of the Delhi Cricket Association. In the evening, we visited the tomb of the great Muslim saint Hazrat Nizamuddin Aulia, and offered *fateha*. We also visited the *samadhi* of Mahatma Gandhi and placed wreaths on it. At night, we attended a dinner hosted by Shoaib Qureshi, our high commissioner in India. He advised us to demonstrate the best of our qualities in the field. He seemed concerned about the outcome of the series.

Lala Amarnath won the toss at the Feroze Shah Kotla ground and elected to bat on the slow turf wicket. There were some visible rough patches on the wicket at the end of the first day's play. This assured me that the Indian batsmen would probably find it difficult to score on the second day. The next day, when we reached the ground and saw the condition of the wicket, it was astonishingly flat. All the rough patches had been removed. India scored 372. With the exception of Hanif, who scored a patient 51, we batted poorly in the first innings and consequently followed-on. Our batsmen succumbed to Mankad's deadly spell. We did not do any better in the second innings either. Vinoo was simply unplayable. Only Kardar with 43 not out, Imtiaz (41), and myself with 27 could reach double figures. We lost the first Test match in Delhi. It was painful.

We entered the Lucknow Test without Khan Muhammad who was unfit, but with Mahmood Hussain who was given his first Test cap. India won the toss and elected to bat. Maqsood opened the bowling attack and gave us an early breakthrough on the jute matting wicket. I was bowling as first change and got rid of Roy. Then wickets began falling at very short intervals. The whole Indian team was out for 106 runs. I took five wickets. Mahmood Hussain gave me tremendous support from the other end by claiming 3 for 35. I remember one beautiful leg-cutter that I bowled to Manjrekar. It came in sharply with the seam and uprooted his off stump. Nazar Muhammad dominated the whole second day and the first half of the third day with his fine batting. The wickets tumbled at the other end, but he stood firm at his crease scoring 124 runs. He was saved once in his innings when Gul Muhammad caught him on Hiralal's ball but, in the process of completing the catch, Gul rolled over and the ball touched the ground. The Indian batsmen did not succeed in the second innings either. Mahmood Hussain got Roy. I got Manjrekar, Gaekwad, and Kishenchand. Umrigar put up some resistance but could not change the outcome. If Zulfiqar had not dropped Amarnath on my bowling in the early part of his innings, we could have won the match on the third day as Amarnath showed great restraint and remained unbeaten with

61 when India was all out for 182. We won the match by an innings and 43 runs. The series stood level at Lucknow. The crowd could not accept their team's defeat at Lucknow. After the match, a mob manhandled some Indian players and attacked the bus that was carrying them to the hotel.

One episode that contributed considerably to our victory must be mentioned. As the Pakistan team emerged from the bus that carried us to the Gomti ground on the first day of the match, some college students, of both sexes, told us not to worry as they would wholeheartedly support us during the course of the play. They were all Muslims and I must admit that whenever our bowlers appealed against any batsman, these students supported them with loud voices from the boundary.

We did not play well on the slightly soggy turf at the Brabourne stadium, Bombay in the third Test. However, Hanif and Waqar Hasan excelled in both innings. They both tackled the guile of Mankad, Gupte, and Ghulam Ahmad with extreme confidence on the dew-effected turf on the third day. Poor Hanif missed his century by only four runs in the second innings. We lost the match. Had our other batsmen not taken liberties with Mankad, and our fieldsmen not done the same with Hazare and Umrigar, who scored centuries, we could have won the match. I did not take any wickets in this match.

Amarnath's strategy also played a very important role in India's win. On the third day of the match, he declared India's first innings at 387. It seemed adventurous, but he had weighed the situation correctly, and was able to exploit the fatigue of our batsmen who had been on the field the whole day.

The fourth Test at Madras (now Chennai) truly belonged to Zulfiqar and Amir Elahi. Kardar scored 79 runs in the first innings and a most productive last wicket partnership between Zulfiqar and Elahi produced 104 runs. Pakistan succeeded in amassing 344 runs. Zulfiqar remained unbeaten on 63 while Elahi made 47 valuable runs. During the early course of this partnership, the Indian captain Lala Amarnath avoided batting in the crucial period and asked his bowlers to take things easy. Amir Elahi overheard Lala's instruction to the bowlers and told him in a friendly fashion, 'If you can't get us today, you will find it difficult to get us tomorrow.' This proved very correct as they put in 104 for the last wicket. We were in a winning position at Madras but rain on the third day ruined all our hopes. We got 6 Indian wickets for a paltry 175 runs. The conditions at Madras suited me. I was bowling on turf with the breeze at my back. Imtiaz kept wickets for the first time in Test cricket at Madras.

We entered the fifth and final Test at Calcutta determined to win. Lala Amarnath won the toss and put us in to bat. We scored 230 runs for the loss of five wickets at the close of first day's play. The second day began with very poor batting by our tail-enders. Phadkar and Ramchand bowled just seven overs between them, and we were all out after adding only 27 runs to our overnight score. India finished the second day at 179 for 6. During lunch, Lala Amarnath said to me, 'You are a wonderful bowler. The great ball that you bowl is the leg-cutter but one can make that out when you come close to the stumps.' After lunch, the match started and we both had an interesting encounter. Lala was very watchful. I bowled a leg-cutter from the return crease and Lala was caught out brilliantly by Maqsood Ahmad.

The third day belonged to the new Test cap, Deepak Shodhan, who scored a splendid century and India took a lead of 140 runs. We were soon in danger of defeat but young Waqar Hasan saved us. After the departure of Nazar, with Imtiaz, Kardar, Maqsood, and Anwar Hussain out and the addition of only 50 runs to our total, Amarnath and his men were keyed up for victory. Waqar remained quite unperturbed, carrying on with the difficult task of pulling his team out of danger. His memorable knock of 97 was a demonstration of courage, determination, and patience. He completely dominated the good-length and well-flighted bowling with an immaculately straight bat. His powerful drives, hooks, and cuts were a delight to watch. He was never in trouble. In my opinion, he played the best innings of his career. I am sure that the cricket fans of Calcutta still have memories of Waqar's batting. Finally, a seventh wicket partnership of 64 between Waqar and myself saved the match. Indeed, the dew-topped heavy turf at Calcutta assisted the Indian swing bowlers, Phadkar and Ramchand, but our batsmen became victims of risky shots.

When India started its first innings on the second day of the match, none of their batsmen could play either Mahmood Hussain's fiery bouncers or my accurate cutters or out-swingers with any confidence. With slightly better luck and alert fielding, we could well have run through the Indian team before the drawing of stumps. The pendulum swung heavily in India's favour on the third day. Deepak Shodhan made a magnificent 110. India made 397, and gained a lead of 140 runs. The courage and determination with which I was pegging away at the stumps can be determined from the fact that my sixty-fourth over, which brought Shodhan's wicket, was a 'maiden'. It was bowled with the same accuracy which had characterized my earlier overs. I must give credit to Mahmood Hussain as well, who literally bowled his heart out. Amir Elahi was handicapped with an inflammation in his eyes, which limited our attack. Kardar was also unable to bowl because of his injured left-hand. Amir had received the news of the birth of his first son in Lahore. He was very happy and, to celebrate, he had dyed his grey hair to look younger. The next day, his eyes were swollen due to a chemical reaction from the dye.

Although Pakistan lost 2–1 in the series, the Lucknow victory gave us enough confidence to play competitive cricket. There were a couple of tactical mistakes which could have been avoided. Young Waqar was originally selected in the team as a one down specialist batsman, but surprisingly, in the Delhi Test, he was sent in at number eight in both innings. Again in the third Test, Waqar was included in the team only when the vice-captain, Anwar Hussain, declared himself unfit at the start of play.

We enjoyed the Indian tour both on and off the field, and were simply overwhelmed by the friendliness of people at the centres. They welcomed us with open hearts, especially at Nagpur where we played a three-day match against the Central

Zone. India's all time greats C.K. Nayudu and Syed Mushtaq Ali played in this match. C.K. was celebrating his fifty-eighth birthday. I believe he was probably the oldest cricketer of the subcontinent to play a first-class match. In Nagpur, the people would stand by the roadside as our bus drove past on its way to the cricket ground. During the bus journey, it was usual for us to sing 'Dil mein sulagtai hain armaan', 'Aa ja balam aayee baharen', and 'Lagh ghia kisi day nainan da nishana'—some of our favourites. Nazar would lead the chorus and Maqsood, Waqar, and I would join him. During a reception in Nagpur, there were requests for us to sing. We obliged. Nazar led the chorus, singing songs like 'Bach ja mundia mor tohn' and 'Chandni ratein'.

We also met our old friend Chuni Lal in Nagpur. He was a former NICA cricketer and had lived in Lahore before Partition. He was the moving spirit behind most of the parties and functions in the city. He spared nothing to make our stay happy and comfortable. In Lucknow, our singing was very popular. The cricket fans, in their typical Lucknow style, would request us to sing a song with every autograph. We thoroughly enjoyed this. The Maharajakumar of Vizianagram and the Uttar Pradesh government made sure our stay in Lucknow was comfortable and enjoyable.

While we travelled from Ahmadabad to Bombay, cricket fans greeted us at almost every railway station. In Surat, they did not let us sleep at night. When the train stopped at Surat, some people constantly knocked at the windows of our compartment. It was two o'clock. When one of us opened the window, they said that they only wanted to garland the players and had been waiting several hours for us. It was impossible for the players not to reciprocate their sentiments. We accepted the flowers, and the train moved on.

In Bombay, a grand dinner party was arranged in our honour. The celebrities of the Indian film industry were also invited. After dinner, Talat Mahmood sang a number of songs for us. Nazar also contributed his melodies.

In contrast to the warmth, there were some hostile elements who did not like our visit. In Nagpur, some members of the

Hindu Mahasabha welcomed us with anti-Pakistan slogans. We took it sportingly. In Amritsar, the most badly affected city during the bloodshed that accompanied Partition, the local administration was extra cautious about our safety. They did not allow us to visit the city but took every bit of care for our comfort and food.

6

Pakistan in England: 1954

The England & Wales Cricket Board had invited BCCP to play a four-Test match series in the summer of 1954. The BCCP organized an inter-provincial Jinnah tournament in 1953–4. This first-class tournament was organized on the pattern of the Ranji Trophy in India. After the tournament, the BCCP asked about forty-five players to play trial matches in Bahawalpur. When the BCCP announced the team after the end of the trial matches, there were some unbelievable omissions, and additions. Muhammad Amin, who had taken eight wickets in the trial match was omitted. He was a product of the Mamdot club and Kardar did not like the players from Mamdot. Both Munnawar-ul-Haq and Yawar Saeed were very good all-rounders and fielders but were not selected. Yawar later played for the English county Somerset against Pakistan and got four wickets. A couple of cricketers were chosen purely on the basis of political influence, and after the England tour were forgotten.

The selected players were asked to join the month long training camp at the Dring stadium in Baghdad-ul-Jadid, the capital of Bahawalpur state. The camp began in the first week of March. We were accommodated in tarpaulin tents installed outside the stadium. There were no five-star hotels in those days but we could have been easily accommodated in a government rest house. Probably, the cricket board wanted us to have a taste of England's cold climate. Our daily training started early in the morning with physical exercises. An army-man had been engaged for this purpose. The training camp, which lasted for three weeks, I believe, was the best of its kind. Besides physical exercises and fielding practice, the players were also acquainted with the English way of life. Some new players who had not gone on the England tour with the Pakistan Eaglets team were taught table manners.

I had spent about two weeks in the camp when I learnt of the sad demise of my beloved mother and had to rush to Lahore. My father was very sad and I tried to console him. Fate had deprived me of the affection and love that only a mother could give to her child. It was a great loss for me. She was a constant source of strength for me and would pray for my safety and success.

A day before the team's departure for London, the Karachi cricket association hosted a dinner. Various people spoke on the occasion. A message from the former Indian captain Vijay Merchant was also read out. It said: 'If Pakistan draws ten and wins four or five county matches in England it should consider its tour a success.' I vehemently rejected Merchant's views and maintained that Pakistan would win at least one Test. Many considered it a boastful claim. Well, it might have been presumptuous but probably I was the only person who was confident and determined to beat England.

Our ship, the SS Battery, left Karachi on 12 April. A large number of people bade farewell to us. I shared a cabin with the assistant manager, Salahuddin, and Kardar. Next morning, we drew up a programme for daily physical training and fielding practice on the deck. We were to disembark in the first week of May and did not want to waste this time. But, we were able to carry out fielding practice for only a couple of days because the balls that the team had brought along were knocked into the deep sea by our batsmen. However, the physical training continued. Some players enjoyed playing table-tennis on the ship. My daily routine was to get up early in the morning and briskly walk around the deck thirty-five times which came to about three miles. Short sprints enabled me to keep fit and swimming the breast stroke kept my muscles in shape. My waist was nineteen inches, chest thirty-four, and the expansion was eight inches, making it forty-two inches.

After a wonderful 'holiday' on the SS Battery, and a rough passage in the English Channel, we reached England on 8 May. Even as it entered the Southampton docks, fifteen feet high sea waves were breaking over its bows. From Southampton, we boarded a train and arrived at the Waterloo station, where officials of the England & Wales Cricket Board, Alf Gover, and Sir Leonard Hutton received us.

In England, we were given wide publicity in the press and were interviewed on television. But, as far as our playing talent was concerned, the sports critics did not take it seriously and dubbed us the 'babes of cricket'. It was generally assumed that our standard was approximately equal to that of an average English county team. They considered it unwise that Pakistan had been given a full Test status. Their patronizing attitude towards the Pakistani team was rather disconcerting. The Indian team in earlier Tests against England had in many instances not played as well as we had, but such an attitude was never adopted towards them. Nevertheless, there was the lone voice of Alf Gover, the ex-England fast bowler, who had forewarned the critics in a newspaper column that 'Pakistan will win at least one of the four Tests'.

During the three-and-a-half month tour, we were to play four Test matches and a number of county matches. The first county match against Worcestershire was exciting, particularly on the last day. Till lunch it seemed that the match would be drawn. Worcestershire's score was 156 for one at lunch. They needed only 54 runs to save an innings' defeat. While we were having lunch and discussing the fate of the match, Shujauddin, a team-mate, remarked that 'the match, was drawn'. I was struggling hard in the middle, so naturally I did not like that remark. My first over after lunch completely transformed the match in our favour. I got Kenyon and Bird out on successive balls—the new batsman, Broadbent, calmly played my next ball and averted the hat-trick but was trapped leg-before the next ball. About half an hour before the tea interval, Worcestershire was all out for 244. When we returned to the pavilion, Shuja was still enjoying his soup. 'Is the match drawn?' he asked. 'No, we have bowled them out and now we need a few runs to win the match,' I told him. 'Impossible,' he said. But, it was true and we beat Worcestershire by 8 wickets. My contribution in the match was 11 wickets, 2 catches, and 68 runs!

After our victory against Worcestershire and Oxford University, and drawn games with Cambridge University, Leicestershire, and MCC, the same critics started saying that 'England should not take Pakistan lightly.' The English selectors took no chances in selecting their team for the first Test. They fielded their strongest possible side at Lord's. This was a compliment to our performance against the county sides. We were not over-awed by the great names in the England team and were mentally prepared to take them on.

Rain dominated the first three days in the Lord's Test, and the match started on the fourth day. We were all out for 87 runs. England declared its first innings at 117 for 9. Khan Muhammad got five wickets and I got four. However, I shall remember the Lord's Test for the meeting with Her Majesty Queen Elizabeth II at the Buckingham Palace. Because of rain, the customary ceremony was held in the Palace, which was a rare occasion. All the members of the Pakistan team were introduced to the Queen. When my turn came, the Queen, while shaking hands with me, looked into my eyes and went on to meet the other players. After shaking hands with the last player in the queue, the Queen came back to me and said: 'You are a Pakistani. How do you have blue eyes while the others do not?' 'Your Majesty, the people coming from the northern areas of Pakistan do have blue eyes,' I told her. The Queen was amused. Later, I was also invited to attend the Queen's garden party.

The Lord's Test was a financial disaster. Three days were lost because of rain. After lunch on the fourth day, an understanding was reached between our team manager, Syed Fida Hussain, and the MCC that spectators would be admitted at half the normal charges. The move was to encourage more people to watch the match. However, public interest was so strong that on the third morning an ardent cricket enthusiast telephoned the ground staff at frequent intervals from Leeds hoping to be told that play would start. He had chartered a small plane and wanted to fly to London in case the match began.

I pulled a muscle in my left leg during the match with Nottinghamshire. It was not serious then, but in the second Test at Trent Bridge, while I was bowling my last over of the day to Compton, my front foot slipped on a small crack on the bowling crease and I pulled the same muscle. I reached the hotel and massaged my whole body with 'ambrocation' cream. Then I took a hot bath and went to bed. Next morning, when I got up it was still giving me trouble. After consultation with the doctor, I strapped myself up from knee to thigh and had to cut my run-up and pace. Imtiaz Ahmad was my runner in the second innings.

We lost the Nottingham Test. Maqsood Ahmad was playing extremely well in the second innings and we thought that defeat could be averted. But, after a while Maqsood started playing wildly. He lofted Appleyard hard but Statham dropped the catch. Still Maqsood did not change his carefree style and again lofted Appleyard high in the air. Seeing Peter May catching the ball, Maqsood started to walk off the field. However, after completing the catch, May looked down at his feet and saw that they were on the ropes. He signalled a six to the umpire and Maqsood was called back. May's attitude was a most noteworthy display of sportsmanship. Unfortunately, sanity did not prevail and Maqsood played him in the same way again, but this time Statham made no mistake and he was out for 69.

After the match, Syed Fida Hussain told me that he had contacted Dr Tucker through Alf Gover, and that he would drive me to London. Dr Tucker was himself an international rugby football player. After two week's treatment, I was able to run again. I missed the matches against Derbyshire, Surrey, Northamptonshire, and Lancashire.

Our next match was the third Test at Manchester. England declared their innings at 359 runs. The second day's play had to be abandoned due to rain. Aslam Khokhar and I went out and did plenty of shopping and bought some woolies. When

Pakistan started their innings, the condition of the wicket had deteriorated. I was waiting for my batting turn amid the tumbling of wickets when I heard Peter West's voice on the air. He was offering his expert comments on the condition of the pitch. 'There is nothing wrong with the wicket except that the ball takes a turn after touching the surface,' he said. His absurd remarks pained me. During the game I had discussed the wicket with Compton, Graveney, McConnon, and Evans. They all agreed that the wicket was unplayable for the batsmen. When I told them about the comments of Peter West, they too appeared to be puzzled.

It was this England tour which made the BCCP prosperous. We earned about £ 16,000, and of this £ 10,000 were spent on our training and travel in England.

7

History at the Oval in 1954

Whenever the history of Pakistan cricket is written, the glorious victory that the 'babes of cricket' achieved at the Oval cricket ground on 17 August 1954 would not be forgotten. Indeed, the Oval Test match deserves a special place not only in my career but also in the history of our country. My performance in the Oval Test gave me personal glory, and I was selected as one of the five best cricketers of the year for *Wisden*, the cricket Bible. It was only after this victory that Pakistan became known all over England. Until then, the common Englishman held the mistaken belief that Pakistan was a state of India. After this victory, they learnt that Pakistan was an independent and sovereign state. This was a change from our arrival in England when we were coming out of the docks at Liverpool and a porter asked, 'Oh, you are here again, were you not here last year?' Abdul Hafeez replied, 'No, it was the Indian team, not us. We are from Pakistan.' The porter showed his ignorance about Pakistan by saying, 'To me, you are the same, from India.'

The English team was magnificent. Each player seemed better than the players of other teams. Sir Leonard Hutton, after missing the Tests at Trent Bridge and Manchester, was leading England in the Oval Test. He was a world record holder. Peter May would play very hard with a straight bat. Denis Compton was a killer. Godfrey Evans was marvellous. McConnon was considered a great off-spinner. Johnny Wardle would bowl the chinaman and googly very effectively. All these players were living legends.

In 1953, when I was in England with the Pakistan Eaglets, I witnessed the great Sir Len Hutton receiving applause from the crowd on the Oval balcony. I had a strange feeling that in the coming year, I could be jubilantly standing on the balcony of the Oval pavilion receiving the same ovation from the crowd. This proved to be true.

I entered the Oval ground in 1954 with a strong determination to win. A few days before the start of the match, I had pledged to some top British politicians that 'given a chance we are capable of performing.' Moreover, I had promised my friends in Lahore that we would give England a very tough fight. Few had taken me seriously, and I was hard pressed to prove myself right.

The match started after lunch on the first day because of rain. Although rain had stopped at about the time the game would normally have started, the ground staff began their efforts to make the ground playable. Three motor suction driers were used to draw up the moisture on the square. But, in the absence of sun and wind, with the sky still dark and threatening, the process took time. Kardar won the toss and decided to bat. The wicket was partially dry. England's fast bowlers did a tremendous job on the soft wicket which gave little help to them. Hanif played five balls from Statham comfortably, but on the sixth was late with an attempted pull shot and was out lbw. Tyson, making his debut, opened from the other end with three slips and a cluster of short legs. He was described by experts as the fastest bowler since Larwood. His third over gave him his first and second wickets in Test cricket. He clean bowled Alimuddin and Maqsood Ahmad on his third and fourth balls. It was Imtiaz Ahmad who left the fifth ball alone and denied Tyson his hat-trick. Imtiaz played some daring strokes before failing to hook a short ball from Tyson and was caught behind the stumps. Then Wazir was run-out and I was caught behind off the bowling of Loader. At one stage, Pakistan was 51 for 7. However, Kardar and Shuja played with great confidence. Kardar, with his individual score of 36, fell victim to a Tyson ball that pitched on a perfect length. Zulfiqar joined Shuja and they faced the English attack with courage. Shuja was content to defend. The ninth wicket gave us a valuable partnership of

29 runs. Mahmood Hussain joined Shuja after the fall of Zulfiqar, and soon he started hitting McConnon so hard that Hutton was forced to bring back Tyson. Mahmood struck out at the first ball from Tyson and got four runs. He was beaten on the next ball and the third delivery took his leg stump. He scored 23 runs. Pakistan was all out for 133 runs. Shuja remained unbeaten with 16. In the remaining few minutes, England scored one without loss.

The second day's play was washed out. The third day of the Test match was also Pakistan's independence day. I wore the old kit that I had worn in the Lucknow Test of 1952, in which I had taken twelve Indian wickets, hoping that this would bring me luck. The third day's play started forty-five minutes late because of overnight rain. The sun was shining brightly when I started my first over of the day. Both Mahmood Hussain and I had set an attacking field, and under the prevailing conditions, 133 looked like a good score. Mahmood Hussain struck the first blow in his second over when Simpson failed to get his bat away from the ball and offered a simple catch to Kardar. Peter May joined Hutton, and between overs they both held conferences and naturally decided to attack in order to make as many runs as they could before the pitch became more vicious. Hutton, usually calm at the beginning of an innings, first steered Mahmood through the leg trap and then lofted me over cover for four. England's score reached 26 when Hutton stepped out to drive me again through the covers. He mistimed the ball, which rose high far behind the wicket. Imtiaz Ahmad raced almost ten yards in the direction of third-man and took the catch over his head. Denis Compton, who joined May, tried to disturb Mahmood by marching down the wicket, but Mahmood gave him a slow yorker which almost got through. After that, both batsmen adopted a defensive approach. I bowled eleven maidens in my first fifteen overs. After lunch, I got Peter May, who played forward to a rising ball that glanced off his bat and went to Kardar fielding at gully. Then came Graveney, who offered a simple catch to Hanif off my bowling. By now, the pitch had dried sufficiently and had become nasty for the batsmen. Evans too did not survive long. He mistimed a bouncer from Mahmood and was caught by him at short-leg. With wickets falling at the other end, Compton began to take more risks. Time and again he rushed down the wicket to hit Mahmood Hussain and me. When on 31, Compton skied a ball back to me. I ran back a few yards and put my hand to the ball but dropped it. On my next ball, Compton was again dropped at long-on by Wazir Muhammad. At 38, Compton gave Wazir a possible chance in the deep, but he failed to hold the catch at the second attempt. I got both Wardle and Tyson through Imtiaz behind the wickets. Compton's resistance ended when his score was 53. He went down the pitch to steer me through the covers but played inside his intended off-drive and Imtiaz collected the ball behind the stumps. The England tail-enders offered no resistance and the whole team was out for 130, giving us a three run lead. This gave us a psychological edge over England. My figures were 30-16-53-6. Mahmood Hussain gave me tremendous support at the other end by getting four valuable wickets.

Pakistan started their second innings this time with Shuja opening with Hanif. Shuja had shown wonderful courage in the first innings. The wickets started falling at short intervals. Hanif took-off brilliantly by hitting three fours off Statham. But, at 19 he edged Wardle, and Graveney made no mistake in the slips. Shuja played defensively but at 38 he, too, became a Wardle victim. Then McConnon got Maqsood out, caught by Wardle, and Waqar Hasan was smartly run-out by Hutton. At this stage Hutton brought on Tyson. He bowled very fast and got Imtiaz at short fine-leg. Kardar scored 17 valuable runs. Alimuddin got a duck and I attempted a cross-bat stroke to McConnon and was bowled. Pakistan was 82 for 8 at this stage. McConnon dislocated a finger on the right hand and could not bowl for the rest of the Test match. Then came a very fine partnership of 58 runs between Wazir and Zulfiqar which brought respectability to the Pakistani score. Both batsmen played defensively and occasionally got runs pushing through the covers and playing into the fine leg area. Wazir, particularly, defied the England attack without trouble for about three hours, showing tremendous concentration and impeccable defence. With the score at 140, Zufiqar's courageous knock ended when he edged Wardle and this time May made no mistake. Mahmood Hussain joined Wazir Muhammad. The latter twice drove Loader through the covers. With the fall of Mahmood's wicket, Pakistan's second innings ended. Wazir was 42 not out, having played sensibly in very difficult conditions. England was left to score 168 runs to win. Johnny Wardle had been marvellous. He was the main wrecker, and finished with 7 for 56.

When Hutton and Simpson started England's second innings, the odds appeared to be favouring England. But, after managing to oust Len Hutton, Denis Compton, Graveney, and Peter May in the first innings, I was confident that they would offer little resistance in the second innings. This time I had adopted a new strategy. I would change the line of the ball every now and then. For instance, I would bowl the leg-cutter from the return crease which was a wicket-taking ball. There was also a hidden in-swinger from the return crease, an in-swinger from the middle of the crease, and an in-swinger from close to the stumps. The particular ball which induced Hutton to play forward was well concealed and I knew that I would get his wicket with it. I would bowl that ball with deadly accuracy, he would come forward, try to drive, and the ball would find the edge.

In the Oval Test, Len Hutton could not read my in-cutters or leg-cutters. He was repeatedly beaten and was not comfortable. He could not understand the intricacy and the combination of in-cutters and leg-cutters. The duel began. In one over, Hutton was rapped on the pads three times in four balls. He then used the long handle, hitting wildly and the ball went over Waqar Hassan standing at cover position. He jumped but the ball just glanced his fingers. While Hutton was running in between wickets, he came to my end. I applied psychological pressure and looking at him, said, 'This is not Hutton like.' He had a good look at me—naturally the greatest batsman of his times would not take kindly to such a remark from anybody. When he went to the other end, I decided to bowl that special concealed ball, knowing that if I were to miss I would not be able to tame the lion. So, I maintained my accuracy, speed, and rotation of the ball, inviting him to play into the covers, yet giving some room in between bat and ball. Hutton played through the covers, but the ball found his outer edge and went into the safe hands of Imtiaz. I was jubilant. My appeal was apparently very closely listened to in the dressing room and in the streets of Pakistan, particularly in my hometown Lahore. I had bowled twenty-seven different deliveries to Len Hutton in the Oval Test. It was carefully planned to the last detail. Hutton was tamed twice. His Test record against Pakistan is his worst against any country. In three Test innings he scored 19 runs.

Peter May joined Simpson, and they both carried the score to 66, when the latter gave a simple return catch to Zulfiqar. Then Compton joined May, and both played forcing strokes. May hooked Mahmood Hussain twice for fours. They were enjoying hitting the Pakistani bowlers and it seemed as if they wanted to finish the match before the close of the day's play. The score reached 109 for 2, and Kardar's gestures showed that he was thinking of replacing me. After the end of Mahmood's over, the ball went to Kardar. I approached him and literally snatched the ball from his hands saying, 'Do you want to lose the match?' He looked surprised. At that time, he did not think that Pakistan could win the match. He replied: 'Let the match go on till tomorrow. It might rain overnight and the match may end up in a draw.' Those were his words. 'Where should I stand?' he then asked after giving me the ball. I wanted to bowl one ball quickly lest he change his mind. I immediately pointed towards a position and said, 'Stand there.' I bowled to May with only half a start, and as luck would have it, I got Peter May out at gully caught by Kardar.

At this stage, Hutton changed the batting order and sent Evans in place of Graveney, which showed that they really wanted to finish the match before close of play. He was a good hitter of the ball. He came in and took guard and I knew that he would go flat out to hit me. I saw that while playing a stroke, he left his leg stump open. So with great accuracy, speed, and rotation of the ball, I bowled at him far outside the leg stump, slightly short of his front foot. That kept Evans quiet for a time and set the dressing room thinking. Then Evans was bowled round his legs. Graveney followed Evans. Shuja had him adjudged leg before for a duck. Now Compton was the only recognized batsman left. By then I was confident that Pakistan could win the match. But, the captain did not seem to feel the same. I was bowling the second last over of the fourth day when I had a dig at Hafeez Kardar, 'Hafeez, what if I get Compton out?' He replied in typical Punjabi—'Fere tha jith janwan ghain', meaning in that case we can win the match. I bowled a very fast in-cutter to Compton, which found the outside edge of his bat, and he was caught behind. The match had been virtually won. At the close of the day's play, England were 125 for 6.

I went back to the hotel, had a good hot bath and was relaxing when Kardar came to my room. After an exchange of greetings, he asked what I thought about the match. What should be the line of action? I said that he was the captain and that he should know better. I was a little angry. Nobody was apparently expecting that we could win the match. I thought we could win so, naturally, I was disturbed when others did not agree. I said, 'Well, you look after Zulfiqar and take care. There is Wardle in the middle and he can have a shy against a slow bowler. Even a miss-hit could be a six.' Kardar said, 'You relax, I shall come again,' and he left the room. Syed Fida Hussain, who was the manager, then came to my room and gave me a little sermon. I replied vehemently: 'Sir, instead of giving me this sermon give it to Kardar so that he should conduct himself like a captain who believes he can win.'

The final day's game started in a tense atmosphere. The odds were on Pakistan that morning. England needed 43 runs to win. The people, the newspapers and the remaining English team were banking on John Wardle to save the game. 'Oh Johnny can you save England?' were the headlines in most British papers. In spite of the intriguing state of the match, only a few hundred spectators were present at the Oval ground, mostly Pakistanis and Indians who were backing us. There were ladies reciting religious verses on their rosaries. Whenever an England batsman was beaten, the whole crowd would appeal in sheer anticipation. That gave us a lot of encouragement. Alimuddin dropped Wardle at second slip off Mahmood Hussain. It was an easy catch. But, from the other end I got Tyson's wicket. I bowled a leg-cutter which turned like a well spun leg-break from a good length. Tyson stretched forward, but edged the ball giving Imtiaz Ahmad his seventh catch of the match. At this stage, Wardle tried to bat from both ends. Loader came to the crease and pushed me to deep mid-on for four. The next ball, he scored a single in the covers. Now Wardle came to face me. I knew that Johnny would try to play forward. My leg-cutter would this time be an in-cutter. I placed Shuja at a marked point at backward short-leg. I knew that Wardle would offer a catch right there. 'You put your right foot here, left foot there, unfold your hands and stand ready for a catch. The ball will come right into your hands and you just grab it,' I told Shuja. It happened exactly like that. Shuja was almost hysterical. He was appealing while he held the catch.

Then came McConnon. He was suffering from a dislocated finger on his right hand, but was determined to bat. He played the last ball of my over safely. Mahmood Hussain got Loader out when Waqar Hassan held the catch. England now needed 30 to win as the last man, Brian Statham, came in. McConnon decided to take most of the strike. He played the first five balls of my over calmly. The last ball McConnon wanted to steal a single in order to keep the strike. He pushed the last delivery of my over into the covers and called Statham for a sharp single. Statham got home easily, but McConnon was smartly run out by Hanif.

Pakistan had beaten England on her soil. As the umpire raised his finger, I ran towards Hanif and hugged him. We were all jubilant. It was a memorable occasion, not only for us but also for all the Pakistanis who were present at the Oval ground.

8

Laurels with Victory

We returned to the pavilion extremely excited after the win. What India probably achieved in the 1960s—Pakistan had achieved in 1954. The then Pakistan army chief, General Ayub Khan, Lt. Gen. Azam Khan, former president of the BCCP Justice Cornelius, and Mian Mohammad Saeed (first captain of the Pakistan cricket team in the unofficial Tests and my father-in-law) were there. They all hugged and congratulated me. Justice Cornelius was overjoyed, and kept saying, 'Call Hutton, call Compton and tell them to learn from Fazal how to play cricket.' 'We want Fazal—We want Fazal' was the demand of the crowd that had gathered under that very balcony where Hutton had stood jubilant in 1953. Since then, I had been determined to stand on the same balcony and by the grace of God my desire had been fulfilled. I appeared on the balcony—waved my hands to the emotional crowd and left, but had to reappear because the people wanted to continue applauding me.

While sitting in the dressing room after the match, I received a call from Lord Hastings, 'Fazal, congratulations. Not because you have beaten England but because you have proved your point that "Given a chance we are capable of performing."' This had been my answer when Lord Hastings asked me during dinner a couple of days before the Oval match what the people in Pakistan thought about Kashmir. I told him that because the majority of Kashmiris were Muslims, they should be Pakistanis. Lord Radcliffe was sitting besides Lord Hastings when I said, 'In India, we were denied chances, denied opportunities. The composition of the Indian team was twelve Hindus, four Muslims, and one scheduled caste. Sir, given a chance we are capable of performing.' And, we did perform at the Oval that day.

Alf Gover was also very happy. He was a commentator for the match and after our victory he shouted, 'We have won—we have won,' completely forgetting that he was British. He came on to the field and asked if he could have a photograph with me. He enjoyed our victory as if he were a Pakistani.

The tradition was that after the match both captains cut a cake and exchanged greetings with each other. Kardar asked me to cut the cake and the ceremony was performed by Peter May, the vice-captain of England, and myself. Well, I deserved it because I had led Pakistan to victory.

When we came out of the Oval ground, I was surrounded by fans. We could barely reach our hotel. That night there was a very big function at the Pakistan high commission. An English girl from the high commission staff kissed me on the cheek and left. This was British culture and not ours. It was photographed. I requested everybody around not to send it to Pakistan, but it appeared in all the papers anyway.

Indeed, conditions favoured me at the Oval. The sky remained overcast and the atmosphere was heavy most of the time. These were ideal conditions for me. I swung the ball late and moved it both ways. And, I was absolutely sure that we would win the Oval Test. I had that kind of a feeling, backed by determination, perseverance, application, concentration, and motivation, and I knew we could turn the tables on England. The only suggestion that I offered to Hafeez Kardar on the last day of the match was to advise Mahmood Hussain to bowl within the stumps, slightly short of a length. The England batsmen would be panicking as they needed to get runs, and our efforts would be to frustrate them.

Before our tour, we had received a message from India's Vijay Merchant, who had opined that, 'If Pakistan could win some county matches their tour should be considered successful.' India wished this because they had not dreamt of beating England in England. I had already visited England with the Pakistan Eaglets and had played against the best of players—

Everton Weekes, Frank Worrell, Clyde Walcott, and others. I
had given very clear indications to my teammates on the
penultimate day of the match that my first over on the last day
would determine the fate of the Test match. My first over was a
maiden and I bowled another maiden, and that was it. Would I
concede a run that day? If I had to hit a penny on the ground on
that day, I would have done it at least five times out of six.

When I recall the Oval match, instances of our erratic,
sometimes even comical, fielding come back to mind, and those
memories make me laugh. Compton played a wild shot, the ball
went up in the air, and we saw my old friend Wazir running
and coming under the ball. He came towards the ball to catch it
with open hands, but the ball landed on his forehead. Compton
played another uppish shot over mid-on. Wazir turned, but
could not sight the ball which fell at his feet. I consoled him by
saying that the ball would come to him again. Compton again
played a wild shot and the ball went up in the air. Wazir saw
the ball and started running, but in the opposite direction to
where the ball was. We shouted at him to turn. He did and got
to the ball, but dropped it. Wazir, the elder brother of Hanif
Muhammad, was a very good batsman and a great friend of
mine.

Zulfiqar was another fielder with a difference. His display of
frustration after dropping a catch cannot be described in words.
He would not scold himself but berate the bowler. 'I was not
ready and you delivered the ball,' he would say.

However, Imtiaz Ahmad and Mahmood Hussain were a great
help to me in the Oval Test. Imtiaz was the only safe fielder of
the team. I always had a tremendous understanding with him,
and in the Oval Test this was at its peak. He knew exactly what
kind of a delivery I was to bowl and would adjust his position
accordingly behind the stumps. He was always prepared to take
a catch. My friend Mahmood Hussain bowled with extreme
determination throughout the Oval match. He generated pace
and was always on target. If I was containing the English
batsmen, Mahmood, too, was not allowing them any liberty. In
England's second innings, I was confident that Mahmood

Hussain would not allow the English batsmen to take the required runs. During the course of play, whenever I approached him with advice, he listened. If Mahmood were to bowl slow, I would tease him by calling him Marilyn Monroe, and after that he would hitch up his trousers which was an indication for the slip fielders to fall back by at least one yard since he was to bowl real quick.

After the Oval Test, the team was invited to a reception at the Victoria League by the Joint Empire Societies. The team members were interviewed on BBC television. Later in the night, we saw our faces flashing on the television screen in the popular programme *Sports Review*. We also saw the film of the Oval Test at the Pakistan House during the reception hosted by High Commissioner M.A.H. Ispahani. It was wonderful watching ourselves in action.

After our defeat in the second Test at Trent Bridge, an article by Daniel Bachelor had appeared in the *Picture Post* under the heading 'Two Cheers for Pakistan', maintaining that there was one bowler, Fazal Mahmood, and one batsman, Hanif Muhammad. The paper also published our photographs. The article suggested that Pakistan was awarded Test status a bit too early. But, when England conceded a three-run lead in the first innings of the Oval Test, the same British press showered great praise on the Pakistan cricket team. Sir Jack Hobbs, the legend of English cricket, wrote in the *Sunday Express* that Pakistanis were very nearly, if not quite, England's equals. Harry Ditton in the *News of the World* said, had Compton been dismissed on the first chance, Pakistan would have been more than a 100 runs ahead. He wrote, 'Fazal had bowled so well that he could scarcely hope ever to have a better day. His accuracy and stamina were things to marvel at, and that judged by any standard, he was a great bowler.' The British media gave warm and unstinted praise to the Pakistan team. The *Daily Herald* said, 'An England Foozle—no they were well and truly Fazaled. We mint the dreadful new verb from the name of Fazal Mahmood whose bowling helped Pakistan to victory in the Test and gave them a draw in the series.' The *Daily Sketch* wrote, 'Glory in the skill of the tall handsome policeman and an amateur cricketer.' In the same paper, Tony Stevens wrote, 'Throw aside our partisan feelings. Admit and give honour that one of the most underrated touring side ever to play in England could overcome rain and ridicule to rub the old lion's nose in the dust.'

Former England and Surrey captain A.E.R. Gilligan, in his exclusive column to *The Pakistan Times*, wrote:

> Pakistan's victory stamped Fazal as a bowler of world class. It is many years since I have witnessed such a wonderful bowling performance in both innings. It is perfectly true to say that Fazal never sent down one bad ball in the 60 overs he bowled. It was inspired bowling at his best. And when England with 168 to win had actually scored 109 for 2 he rose to his finest hour unleashing every thunderbolt at his command. Within half an hour by dismissing Peter May, Denis Compton and Godfrey Evans he had transformed what had looked like certain defeat into an amazing and dramatic victory. It was well-nigh super-human bowling by Fazal. I place him at almost top of the great bowlers in the world today. His performance in the Oval Test puts him to my mind, on the same pedestal as my 1924 colleague Maurice Tate.

Dr Tucker, the renowned physician and the most expensive—his consultation fee then was about £ 50—treated me free for a pulled thigh muscle in the Trent Bridge Test. A year later, when he was treating Nazar Muhammad, he asked him if he knew Fazal. When the reply was in the affirmative, he said, 'If you know Fazal then my treatment is gratis for Fazal's sake.' Then jokingly he told Nazar that 'had he known that Fazal was about to beat England he would not have treated him.' However, Dr Tucker took pride in the fact that he treated me, put me back on the field, and then it was England who were beaten at the Oval. The former president of the cricket control board of India, Subbarayan, while congratulating Pakistan, compared the Oval victory to the first victory of Australia over England on the latter's ground. 'Replace Spofforth by Fazal Mahmood and there you have the parallel,' he remarked.

It would be unfair to one unknown little girl if I do not mention her. One morning, after the Oval victory, I received a novel gift from a six-year-old school girl in the form of a letter with eleven pennies saved from her pocket money. This was the sweetest gift I ever received in my life. I immediately bought a doll from the bazaar and sent it to my little fan. I also received a special award of a 'County Silver Cup' and a cheque of 100 guineas from the makers of the famous Brylcream.

After the Oval Test, the players were impatiently waiting to return home. We departed from London on 24 September for Southampton. From there, we once again boarded the SS Battery and left for Karachi. We reached Karachi on 11 October where a large number of people welcomed us. After staying a couple of days in Karachi, Aslam Khokhar, Mahmood Hussain, and I left for Lahore by Khyber Mail. The train had to stop at various stations at least five to seven minutes more than the scheduled stop, because people wanted to garland me. The train was stopped even on those stations where it was not scheduled to. People just lay down in front of the engine to make it stop. I felt honoured. These were the kind of feelings which cannot be explained in words. When the train reached Lahore, people thronged all the platforms. As I was getting down from the train, one elderly person approached me and whispered in my ear in typical Punjabi, 'Phal ous darakht nou lagda hey jarah jukhda ay' (humility is ultimately rewarded). I remember it till today and try to be modest.

The Oval win was not a victory in cricket but something altogether different. The myth of British supremacy had been broken. England was beaten on its soil.

9

Pakistan Host India: 1954–55

The Indian team made its maiden tour of Pakistan in 1954–55 to play a five-Test series. There was great interest and enthusiasm among the people as it was the first tour of an Indian team to Pakistan after Partition. All the Test matches were to be of four days' duration.

The first Test at Dhaka in the former East Pakistan (now Bangladesh) was drawn. My bowling figures were 25-19-18-0 and 23-11-34-0. After the match, I went to India on a private visit and returned three days before the start of the second Test at Bahawalpur.

India won the toss at Bahawalpur, and Roy and Punjabi came to open the innings. In my first over, Roy was beaten by a sharp turning leg-cutter. He went forward defensively, but looked back to see the bails flying off. The matting wicket was not fast but cloudy weather and overnight dew helped me move the ball either way. Mankad came in and swung his bat dangerously at my bowling, missing each time. Mankad did not last long and with an individual score of 6, he edged me into the safe hands of Imtiaz. Mankad came to Pakistan with the reputation of being one of the greatest all-rounders of his time. But, he got involved with a lady from high society and played with divided concentration. Hanif after scoring a century at Bahawalpur, became the first Pakistani to score a hundred on home soil.

Maqsood played a remarkable innings in the Lahore Test. He exhibited wonderful strokes, well-timed square-cuts and placings. He kept the spectators spellbound as long as he stayed at the crease. But, if a batsman could be said to be unfortunate, it was him. His score reached 99 and he needed only one run to complete his maiden century in Test cricket. But, he seemed over-eager to get that very important single and tried to push Gupte. He was deceived with the spin and Vijay Tamhane did the rest. The tragedy did not end here for the next day we heard that a cricket fan from Nawabshah had died of a heart attack. He was listening to the running commentary on the radio when the commentator broke the news of Maqsood's dismissal for 99. The fan died on the spot.

There was speculation during the Lahore Test that Lala Amarnath would play the fourth Test at Peshawar, and the BCCI president, Maharajakumar Vizianagram, along with the Indian captain, Mankad, had indeed persuaded Lala to play in the Peshawar Test. Lala played a three-day match against The Services XI at Rawalpindi, scored an unbeaten 55, and took two wickets. However, he did not play in the Peshawar Test.

After the Lahore Test, I was asked to lead the Punjab cricket team in a three-day match against India at Sialkot. On the opening day of the match, I injured my right foot while stopping a full-blooded shot off my own bowling. The x-ray showed injury to my bone and the doctor advised me ten days rest, causing me to miss the Peshawar Test.

We displayed the most pathetic batting performance of the series on an easy Peshawar turf. Both Gupte and Mankad did not allow our batsmen to take any liberties. Had there not been a steady third-wicket partnership between Waqar and Maqsood, we might have been out for under 100 runs. We made 129 runs by the end of the first day. Play on the last day of the Test, however, was full of excitement. India was on top when play started. Waqar, Wazir, and Kardar followed each other into the pavilion, and it was then left to Imtiaz and Maqsood to guide Pakistan out of danger. They played a match-saving fifth-wicket partnership. Imtiaz was in a vengeful mood. He attacked the Indian bowling when it was right on top and scattered the fielders helter-skelter. Till his arrival, the match had seemed firmly in India's bag. Imtiaz's innings was full of aggression and he was particularly severe on Gupte. Maqsood, on the other end, sacrificed his natural style and put up a dogged fight to save his team from clear defeat.

Our first innings total in the Karachi Test was 162. The bowlers had a difficult task to restrict the Indian batsmen within this total. However, the prospects of a decision in this Test became probable when we bowled India out for 145 runs and scored 69 for two at the close of the second day's play. Overnight rain delayed play for about three and half hours on the third day. When Pakistan started its innings, the Indian captain went on the defensive. Pakistan's score reached 200 for five after lunch on the fourth and last day. With the addition of 17 runs as a first innings lead, 217 was not an easy target to achieve in about three hours time. But, Kardar thought otherwise and delayed his decision till he was out on 93, with the total score of 236, and then waited for Alim to complete his century before finally declaring the innings at a total of 241.

The conditions in the Karachi Test were conducive to my kind of bowling. In spite of the fact that I was not given the new ball, I was confident that the Indians would not be able to score more than 150 runs. My plan was very simple. I would request Khan Muhammad and Mahmood Hussain to bowl with full fire and attack the Indian batsmen, whereas I would, for now, allow them to take any liberties with my bowling. But Kardar, perhaps, had lost confidence in his bowlers and that swayed his decision in favour of delaying the declaration. He probably thought that to score a run in a minute would be easy for the Indian batsmen but forgot that it needed courage, which they lacked. This was proven when in the remaining two hours India scored only 69 runs for the loss of two wickets.

The people in Pakistan showed great interest in the Test series with India. They thronged the grounds where the matches were played. When 47-year old Miran Bukhsh clean bowled Manjrekar in the Lahore Test, the crowd danced with joy, waved their handkerchiefs, and shouted in excitement. The total attendance during the Lahore Test was more than 50,000. A few thousand Indian citizens also came from Amritsar, Jallundhar, and Ambala to witness the match. The Lahorites received them with open arms and not a single anti-India slogan was raised.

The series with India was not free from some minor controversies involving the cricketing authorities of both countries. During the Lahore Test, the BCCP proposed that the fourth Test at Peshawar be played on matting instead of turf. Lala Amarnath, the manager of the Indian cricket team, objected to the proposal. The BCCP's stand was that when the tour was being arranged, the BCCI had been informed that this match may be played either on turf or on a matting wicket. Lala had agreed to play on matting, but later learnt that the BCCI president was arriving in Lahore to discuss the matter. Then there were reports that the venue of the fourth Test might be shifted to Lahore if the turf wicket was not available at Peshawar. However, the match was played on the turf wicket of the Peshawar club ground. After the drawn Peshawar Test, the BCCP proposed to its counterpart to extend the fifth Test at Karachi to five days, but this was not accepted.

Before the Karachi Test, Lala had expressed his reservations about the umpiring in Lahore and Peshawar Tests, which, according to him, was unsatisfactory. However, he gave no examples to substantiate his point. The umpire, Idrees Baig, reacted to Lala's statement and requested the BCCP to drop his name from the Karachi Test. The BCCP changed umpires to take into account the sensitivities of the visitors.

10

MCC-A and Australia Visit Pakistan: 1955–56

The England cricket board sent its MCC-A team to Pakistan in the winter of 1955–56 to play four unofficial Test matches. Our players were visibly disturbed about the unofficial status of the Test matches that were to be played at home. They had already played official Test matches against England on their soil and had beaten them in at least one Test at the Oval. Perhaps the England cricket board wanted to avoid further embarrassment. They had not yet gotten over the Oval Test defeat and did not want to risk sending their Test team fearing that it would be badly exposed in Pakistan. On arrival in Karachi, Donald Carr, the MCC captain stated: 'I will not touch the shores of England until I avenge the Oval defeat.' They seemed to be still nursing their injuries. However, Pakistan easily beat the MCC and won the series.

In October 1956, after losing the Ashes series, Australia stopped over in Karachi to play a one-off Test. The BCCP had proposed to the Australian cricket board a two-Test series, but because of their own domestic commitments they agreed to only one. The Australian team was studded with world-class cricketers—Keith Miller, Neil Harvey, Ray Lindwall, and Alan Davidson. It was not easy for the BCCP to field a strong team against the Kangaroos. Gul Muhammad, an All-India Test cricketer was back in Pakistan. After prolonged discussions, he was included in the team.

The match was played on a lifeless matting wicket. The ball came off with little pace, but lifted occasionally from a good length. Khan Muhammad and I bowled unchanged for nearly four hours. Ours was a sort of combined operation in which we did not allow the batsmen any opportunity to relax. They had to play each and every ball. I got the wickets of the first six batsmen, while Khan took the remaining four. While I never wavered in length and direction and attacked the stumps vigorously, Khan's sustained accuracy always pinned down the batsmen. The Australians were all out for a paltry 80 runs on the first day of the Test.

Our batting was pathetic. We lost five wickets for only 70 runs. It seemed that the achievements of the first day were wasted. However, a defiant partnership between Kardar and Wazir gave us the lead. Kardar's attacking knock was morale boosting and we scored 199 runs. The Australians again struggled for runs in the second innings. The great Keith Miller had no clue to one complete over that I bowled to him. He was lucky to be dropped by Khan Muhammad at square-leg. Burke cut me violently and the ball went like a bullet towards Wallis, who held a spectacular one-handed catch to dismiss Burke. The sixth-wicket partnership between Benaud and Davidson denied us an innings victory. Though Benaud scored the highest runs in Australia's second innings, it was Davidson who played the more polished innings. His strokes were masterful. Some of his cover-drives were a treat to watch.

Australia was all out for 187 runs just after lunch, leaving us to score 69 runs to win in about three hours. Though it was not a difficult task, but our batsmen were subdued by the accurate bowling of Miller, Davidson, and Lindwall. The scoreboard moved at snail's pace and it almost exhausted the patience of the crowd. They started booing at the batsmen. At one stage the booing increased to the point that Alim jokingly offered his bat to the crowd. We finished the fourth day needing six runs to win. Had our batsmen showed a little more courage we could well have won the match on the fourth day. More than 20,000 spectators who had paid to watch the game, waited impatiently. They yelled at our batsmen. It was a rare occasion that the batsmen leading their team to victory were booed on their home ground. However, a fairly large crowd saw Pakistan beating Australia by nine wickets on the last day.

Although I got 13 wickets in the match, I was unlucky to miss a hat-trick. In Australia's second innings, I bowled Benaud fifth ball and trapped Lindwall leg before the next ball. In my next over, Johnson survived the first ball and was bowled the second delivery. Archer luckily escaped. He was beaten, and the ball hit the stumps but the bails did not fall off.

Before the visit of the Australian cricket team in 1956, Kardar led a team under the name of 'The Writers Club' to Kenya. Almost all the Pakistani Test cricketers were in the team. I refused a go to Kenya as it was a 'dinner dance' trip. Kardar tried to persuade me, but I wanted to prepare myself for the Australians. I went to Murree and stayed there for one month at Sams Hotel. My daily work drill was climbing up and walking down the mountains for twenty to twenty-five miles. I would eat fresh fruit and vegetables. Sultan, the owner of the hotel, watched me with great interest. He was amazed by my daily routine. On the second last day, he asked me why was I doing all those exercises. When I told him, he asked me what I thought of the Australian team. 'I will get them out under 100 runs,' I said. 'Impossible', was his reply. Then he said that if the Australians were dismissed for under 100 runs he would withdraw the hotel bill, otherwise he would charge double. When the Australian team was bowled out for 80 runs in the Karachi Test in October 1956, I received a telegram from him which said, 'QUITS.'

The victory against Australia marked the end of the first chapter of Pakistan's cricket history. It was the end of its childhood. After beating the two giants of the cricket world— England and Australia—Pakistan successfully ended the so-called teething stage of a precocious child. The cricket toddlers of four years ago, who tumbled an astonished elder at the Oval, were now full-grown adults. Though it remained, of course, the youngest cricketing nation, yet it had earned a place among the strongest.

11

Playing the West Indies at Home and Abroad: 1958–59

After defeating England at the Oval, Pakistan was recognized among the top cricket playing nations. We had also easily beaten Australia at Karachi in October 1956. This was not a small achievement for a young side who had gained ICC membership only four years earlier. Now every Test playing country wanted to play with Pakistan. The West Indies cricket board was also eager to invite the Pakistan team. It had been the first team that had visited Pakistan soon after its independence. Besides this, it had supported Pakistan at the ICC meeting, which was to decide on Pakistan's application to be given the status of a Test playing country. Both the BCCP and the West Indies cricket board agreed to play a five-Test match series. They also agreed that the Test matches would be of six-day duration.

The BCCP consequently organized a training camp at Bahawalpur. Maqsood, Zulfiqar, and Shuja were invited to the camp, but were not included in the final squad. The selectors included three new faces in the team, namely Saeed Ahmad, Haseeb Ahsan, and Nasimul Ghani.

The Pakistan cricket team embarked on the West Indies tour in January 1958. This series was a real test of the Pakistani cricketer's calibre, endurance, patience, attack, and defence. After playing three representative matches, Pakistan played its first Test against the West Indies at Bridgetown. This match shall always be remembered as Hanif's match as he played the longest innings in Test cricket history. The West Indies piled a huge total of 579 runs. In the second innings, Pakistan needed

473 runs to avoid an innings' defeat. Imtiaz and Hanif scored
152 runs for the first wicket. Imtiaz played a daring innings
when he mercilessly hooked and pulled Gilchrist. One of
Gilchrist's bouncers glanced Imtiaz's chin and we thought that
perhaps it had hurt him badly. But, Imtiaz stood his ground
with great determination and courage and the next bouncer
from Gilchrist was hit hard across the ropes. Gilchrist was tamed
after this and he was no longer a threat to our batsmen. At the
other end, Hanif calmly guarded his fort. He put his head down
and dominated the crease, scoring at a snail's pace, as was the
need of the time. Saeed, too, made a useful contribution of 65
runs. At the age of sixteen, Nasim became the youngest player
in the history of cricket to make his Test debut. Hunt and
Weekes excelled from the West Indies side. They both scored
centuries. Weekes missed his double century by three runs. In
fact, this innings brought much relief to Weekes who had scored
only 17 runs in five previous Test innings, including a duck at
the Oval against England.

The second Test at Port-of-Spain was a close match, most of
the time, though we lost by 120 runs in the end. Kanhai, Weekes,
and Sobers were the run-getters, while Gilchrist tormented our
batsmen with his pace and Smith baffled them with his accurate
off-spin bowling. Wallis Mathias and I made 73 and 60 runs
respectively in the first innings, while Hanif and Saeed excelled
with 81 and 64 runs in the second innings.

The third Test was played at Kingston. Mahmood Hussain
pulled his thigh muscle after bowling only five balls in the West
Indies' first innings and could not continue. In the second Test
at Port-of-Spain, a bouncer from Dewdney had glanced Hanif's
nose. It seemed that it had hit him badly, but it actually had
not, although his confidence was shaken. At Kingston, Hanif
dropped down from being the opening batsman to the middle
order. Kardar was playing the match with a broken left hand
finger. Nasim was also not fit. However, Khan Muhammad was
back in the team after missing the first two Tests.

The West Indies established its supremacy in all aspects of
the game. Sobers made history by overtaking Sir Leonard

Hutton's record of 364 against Australia in 1938. Hunt, too, made a double century and the West Indies scored a total of 790 for 3. My bowling figures were 85.2-20-247-2. Imtiaz and Wazir scored centuries for Pakistan, and Mathias, Saeed, and Kardar scored fifties. Both Mahmood Hussain and Nasim did not bat in Pakistan's second innings because of injuries. We lost the match by an innings and 174 runs.

By the start of the fourth Test at Georgetown, I was the only fit attack bowler as both Khan Muhammad and Mahmood Hussain were on the injured list. Kardar shared the new ball with me. With the West Indies winning the fourth Test at Georgetown, they had scored three wins in a row. However, our batsmen made useful runs against a very fiery attack. Saeed played a dashing innings of 150. His innings was a blend of aggression and power. He hit every West Indies' bowler hard. His hook shots against Gilchrist and Dewdney were simply classic. Wazir played a courageous innings in the second knock. He ran short of partners and missed his century by three runs. Kardar made 56. I was hit on the knee by a Gilchrist delivery and had to be given several injections in the hospital, but the pain was intolerable. In the West Indies' second innings, I could bowl only four overs and was forced to leave the field. Sobers was in great form in the match and made centuries in each innings of the Test, while Walcott and Hunt also did the same.

Pakistan won the fifth Test at Trinidad, and salvaged some of its lost pride by defeating the West Indies by an innings and one run. The West Indies were dismissed for a moderate score of 268 in the first innings. I took 6 wickets for 83 runs. The remaining 4 wickets were shared equally by Khan Muhammad and Nasim. Wazir Muhammad's masterly innings helped Pakistan gain a lead of 228 runs. Saeed missed his century by three runs. In the second innings, Nasim did not allow the West Indies batsmen to take liberties with his bowling. Only Walcott faced him with confidence. Nasim got 6 wickets including that of Sobers, Hunt, and Walcott. Haseeb, too, bowled well in the second innings and got the valuable wickets of Weekes and Kanhai.

This West Indies tour was very difficult for me. I was fighting against all odds within the team and faced external pressures. I was given a leather ball sewn with fine cable-wire which would pierce through my finger. I could not rotate the ball. Rotation with speed was my main weapon. I had been denied my leg-cutter which was a wicket-taking ball. I had to grip the ball from the centre and it let me down. I protested, but the skipper did not agree. The manager, Brigadier Haider, had not the faintest idea about cricket. He was always busy in his off-the-field activities and so there was no point in complaining to him. I had no option but to opt for a variation of pace and the use of the crease. However, in the last Test, a thread-sewn ball was used and Pakistan defeated the West Indies.

Saeed Ahmad was the find of the tour. This attractive young batsman treated the West Indies pace battery mercilessly and was the most consistent batsman on the tour. By beating West Indies, Pakistan maintained its record of beating every Test cricket playing country on its first foray—India at Lucknow (1952), England at the Oval (1954), New Zealand at Karachi (1955–56), Australia at Karachi (1956), and the West Indies at Port-of-Spain (1958). The tour also marked the end of Kardar's career. After the end of this series, he announced his retirement from Test cricket.

The umpiring in the West Indies was not good. Whenever any local batsman would cross 90, the umpire would perform the sacred duty of helping him complete his century. The umpire would be lucky if the batsman was bowled, because otherwise the spectators would not have spared him. Almost all the visiting teams had expressed their reservations about the umpiring in the West Indies. When England visited that country in 1955, the crowd not only beat an umpire who had given an unfavourable decision against the home batsman but also burnt his house.

In the first Test, Imtiaz was out to a controversial leg before decision when he was 9 short of his well-deserved century. During the second Test at Kingston, the umpires did not give a couple of decisions in our favour. I remember that after the end of the match I casually asked the umpire, 'What do you think about those decisions?' Back came the reply: 'Fazal, when are you going back home?' 'After a couple of weeks,' I answered. 'Well, I have to live here,' the umpire mumbled. After the West Indies tour, the Pakistan team flew to the USA to play some festival matches there and in Canada. I did not join the team because of my professional commitments with East Lancashire, so I left for London.

After defeating India 3–0 in a five-Test series, the West Indies again arrived in Karachi in February 1959 to play a three-Test series. The BCCP invited me to lead the team. Although I had not lobbied for the job, I knew it would come to me. After Kardar had announced his retirement from Test cricket, I was the obvious choice. Kardar was made the chairman of the selection committee. However, I had clearly told the BCCP that I would not allow the selection committee to impose its team on me and that I should have a definite say in the selection.

Before the arrival of the West Indies team, the BCCP organized a training camp at Karachi. Tarpaulin tents were installed outside the National Stadium, Karachi, and we were supposed to live in those tents. This was normal in those good old days, and it was fun. Besides batting, bowling, and fielding practice, the players were also given extensive physical training. I found out that some boys were coming back late at night, so the next day I ordered everything doubled. The daily workload went up from ten to twenty miles with the result that the boys came back in time and became even fitter.

One day we were informed that President Field Marshal Muhammad Ayub Khan would visit the training camp and meet the boys. Ayub Khan was a keen sportsman and took a deep interest in the development of sports in Pakistan. He came to the camp and watched the players practising and spoke some words of encouragement to the players, 'When war is not on, the best place for the promotion of team spirit is the sports field. The West Indies is a tough side but you all look good too.' He declared that he and his staff would purchase tickets and watch the match. After his announcement, the gate receipts were very large as the complimentary passes and tickets disappeared.

There were reports that the West Indies cricket board had asked Sir Frank Worrell to lead the team in Pakistan. He was willing, but his tutor at Manchester University had advised him not to accept the invitation as it would badly affect his chances of success in his exams. So, he informed the board of his unavailability. In his place, Alexander captained the team.

The morale of the West Indies team was high before the start of the first Test at Karachi because only a couple of days before they had convincingly beaten India. Despite the fact that the West Indies team was packed with world-class batsmen, I had complete faith in my bowlers. We won the toss, and put them in to bat. We got an early breakthrough when opener Conard Hunt edged my leg-cutter into the hands of Imtiaz. Kanhai and Holt played defensive cricket. They were careful, avoided playing strokes, and built a good partnership for their team. Nasim got us a breakthrough, and after that it was hard for the West Indies batsmen to stay at the wicket. They were 62 for 2, 63 for 3, 117 for 8, and 146 all out. Nasim bowled a teasing length. The batsmen were extra cautious on my bowling, but they tried to take liberties with Nasim, and the result was that either they were caught in the middle or stumped.

Hanif with 103 and Saeed with 78 put us in a good position, and we gained a lead of 158 runs. Because of some dropped catches by the West Indies, we managed 245 runs in the second innings. Butcher with 61 and Solomon with 66 tried their best to salvage the situation. In our second innings, Hanif retired hurt. His injury was mysterious. First, it was reported that he had a knee injury, but the press later reported that he had a fractured finger. However, Ijaz Butt scored well and Pakistan won the match by 8 wickets.

We played the second Test without Hanif Muhammad which weakened our batting considerably. The West Indies won the toss and put us in to bat. Our batsmen could not face the fiery spell of Wes Hall. At one stage we were 22 for 5. But, Wallis Mathias and Shuja then got together and their fighting partnership saved us from utter humiliation. We were all out for 145 runs in the first innings. When play ended on the first day, the West Indies had lost two wickets for 20 runs. When the team reached the hotel, I confined myself to my room and began planning our strategy for the next day. Though 145 runs were not an easy total to defend, yet I was confident. I knew that at the Oval, Pakistan had scored 133 runs and yet we had gained a three-run psychological lead. Imtiaz, Mahmood Hussain, and Wazir Muhammad joined me in my room. Together, we discussed and finalized our strategy.

The second day of the match was very exciting. The West Indies batsmen fared even worse than us. They were forced to play according to our set plan and their last six batsmen were out with the addition of only 11 runs. It was amazing. The West Indies were all out for 76 runs. We did not bat well even in the second innings. Mathias once again played a courageous innings of 45 runs, and Pakistan was all out for 144 runs. The West Indies needed 214 runs to win the match.

During tea interval on the last day of the match, the governor of East Pakistan and the foreign minister, Manzoor Qadir, approached me and asked: 'Fazal, where do we stand in the match?' I looked at the clock and said, 'Sir, I shall be back from the field after one hour.' 'I hope with victory,' remarked the foreign minister. 'The victory is in our pocket, sir,' I said firmly. It is said that when a batting pair is well set and is on a scoring spree, lunch and tea intervals become good bowlers. The batsmen continue to believe that they are well set whereas they are not. Mahmood Hussain and I proved too good for them. They were all out for 172 runs, and Pakistan won by 41 runs.

After winning two Tests in a row, I was a satisfied man. Now I could take risks in the third and final Test at Lahore. I wanted to play Mushtaq, and the younger brother of Hanif Muhammad then a young lad of fourteen. His name was missing from the team list that the selectors had given to me. Mushtaq had scored a fine 53 in a three-day match against the West Indies. The youngster had flair and promise. On my insistence, he was included in the team. When the selectors had earlier announced the team, Mushtaq decided to return to Karachi, and took the train back the same day. When his name was finally included, he was not around. A man was rushed to the railway station, with very little time left for the train to depart. After much difficulty, he managed to locate Mushtaq. The youngster was lying on the berth in one of the compartments. Mushtaq was brought to the field to play in the Test match.

Dropped catches by our fielders allowed the West Indies to pile up 469 runs, batting first after winning the toss. Kanhai scored a double century. We followed-on as Wes Hall ran through our middle order batting. He even got a hat trick. In the second innings, our batting again crumbled against Atkinson, Gibbs, and Ramadhin, and we suffered an innings defeat. Two factors went against us. We batted in conditions made difficult by a combination of poor light and drizzle. Poor light helped Hall to complete his hat trick.

BENEFIT MATCH

After Pakistan defeated the West Indies 2–1 in the home series of 1958–59, some enthusiasts and diehard fans in the government and business community, decided to organize a benefit match for me. A committee was formed by Qamarul Islam (a senior bureaucrat known as the wizard of taxation) and Fakharuddin Valika (he set up the first mill at Karachi after Partition which was inaugurated by Mr Jinnah). The committee headed by Qamarul Islam concluded an agreement with the then BCCP for the holding of a Fazal Mahmood Benefit Match. The BCCP allowed the National Stadium, Karachi as the venue of the match. The enclosures were fabricated and were sold out to various business groups. As far as possible all administrative formalities were completed.

The committee invited almost all the leading cricket celebrities to play in that match and they all gladly accepted. To name a few: Sir Don Bradman, Sir Len Hutton, Keith Miller, Dennis Compton, Jim Laker, Lala Amarnath, Vijay Merchant,

Frank Worrell and Everton Weekes. Two teams were raised—
one led by Sir Len Hutton and the other by Sir Don Bradman.

As the committee was in the process of finalizing the dates of
the match Abdul Hafeez Kardar jumped into the arena on an
identical pattern—the way he was made the captain of the
Pakistan team. His suggestion was that his name also be
bracketed with mine. Kardar had the backing of then BCCP
secretary Mir Muhammad Hussain who wrote a letter to the
organizing committee insisting that Kardar's name should also
be bracketed with Fazal Mahmood to which the committee
declined. The BCCP had no right to interfere because it was in
agreement with the organizing committee for the holding of a
Fazal Mahmood Benefit Match. It was a flagrant breach of
agreement. It was not justice. I was furious as it was all 'take
the cream of the milk and brag about it'. However, Mir
Muhammad Hussain manipulated things on behalf of Kardar
and gave the impression to the organizing committee that he
was doing all this on the instructions of President Muhammad
Ayub Khan, the then chief of the BCCP. The match was
abandoned with regrets to all the invitees. Pakistan cricket
would have gone sky high were that match had played and all
the players participated in it.

12

Captaining in India: 1960–61

The Australians came to Pakistan in November 1959 to play a three-Test series with Richie Benaud as the captain. He had been a member of the Australian team that visited Pakistan in 1956 and had lost the one-off test at Karachi. This time the Australiens were well prepared.

The first Test was played at Dhaka. Richie won the toss and put us in to bat. Except for Hanif, who made 66, and new Test cap, Duncan Sharpe, with 56, no other batsman could handle the Australian attack. However, apart from a very responsible innings of 96 by Harvey, the Australians too did not respond confidently. They were 151 for 8 when a fine duel between Harvey and myself ended with his dismissal. At this stage it seemed that we would take a thirty plus first innings lead, but wicket keeper batsman Wally Grout's glorious innings shattered our hopes, and, instead, the Kangaroos took a 25-runs first innings lead.

We batted poorly in the second innings also, and succumbed cheaply to the guile of the medium-paced off-breaks of Ken Mackay, who took 6 wickets. Benaud grabbed the other 4 wickets. Duncan Sharpe again scored a polished 35 runs. We made 134 runs. The Australians, needing 110 runs to win, achieved the target by losing just two wickets.

I missed the second Test at Lahore because of a thigh injury. The match was played in the newly built Lahore (now Gaddafi) stadium. Imtiaz led the Pakistan team in my absence. This Test would always be remembered as the Saeed-Shuja match. There was a heroic partnership between them, but fine bowling by

Kline on the last day resulted in another victory for the Australians in the closing minutes of the game.

I was back in the third and final Test at Karachi. Pakistan were two down in the series. My endeavour was to stop the Australians from making a clean sweep. We tried out Intikhab Alam, a 17-year-old youngster in the Test. He created history when he clean bowled Colin McDonald who played the first ball from him as a leg-break but which was, in fact, a straight ball. In the second innings, Hanif scored a match-saving century and the Test was drawn.

Every tournament and Test series has its own significance, but the Pakistan cricket team's tour to India in 1960–61 was the most difficult and painstaking tour of my whole career. I had already led the Pakistan team in the two home series against the West Indies and Australia. Pakistan won the series against the West Indies and lost to the Australians. But, leading the Pakistan team against India was a difficult task. Test matches between these arch rivals are very closely watched and hotly contested to this day. Neither side wants to lose the match or the series. The Indian team had won in their first ever visit to Pakistan in 1954–55. With this background, the Pakistan cricket team arrived in India in November 1960.

I had damaged my knee by over bowling, well before the start of the Indian tour and I went to England for treatment. When I came back, the training camp for the selection of the team was in progress at the Lahore stadium. I was absolutely bewildered to see what was happening in the camp. It was a routine kind of net practice, much like what was done in the 1930s. When I tried to make some changes, I was told to stop. Thus, I had to do my own training and practice in the Bagh-i-Jinnah cricket ground.

Kardar had come out of retirement. Both Kardar and I were mentally, physically, and outwardly not only on trial, but the loyalties and the association of other players were also divided. Prior to the selection of the Pakistan team, a three-day match was organized at the Bagh-i-Jinnah cricket ground. Hafeez led one side and I led the other. This was a test in the true sense of the word. During the course of play, it was announced that I would be captain of the touring team. I was called to the selection committee meeting. Mian Muhammad Saeed, Dr Jahangir Khan, and another person were sitting in the room. They showed me a list of some fifteen players that they had already selected. For the sixteenth player, they gave me two names, asking me to choose—Shafqat Rana and Zafar Altaf. My answer was pretty straight, 'You have picked the team. This trivial issue can also be resolved by you.' Zafar Altaf was picked to go on the Indian tour. The five-Test match series ended in a draw amidst controversial umpiring decisions. Out of a total of thirty-two umpiring decisions twenty-eight went against us. I cannot forget some of those decisions even after four decades have gone by.

THE FIRST TEST: BOMBAY

After playing a couple of side matches, the Pakistan team arrived in Bombay to play the first Test. Before the match, Nari Contractor, the captain of the Indian team, and I had a meeting about the playing conditions. The Test matches were being played under the MCC rules. I knew that the Indian team was depending, and rightly so, on their batting. It was decided that since proper covers were not available, the wickets would not be covered during the Test matches. It was also decided that because of the hot weather, drinks would be served on the ground every forty-five minutes instead of every hour. Interestingly, these two points went in Pakistan's favour. Without covers, the overnight dew favoured our bowlers. The Indian batting became timid, and in the morning session their batsmen were more vulnerable to our bowlers. Their run rate in the five Test matches was nearly 120 runs a day as compared to Pakistan's 170. I remember teasing Lala Amarnath, 'Amu, 120 runs a day and you expect to beat us?'

The tour selection committee met on the eve of the Test match but had to adjourn for an hour. The reason was a domestic issue similar to that which had arisen during the Dhaka Test against the West Indies in 1958–59. One of our star batsmen demanded match fee, failing which he had a 'bruised' finger. I had no such money at my disposal. As luck would have it, Malik Mubarik and Malik Bari, two film magnates from Lahore, were also sitting in my room where the conversation was held. Malik Mubarik pulled out his chequebook and handed over a cheque of a few thousand rupees to the batsman. He insisted that he should be paid in Indian currency. It was frustrating. However, the matter was settled and he played the Bombay Test.

The umpiring in the Bombay Test was atrocious. There was no such thing as caught behind or leg before for the Indian batsmen. The umpires disturbed our bowlers by frequently calling no balls. On the second day, when India was playing its first innings after lunch, shortly before the tea break I broke into Nari Contractor's defence and he was clean bowled. Nari started to walk towards the pavilion and then stopped. To my bewilderment, the umpire had pulled his hand out, declaring my delivery to be a no-ball. 'Why didn't you call the no-ball in the first place?' I asked the umpire. 'The chewing gum got stuck in my throat,' came the most innocent reply. Again, on the fourth day of the match, before the lunch interval, Hanif Muhammad, Mushtaq Muhammad, and Haseeb Ahsan argued with umpire Ganguli. Noticing that the umpire called no-ball on a delivery by Haseeb, both Hanif at mid-on and Mushtaq at mid-off decided to keep a check on Haseeb's bowling. When the umpire once again called a no-ball, they rushed to him to convince him that Haseeb had not crossed the line. Ganguli was not convinced.

The Pakistan high commissioner in India, A.K. Brohi, had came to watch the match. He asked me what was happening. I told him about some of the umpiring decisions. That night there was a banquet in the cricket club of India. Nearly one thousand guests attended that dinner. Before the dinner, selected speakers delivered speeches. When it was Mr A.K. Brohi's turn, he rose and made a very interesting speech:

Gentlemen, I have probably become a talking machine since this is my seventh speech today. I hardly know about the game of cricket. I came to Bombay in a double capacity as High Commissioner and secondly because I had promised Fazal that I would watch him in action. While I was having my dinner, Mr Chidambaram on my left, a great business magnate and President of BCCI, and Wala Bahai Koshal Patel on my right, apprised me about the game. They used a phrase 'benefit of doubt' which always goes to the batsmen. These words intrigued me because I am a lawyer by profession and these words are often used in courts. I did not know that the Indian batsmen were such great criminals that every time the benefit of doubt goes to them. Thank you.

The audience burst into laughter.

The Second Test: Kanpur

After the Bombay Test match, we played a three-day match at Nagpur. From Nagpur, we travelled by train to Kanpur, the venue of the second Test match. It was a long and tortuous journey. During the journey, I thought hard of how to neutralize the Indian umpires, and how to counter Indian plans. They had to be convinced to stay within the norms of cricket—meaning fair play. The entire group of Indian and Pakistani cricketers and officials stayed at the Kamlapat Retreat. In the evening, I saw Ram Parkash Latto dining alone. I knew Latto from Lahore. He was a resident of Ghumti Bazar, a locality inside the old city of Lahore. Before Partition, he was a member of the City Gymkhana, a leading cricket club in the pre-Partition days. We had played a lot of cricket together. He was lovingly known as 'Latto' in the cricket circles of Lahore. This name has an interesting story behind it. Ram Parkash was a very good batsman and loved to play the hook shot. He was short, and his stance was very clumsy and he would bend his knees in such a way that the handle of his bat would almost touch the ground. He would hook the ball in such a gawky fashion that his whole body would spin like a 'top'. It was because of this peculiar style of hooking the ball that his friends named him 'Latto', meaning a top.

I joined Ram Parkash Latto at his table. He was then the secretary of the BCCI. During the course of our conversation, I asked him: 'Latto, there was a time when you were my captain in the NICA and you termed the captaincy as a garland of thorns.' I told him that the standard of umpiring was bad. I politely asked him about their designs against us? His response was amazing. He told me in typical Punjabi: *'Ballee, jay braber chala janwany tha jit da sera apna ser samgian'*, meaning 'Boy, if you draw the series then consider yourself a victor.' I gave him a matching reply by saying, 'Latto, defeat is not in my book.' 'What will you do?' he provoked me. I said with confidence and courage, 'Just a few bouncers will decide the issue.'

After the Delhi Test match, an official banquet was held in the Ashoka Hotel which was attended by both the teams and officials of the BCCI. Before dinner, officials of both sides delivered speeches. Being the captain of the team, I was also called to speak on the occasion. I made a very brief speech. My words were: 'When I arrived in India, a very senior member of the BCCI apprised me of the situation here, and said that if I went undefeated, I should consider myself victorious. Now I am going undefeated. Does the honourable member of the BCCI have the courage to come forward and garland me because I am the victor? Thank you.'

The umpiring standard in the second Test match at Kanpur was also poor. On the second day of the Test match, Pakistan were all out for 335 runs. Twenty minutes were left for the close of play when the Indian captain, Nari Contractor, and Jaisimha opened their innings. Nari played a full-fledged cut on the second ball of Mahmood Hussain. Imtiaz leapt at the ball, fumbled at the first attempt but held the catch in the second attempt. All the players appealled in jubilation. Joshi, the umpire, turned his head away. When we pressed that Nari had played the ball and Imtiaz had collected a fair and neat catch, Joshi's answer stunned us. 'I didn't see the ball because the bowler had come in my way,' he uttered innocently. 'We held the catch, and that should have been enough,' I told Nari, but he acted as if nothing had happened. I asked Ganguli, the short-leg umpire, who said that he did not see it either. What could I do? That was not cricket. Had the umpire given Nari out, the Indians would have come under pressure and we might have got a couple of more Indian wickets.

On the third day, soon after the start of play, I beat Jaisimha plumb in front of the stumps, in the area between the bowling and the popping crease. I appealed in jubilation, but the umpire stood there motionless.

THE THIRD TEST: CALCUTTA

We were in an absolute winning position in the Calcutta (now Kolkata) Test. There was a cloud cover on the third morning of the Test match and I was getting some assistance from the wicket. I beat Manjrekar twice, but he survived. However, after lunch, his defence was smashed. He failed to read one of my leg-cutters and left the ball alone. The ball moved in the air and off the wicket, came in very sharply, and Vijay Manjrekar was clean bowled. Soon I got Nandkarni's wicket too. Pakistan was clearly on top. The Indians had already lost Polly Umrigar, probably their best batsman in the series. The Indian batsmen looked helpless in the middle. Desai came to bat after the fall of Nandkarni. At this stage, it began to drizzle. I bowled a straight one to Desai, which rapped him on his pads. He immediately made an appeal for poor light and rain, and was upheld by the umpire, Ganguli. Rain stopped after about an hour, so both Nari and I came out to check the possibility of play. I was eager to start the match as the outfield was all right. However, Nari disagreed with me. The umpires inspected the wicket after the tea interval. Ultimately, they gave their final verdict at teatime– no play. An outside chance to beat India at Calcutta was blocked by the Indian umpires.

There was plenty of rain on the off day of the match as well. On the fourth morning of the match, Nari came into our dressing room and we both went to inspect the wicket. The ground was dry, and while walking towards the middle, he remarked that it had rained overnight. I was speechless. It was clear that the opinions on the condition of the pitch were being dictated by the state of the game, and it was obvious that we both differed. Naturally, I was keen to start the innings, but Nari was resisting. He only saw one end of the field and told the umpires that the wicket was not playable. The umpires made a lengthy inspection and decided to re-inspect the wicket during the lunch hour. According to the rules then, the wicket could be declared unplayable only if the state of the wicket was such that it was likely to cause injury to players. The wicket was not wet. Nevertheless, play remained suspended just because the umpires felt the state of the wicket and the ground was not perfect for the resumption of the match. Almost one day's play was lost. India had not completed its first innings. Amid this controversy, Subramanium, a commentator on the All India Radio, ridiculed the decision of the umpire saying, 'If play was suspended under the kind of playing conditions here in Calcutta, the British would not have enjoyed even one day of cricket in Britain.' A real sad commentary on Indian cricket. After these remarks, Subramanium was not allowed on air for the remaining two Test matches. Nearly 80,000 people watched the game. No one could offer any excuse for not resuming play.

It has been said that war is too serious a business to be left in the hands of the generals. Equally true is that Test cricket is too serious a business to be left in the unchecked control of the umpires. Eventually, the match resumed after lunch. The follow-on was averted, and India was no longer in danger of losing the match. It would not be out of context to mention here the speech of an Indian minister in the central government made during a dinner in Calcutta. 'My heart cries out when I see that we, the politicians, have drawn a line between the two countries. I feel so happy when I see youngsters from both sides of the line sitting together happily, eating from one plate. How wonderful it would be if this line was removed and we could become one as we were in the past.' I asked our team manager, Dr Jehangir, to answer, but he was reluctant. So, naturally, I had to stand up. I did not want the minister's words to be registered without an appropriate response. After complimenting the hospitality that was extended to us, I made particular reference to the remarks made by the Indian minister. Apprising him that his was a political speech, I said: 'We have come to India to play cricket, not to enter into politics. I wish the honourable minister could have said this earlier. We remember how we were treated before the Partition of India. If the honourable minister were to be a big brother, he should have given us our rights which had been taken away.' I believe that my point was well taken by all present.

THE FOURTH TEST: MADRAS

The fourth Test match was played at Madras (now Chennai). This match was played on a placid wicket, and it took five days to play one innings. Here, Imtiaz scored his first century against India. He was so determined at the beginning of Pakistan's innings that he insisted that I send him to open with Hanif Muhammad. His innings was a blend of aggression and contempt. He was particularly harsh on Desai whom he hit for four boundaries in an over. When Imtiaz returned to the pavilion after scoring a scintillating 140 runs, he received an unforgettable applause. An eager spectator garlanded him. Both Hanif and Imtiaz made a very good opening stand of 162 runs. Saeed Ahmad also scored a century. Saeed was a batsman who had no fear of bowlers of any reputation in the cricket world. When he was on a run spree, fielders would scramble all over.

The beginning of the Indian innings was not good. At one stage they were 146 for 3. At 164, we got Nari who had played a risky innings. Nari misread a Haseeb delivery and played it high to square leg. Intikhab Alam sprinted behind and held on to the ball. It was a remarkable catch. Such catches win matches. After Nari's fall, the complexion of the game could have changed in our favour if Haseeb had picked up a snick from

Umrigar off Mahmood. Later, both Umrigar and Borde took command of the situation and pulled their team out of trouble. They scored 177 runs for the fifth wicket. India declared its first innings at 539 for 9 on the fifth day, and in the remaining time Imtiaz and Saeed collected 59 runs.

Haseeb Ahsan would always remember this match for his marathon spell of about 84 overs and 6 wickets in the only Indian innings. It was a brilliant display of bowling on a placid wicket. However, one particular biased umpiring decision would always haunt him. When on 95, Chandu Borde snicked a ball from Haseeb and Imtiaz held the catch. It was a very close bat and pad catch. We appealed, but the umpire, in the mistaken belief that our appeal was for leg before, said, 'He played the ball'. 'I have caught it,' Imtiaz appealed. 'Never mind, I have not seen it. The bowler had come in my way,' replied the umpire. During the lunch interval, umpire S. Pan came to our dressing room and expressed his regret for the decision. His bold confession only served to rub salt into our wounds. However, it was good of the umpire to show courage and accept his mistake which helped Borde complete his coveted century. The wicket was so dull that both teams only completed their first innings in five days.

THE FIFTH TEST: DELHI

The fifth and final Test match at the Feroze Shah Kotla ground, Delhi was perhaps the most unnerving match of my career. I was at the end of my career, and leading the side in India. Defeat was considered a sin in both the neighbouring countries. We were playing amid biased umpiring decisions. The last day of the Delhi Test match would be remembered for a very long time. When Hanif and Imtiaz resumed their second innings, Pakistan was facing a deficit of 120 runs to avoid an innings defeat. The crowd was hostile. From one side of the crowd, flashes of mirrors were directed into the eyes of the batsmen. Imtiaz asked the umpires to have that nuisance removed. The umpires had become players themselves. They were just waiting for appeals from the Indian players. Hanif was bowled by Desai, but Imtiaz was given leg before when he positioned his leg outside the leg stump to play a sweep shot. Imtiaz was astonished. It was unbelievable. Then we lost Burki when he pushed straight to Kumar who fell to the ground in collecting the ball. His back was to the umpire. Raghunath Roy did not bother to even ask the leg umpire or the bowler about the fairness of the catch, and declared Burki out. The match at this stage seemed to be slipping from our hands. The score at lunch was 131 for four. After the loss of Mathias and Saeed, our hopes to save the match began to vanish. I went in to bat after the fall of Intikhab. Mushtaq was at the crease. We both had a brief conference in the middle and decided to spend maximum time at the crease and also keep the scoreboard moving. We evened the score. At that juncture, it seemed that we would see the day through, but soon our fortunes changed. I went forward to play a ball from Desai. My leg was outside the off stump. The ball hit me on my thigh. There was a loud appeal, and Roy answered the appeal in the affirmative. I walked back to the pavilion. It was a very, very long distance for me. As I was changing in the dressing room, I heard a loud noise. This time poor Mushtaq was the victim of a biased umpiring decision by Roy. He was hit on the pad when he had stretched his leg to play a Desai delivery pitched well outside the off stump.

When the match resumed after tea, Pakistan's score was 197 for eight. Former All India Test cricketer Vizzy (Maharajkumar of Vizianagaram) was on the microphone telling the Delhites, 'Come one, and come all to Feroze Shah Kotla ground where you will see Pakistani cricketers being humiliated. It is the day of *holi*. Let's play *holi* with them. Can anybody save them? No, I can say with authority. Come soon as it is a matter of a few more minutes now. Their last batsman is walking in. Both the batsmen at the crease cannot survive against the Indian stalwarts.' I was tense, chain-smoking cigarettes. Renowned sports journalist, the late Sultan F. Hussain, was also watching the match and he told me later that I had cigarettes in both hands. The chances of a draw were ludicrously remote. Defeat looked inevitable. I was concentrating on how to upset the umpires. I called the next batsman, Mahmood Hussain, and gave him some instructions. 'Before you reach the crease and take guard, just go to the umpire and tell him categorically to be honest,' I said. After the fall of the eighth wicket, Mahmood went in with a strong determination that he would come back undefeated. He went straight to the umpire and talked to him. Obviously, Mahmood must have told him to be honest for a change. However, we saw the umpire moving towards the short-leg umpire. They both talked and perhaps decided not to give an unfair decision in view of our weak position. Mahmood also had a conversation with Polly Umrigar, who was leading the Indian team in the absence of Nari Contractor.

Pakistan's score had reached 212 when Haseeb was bowled out by Desai. The atmosphere in the dressing room was tense when the last man, Muhammad Farooq, joined Mahmood Hussain. We kept looking at the clock and the score. Polly Umrigar made a tactical mistake by taking the new ball to quickly get the last wicket. It was a hasty decision. Mahmood played forward and was hit on the pad. The Indian players appealed loudly. However, the umpire did not give him out. I heard Lala Amarnath saying, 'The umpire is stupid. He should have given Mahmood out. Who cares who says what?' Umrigar made another blunder, and brought in the thirdman and other deep fielders close in order to put pressure on the batsmen. That proved the turning point of the match. Both Mahmood Hussain and Muhammad Farooq bravely defied the Indian pace attack. They used the long handle against Desai and Surti. Runs started trickling in first, and then in fours. Both Mahmood Hussain and Muhammad Farooq took the match out of Indian hands and put Pakistan in an absolutely safe position. I was just thinking in terms of declaring the innings as only twelve minutes of play were left when I saw both batsmen coming back as Mahmood Hussain had been bowled by Nadkarni. Pakistan were all out at the score of 250, gaining a seventy-three-run lead. As Mahmood returned to the pavilion, the crowd booed, which was a vivid display of their frustration. Vizzy's voice became hoarse when Jaisimah and Kunderam came to start their second innings. 'Now India cannot score those runs in three overs,' he mumbled.

During the Indian tour, my winning the toss was the talk of the town. I established a world record by successively winning the toss eleven times. Polly Umrigar remarked after the toss in the Madras Test, 'We should either change the Pakistan skipper, or our own.' In this match, even the gold coin given by Vizzy to Nari Contractor could not bring him luck. At a function during the course of the match, Nari acknowledged my supremacy in winning tosses by saying, 'I would like to learn this art from Fazal Mahmood. I hope that Fazal will not mind telling me this after the tour is over.' I replied that the only way I could was for Nari to call: 'Heads you lose, tails I win' in Delhi. In the match against the South Zone at Hyderabad, Ghulam Ahmed, a former Indian Test cricketer who was then the secretary of the Hyderabad cricket association, was so sure that Gopinath, the home team captain, would win the toss that he put a wager on it. When I again won the toss, Ghulam Ahmad presented me a currency note with his signature on it.

Mushtaq Mohammad was undoubtedly the find of the tour. He was first picked in the team that played the last Test match against the West Indies at Lahore in 1958–59, thus also becoming the youngest player to appear in a Test match. Pakistan had already won that series, so I could take chances and picked Mushtaq. He could bowl leg-breaks and the googly, was a fine batsman, and had a cricketing background. I was challenged on my decision from all quarters. Mushtaq embarked on the Indian tour making his first appearance in the Bombay Test with paltry scores in both the innings, followed by 13 in the Kanpur Test. Before the start of the Calcutta Test, his elder brother, Hanif Muhammad, and a member of the tour selection committee, asked me to drop Mushtaq. 'I can drop you, not him,' was my answer. I had full confidence in Mushtaq. All that he needed was a bit of practice to restore his confidence. Mushtaq was given good batting practice in the nets. 'Mushtaq, you are going to play in all the Test matches. So it is up to you to either make or break your cricket career,' I told him bluntly. He scored 61 in the Calcutta Test, and 41 not out in the Madras Test followed by a maiden century in the final Test at Delhi. Later, he captained the Pakistan team against India in 1978, and won the series 2–0.

On completing the Indian tour, the team came back to Karachi. About five thousand people were gathered at the airport to greet us. Mian Anwar Ali, the IG Police, met me at the main entrance of the Hotel Metropole and told me that I had been promoted to the rank of a DSP and transferred to Montgomery (now Sahiwal).

Following the undefeated Indian tour, I had only one desire, and that was to lead the Pakistan team to England and bid farewell to Test cricket from the Oval cricket ground. But, that was not to be. Imtiaz Ahmad was made the captain of the Pakistan team in the three-Test match home series against England. I did not envy his appointment since we were tied up in a 'caught Imtiaz bowled Fazal' combination. He was a long time partner in my adventures on the ground. My name was not even considered for selection for this series. I was not asked by the BCCP whether I was available or not. I knew that my exclusion from the team was the result of a prejudice that had been created against me by Dr Jehangir's report. There were serious allegations against some other senior players also, but the BCCP allowed them to start with a clean slate. That was not fair. If there was any cricket left in me, it belonged to Pakistan and nobody had any right to deprive the country of it.

Pakistan lost the first Test at Lahore. I was just an onlooker. I saw the proceedings of the match from the stands. Suddenly, I was invited to lead a young team against England at Bahawalpur. The team was no better than a mediocre divisional side. Why I was asked to play in the match, I am still not sure. Even though I had not been appointed the captain or considered for the national team, I remained determined to perform. Once again I had to prove that there was still plenty of cricket left in me. I got six wickets for just twenty-eight runs. My performance forced those at the helm of BCCP affairs to include me in the team for the third Test against England at Karachi. My bowling in the Karachi Test was not bad; however, I could not get any wicket. The wicket was tailor-made for the batsmen, besides which a couple of catches were dropped during my bowling. Whenever I appealed, the umpire would dismiss it with a loud 'no.' I knew my fate.

When I recall the Karachi Test, I sometimes think that the MCC players played to a plan to keep me out of the team, believing that I would create problems for them when Pakistan toured England in 1962. They were extra-cautious against my bowling. I sent down 65 impeccable overs in the match and gave away only 90 runs.

During the Test matches against England, the domestic season in Pakistan was also in progress. I wanted to play, but the Lahore division did not include me in their team. I tried to play for Bahawalpur division, but was told by the BCCP secretary, Muhammad Hussain, that I could do so only if I had been transferred to that division. No one in the BCCP had the courage to stand up and say that Fazal Mahmood was not even good enough for a divisional team.

13

Return to Test Cricket: England in 1962

The BCCP organized a camp for the selection of the team for the England tour of 1962. About forty players were invited to the camp. I was not invited. The conspiracy was to keep me out of cricket. It had started with the publication of a report by Dr Jehangir, who had been Pakistan's team manager on the Indian tour. The report appeared in the Indian press. Though there were serious allegations against the senior members of the team that toured India, yet I was made the scapegoat. The BCCP did not bother to find out who smuggled the report to the Indians and brought shame to the country. However, it soon became obvious that the report had been written to pave the way for the captaincy of a favourite. Javed Burki was made the captain of the Pakistan team to tour England. He was Dr Jehangir's nephew and the son of a very senior Pakistan army general and minister in President Ayub's cabinet. I will not hesitate to narrate for the readers of this book how Javed Burki was put in the saddle.

One day, I was sitting in my office when the telephone rang. I picked up the receiver, but an unknown caller was on the line. He said to me, 'Fazal Sahib, there is a telephone conversation regarding you. Please, just listen to it. If by mistake you interrupt, I will lose my job.' I covered the receiver with my hand and listened in on the conversation. The conversation was between an authoritative voice and the then BCCP president. The voice was saying: 'We have helped you reach this position and now you have to appoint our nominee as the captain of the national team.' 'Do not worry, sir, it will be done,' I heard the BCCP president say. 'What about Fazal?' he was asked. 'Do not worry. We will look after him,' the president assured him. The conversation ended. I was filled with anger. I could not sleep for several nights. How I spent those difficult nights can only be understood by a sensitive person. They had humiliated a Pakistani who had brought laurels to the country. It was not frustration but agony.

The team left for England, and I was not in the team. This depressed me for a very short period. But, I soon forgot about it and even tried to forget cricket. I consoled myself by saying that I had had my innings—good or bad, and would allow the people to give their verdict.

The team performed badly in England. It lost three Tests in a row. There was uproar in the country. The people were frustrated. They could not accept defeat after defeat. Cricket lovers openly came out in my favour. The sentiment of the people was understandable. The BCCP was being run by an *ad hoc* committee headed by Justice Cornelius. Initially, the committee disdainfully ignored public opinion. But, it soon began to come under increasing pressure to send me to England to strengthen the team. There were 'Send Fazal' articles in the press when the team needed a replacement for the injured Haseeb Ahsan. I heard that Burki had requested the BCCP to send pace bowler Muhammad Munaf but the irony was that Burki had no knowledge about Munaf's fitness. A couple of weeks earlier, he had undergone a knee operation and needed another two months rest before he could resume cricket. The BCCP first announced that Javed Akhtar (now an umpire in international cricket) was to be flown to England, but then it changed its decision. At this point it considered another promising youngster from Lahore, Bashir Haider, as a possible replacement. Then another development took place in England. Muhammad Farooq underwent an emergency operation for hernia. The manager and captain tried to get the services of some Pakistani cricketers based in Britain, and one such person named Butt, a club cricketer from Lahore, was considered.

Farooq's injury and Mahmood Hussain's sore shoulder further aggravated the situation. Faced with the serious nature of the situation, the BCCP had no option but to bow before public demand and send me to join the team in England.

I owe gratitude to those sports journalists who gave me tremendous support during my ordeal. They wrote columns in my favour demanding that I be sent to join the team. Leading English and Urdu newspapers published strong-worded editorials demanding that 'Fazal should not be allowed to rot and waste at home while the country's honour is at stake in England.' There was an unending stream of letters pouring into the offices of various newspapers, and these were being duly published.

So, one fine morning I was summoned by the BCCP chief in his chamber in the Supreme Court and was asked if I could go to England. I wondered at his words. The same Cornelius had promised to those who mattered that he would take care of me. The humiliation had been difficult for me to forget. 'No, I am not in practice, my fingers are very soft and to go into the Test arena is not an easy task', I said. However, after a protracted discussion, Justice Cornelius was apologetic. He knew my family background, and that I had been brought up by a father who was a nationalist and who, after passing the ICS exams, had refused a job offered by the British government. 'Fazal, can you save Pakistan from utter humiliation?' he asked. On hearing this, I was left with no option but to change my mind. I came home and hurriedly packed my kit and got into the plane for Karachi, and from there took-off for London the next morning.

By the time I joined the team, Pakistan had lost three Tests and there was no life left in the series. Most of the team members were suffering from injuries. I was supposed to retrieve Pakistan's lost prestige. It was a difficult task because I was not likely to get much help from the demoralized players.

I reached London two days before the start of the fourth Test match. The assistant manager of the team received me at the airport. Imtiaz, Mahmood Hussain, Saeed, Haseeb, and Mushtaq Muhammad greeted me as if I were still their captain. They had all been with me on the Indian tour in 1960–61. However, a small group of players, including Burki, did not like my presence in England. At night, a team meeting was held and the team manager, Brigadier Haider, joyfully told the boys, 'Fazal has come. Everything is going to be all right now.' Javed Burki did not speak during the meeting. Mahmood Hussain was not playing in the match because of a shoulder injury. Haseeb had been unfairly dubbed as a 'chucker'. He had bowled in the West Indies, India, and even in league cricket in England without being called for 'throwing'. But, while he was on the England tour in 1962, he suddenly became a chucker.

The English press welcomed me. Perhaps as a token of respect, the British newspapers had headlines like: 'Beware England, Fazal arrives', 'Beware of Fazal—He is England's bogey,' 'Now Fazal will make Lord Ted's men earn their place.' At this time, the England selectors were at Trent Bridge to have a last look at the players before finalizing the team to tour Australia after the end of the series with Pakistan.

I was not the Fazal of 1954. The rules of cricket had changed. Playing conditions had changed. I could not keep more than one man on the right side of the leg umpire. The batsmen were scoring mainly from that area where they would easily glide my leg-cutter. Even bad shots would get runs. My fingers had become as soft as a pianist's. I could not rotate the ball. I had reached Trent Bridge ground only two days before the start of the match. We had nets before the Test match. The attitude of Javed Burki was discouraging during the net practice. His team had lost three Tests in a row, but he did not appear worried. He would come strutting to the field, would whistle, and leave after a few minutes as if he did not care.

Our performance was at its lowest ebb, both on and off the field during the England tour of 1962. I wished they had sent me before Pakistan had lost the series. We could possibly have won or at least drawn one or two matches. But, when we had already lost the series, my only job and endeavour was to prevent England from doing to us what it did to India when it won all the five Test matches.

Before the start of play, I had a little conference with the boys in an attempt to raise their morale. We did some physical exercises and fielding practice. I still remember the remarks of Brigadier Haider, 'Why did Burki not conduct the team the way Fazal has?'

The match started. I knew the limits of my stamina and endurance, but I knew that I could bowl a long spell. I decided to concentrate on my line and length and bowled almost the whole of the first day. The English batsmen were very cautious against my bowling and did not take any liberties. In my first spell comprising of 16 overs, which ended only fifteen minutes before lunch, I had given away only 17 runs. I bowled about 45 overs in the day's play. After a marathon unchanged spell from one end, I was completely exhausted. At the end of England's first innings, my bowling analysis read as 60-15-130-3. I dismissed Ted Dexter, Tom Graveney, and Roger Knight. Sir Len Hutton, in his exclusive column to *The Pakistan Times*, commented: 'Burki, I feel, must have looked around his bowlers and wondered who he would bring on next. His answer always was Fazal—Fazal and more Fazal.'

When Pakistan started its innings, I asked the boys to attack the English bowlers. Saeed scored 43 and 64 in the two innings, and Mushtaq scored 55 and a hundred. Had I been sent to play the second Test, things could have been different. However, I did not disappoint my fans and the match was drawn.

But, calamity struck after the Nottingham Test. There was a gap of almost fifteen days before the fifth Test. Brigadier Haider and the captain forced me to take the team to Ireland. I did not have to go to Ireland, but I agreed as I did not wish to start another controversy. I had been sent to England only to play Test matches. I might have collapsed physically, but I did not. I had the determination and could endure any difficulty that came my way. If I failed at the Oval, it was because of the obdurate attitude of Burki during the match. With the new ball I asked that I should be given a certain kind of field. To my amazement I was denied, I was not allowed to set my field by a haughty captain. Whenever I asked for a fielder to be placed at a particular position, he would arrogantly say, 'Keep on bowling.' What could I do? Javed Burki had pre-conceived ideas about how cricket should be played. He ignored the advice of his seniors who had far more knowledge of cricket than him.

The 1962 tour was humiliating. Pakistan had to endure total disgrace. After the tour, a very high-powered inquiry committee was formed, headed by Justice Constantine. The committee included a very senior bureaucrat and Mian Muhammad Saeed. They were given the task to probe the causes of the national team's ignominious defeat in England, but the findings of that committee were never made public.

Here I want to narrate one interesting incident involving the manager of our team. During the proceedings of the Trent Bridge Test match, Intikhab beat an English batsman with a googly. The manager was sitting in the company of some MCC officials, and exclaimed, 'What a bouncer!' Haseeb, sitting next to him, told him quietly that it was not a bouncer, it was a googly. 'What the devil do I know about cricket? I am a horseman,' the military man replied with a smiling face. The secretary of the MCC remarked, 'Well, Brig, let's call for a drink!'

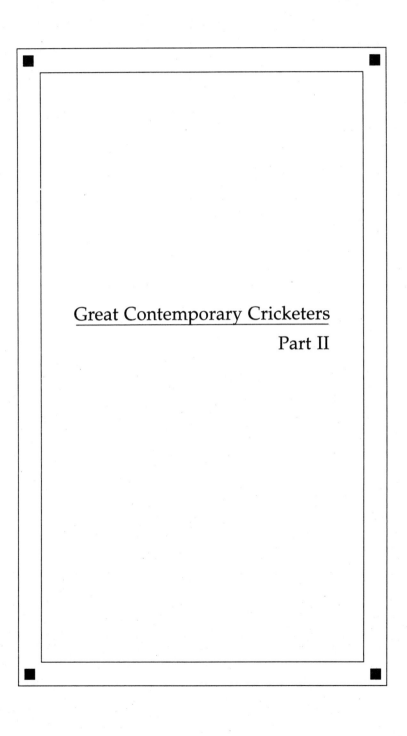

Great Contemporary Cricketers

Part II

14

Sir Len Hutton:
Master Batsman

'This is not Hutton-like'

It was indeed a memorable occasion when I first saw Len Hutton playing at the Oval cricket ground in 1953. I was in England as captain of the Pakistan Eaglets cricket team. In 1953, when Australia was beaten at the Oval, I was at the stand watching the match. Hutton appeared on the balcony after victory and waved to the crowd. The crowd screamed, 'Hail, Len Hutton!' I was exceedingly impressed by the warmth of the jubilant crowd towards this master batsman and world record holder. Even today, I can vividly recall him standing in the Oval balcony in front of a cheering crowd, his face a portrait of simplicity and modesty, and his personality, extremely impressive. I looked at him standing on the balcony and thought to myself that the next year (1954) I would be touring England with the Pakistan team. How wonderful and grand it would be if I were to replace him at that balcony?

When the Pakistan team reached England to play the four-Test series against England in 1954, Len Hutton received us at the Waterloo railway station. That was my first meeting with my school-time hero. We shook hands and exchanged greetings. In the first Test at Lord's, I bowled only one over to Hutton, and in the second over of the match, Khan Muhammad got him out first ball. After the first day's play in the Lord's Test, I came back to the hotel and analysed Len Hutton's batting. His one arm was shorter than the other because of an accident during the war. While playing, his bat would not go across but would always go straight. Thus, whatever shot he would play, he would naturally play with a straight bat. How far his bat would go with that broken arm would depend upon the mobility of the bat. I realized that a ball moving from the leg-stump towards the off-stump, inviting him to play forward, could induce him to make a mistake. However, that ball had to be very accurate so that he would play forward and allow room for the movement of the ball.

After the Lord's Test, Pakistan played a three-day match against Yorkshire. Hutton, who played for the county, missed that match. He didn't play in the next two Tests at Nottingham and Manchester either. We faced each other again in the historic Oval Test. I applied my strategy and succeeded in getting the prized wicket of the great batsman in both the innings. On both occasions, he was caught behind. He didn't look at the umpire and simply walked to the pavilion with his head down. I knew that the greatest batsman of all times would only make a mistake when a very accurate ball was delivered to him, with the ball moving off the wicket or in the air, away from him. I had to bowl twenty-six different types of deliveries, and the twenty-seventh was perfect to get him out.

Hutton had a serious accident in 1941 while serving as a PT Instructor in an army gymnasium. He was hospitalized for more than seven months and underwent a bone-grafting operation. The operation had left his left arm permanently shorter and weaker than his right. Thus, Hutton found it difficult to continue playing in his previous style and was compelled to change his technique.

Sir Len Hutton was a batsman of immense qualities. He would plan his strategy before reaching the crease and never played a thoughtless innings. He had a lot of patience and would wait for the right ball to hit. But, somehow he lost patience in the Oval Test of 1954. The greatest exponent of batsmanship, and my school-day idol, was in an awkward position when facing my leg-cutters. In the first innings, I had him caught behind. In the second innings, he adopted a new technique and used the long handle. The ball went uppishly into the covers. While running between the wickets Hutton came

1. Two-year-old Fazal Mahmood with his great-grandfather Allah Ditta.

2. Professor Ghulam Hussain.

3. Mr and Mrs Fazal Mahmood, July 1948. Fazal married the daughter of Mian Mohammad Saeed, Pakistan's first captain, in unofficial Tests.

4. Fazal Mahmood (seated first from right) with Mian Muhammad Saeed (Pakistan's first captain in unofficial Tests), Dr Dilawar Hussain, Muhammad Nisar and Dr Jahangir Khan (All-India Test cricketers).

5. Pakistan's Governor General Khawaja Nazimuddin with Fazal Mahmood and Abdul Hafeez Kardar after the victory against the MCC in Karachi on 2 December 1951.

6. Fazal with Pakistan's Governor General Khawaja Nazimuddin during a state dinner in honour of the victorious Pakistan team at Karachi on 21 December 1951. Imtiaz Ahmad, Maqsood Ahmad, Nazar Muhammad and Abdul Hafeez Kardar are also seen in the photograph.

7. Indian captain Lala Amarnath welcomes Nazar Muhammad and Fazal Mahmood, at the Delhi Railway Station on 13 October 1952.

8. 'Best of Luck—but you cannot win the match'. Fazal along with Nazar Muhammad and Maqsood Ahmad watching Pakistan losing to India at the Feroze Shah Kotla ground on 18 October 1952.

9. Fazal Mahmood with his fans during a dinner at the Beach Luxury Hotel, Karachi before leaving on the England tour in April 1954.

10. Fazal is jubilant as Tom Graveny is smartly stumped by Imtiaz off Shujauddin in the third Test at Old Trafford in 1954.

11. Fazal returns with the team to the dressing room after defeating England at the Oval in 1954. Mahmood Hussain is behind him.

12. Fulfilment of a dream: Fazal responds to the crowd amidst cries of 'We want Fazal, We want Fazal' after victory in the Oval Test.

13. Former England Test cricketer, Alf Gover congratulating Fazal on his enthralling performance in the Oval Test.

14. Fans congratulating Fazal after the Oval victory.

15. Fazal Mahmood giving autographs to female fans as Denis Compton waits for his turn.

16. Playfair's XI Cricketers of 1954. These were the eleven cricketers of the year, akin to Wisden's Five.

17. Keith Miller, Denis Compton, Godfrey Evans and Fazal Mahmood were all on the Brylcreem advertisements of the 1950s.

18. The Oval Hero leads the welcome procession in Lahore after his triumphant return from England in August 1954.

19. The Pakistan team lined up in the third Test against India in the 1954-55 series at the Bagh-i-Jinnah ground, Lahore on 29 January 1955. From right to left: A.H. Kardar, Fazal Mahmood, Wazir Muhammad, Imtiaz Ahmad, and Maqsood Ahmad.

20. Fazal leads the team off the field after dismissing Australia for only 80 runs at Karachi on 17 October 1956. Fazal's match figures were 13/114.

21. Fazal picks up the coin after winning the toss against the West Indies captain Gerry Alexander at the second Test at Dhaka on 6 March 1959.

22. Fazal bowling in the Dhaka Test between Pakistan and the West Indies.

23. Fazal along with the West Indies cricketers Rohan Kanhai, Butcher, Solomon, Lance Gibbs and O.G. Smith. Dinner party at the Lahore Gymkhana before the third Test in March 1959.

24. Fazal leads the team in the Lahore Test against the West Indies on 26 March 1959. This was the last Test match played at the Bagh-i-Jinnah ground.

25. Fazal and Richie Benaud before the toss in the first Test at Dhaka on 13 November 1959.

26. The US President Dwight D. Eisenhower shaking hands with Fazal Mahmood at the National Stadium, Karachi. President Ayub Khan looks on. This was a rare occasion when a US president witnessed a Test match.

27. Fazal is leading the Pakistan team in the third Test at Karachi on 4 December 1959. Ejaz Butt and Duncan Sharpe are also in the photograph.

28. Fazal Mahmood with Field Marshal Muhammad Ayub Khan and Zulfikar Ali Bhutto at the investiture ceremony held in Rawalpindi. Fazal was awarded the President's Medal for Pride of Performance on 28 October 1960.

29. Pakistan team's group photograph before the Indian tour in 1960-61.
Standing (L to R): Zafar Altaf, Javed Burki, Ejaz Butt, Muhammad Munaf,
Intikhab Alam, Nasim-ul-Ghani, Haseeb Ahsan and Mushtaq Muhammad.
Sitting (L to R): Shujauddin, Mahmood Hussain, Hanif Muhammad, Fazal
Mahmood (Captain), Dr Jahangir Khan (Manager), Imtiaz Ahmad (Vice-
Captain), Alimuddin, Saeed Ahmad and Wallis Mathais.

30. Spinning the coin with Nari Contractor in the first Test at Mumbai. Fazal
called the correct side 11 times out of 12 in the matches he played on the
Indian tour in 1960-61. .

31. Indian film actors Raj Kapoor, Karan Diwan and Gope with Fazal Mahmood at a dinner party in Mumbai on 5 December 1960.

32. Pakistan cricketers Fazal Mahmood (seated fourth from left), Javed Burki, Intikhab Alam, Imtiaz Ahmad and Alimuddin with Indian filmstars Pran, Ashok Kumar and Iftikhar at a reception in Mumbai on 7 December 1960.

33. Fazal introducing Hanif Mohammed to the governor of Calcutta. Imtiaz Ahmad is also seen in the picture.

34. Shaking hands with former All-India Test cricketer C.K. Nayudu after the toss at Indore in 1960.

35. Vizzy's banquet in Kanpur on the eve of the second Test on the 1960-61 tour. Fazal is sitting next to the UP Governor Dr Ramakrishana Rao who is wearing a white cap.

36. Fazal with the Indian President Dr Rajendra Prasad and the BCCI president Chindambaram during a reception in the Pakistan High Commissioner's House, New Delhi in February 1961.

37. The Indian Prime Minister Pandit Jawaharlal Nehru presents a bronze statue to Fazal at a function arranged at the Pakistan High Commissioner's House in New Delhi in February 1961.

38. Dr Jahangir Khan, Fazal Mahmood, Imtiaz Ahmad, Mahmood Hussain and Hasib Ahsan with the Indian Prime Minister Pandit Jawaharlal Nehru at New Delhi in February 1961.

39. Fazal and former West Indies fast bowler Charlie Griffith at the Rawalpindi Club ground before the match between the Commander-in-Chief's XI and the Commonwealth XI. Pindi Club, 22 November 1963.

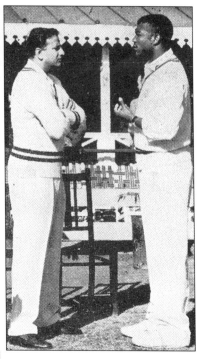

40. Fazal Mahmood: The genial police-man. A caricature by Jawaid Iqbal.

41. Keith Miller: The flamboyant all-rounder.

42. Two immortal West Indians: Sir Frank Worrell and Sir Garfield Sobers walk out to bat in the fourth Test against England at Leeds in 1957.

43. A classical gentle push by Syed Mushtaq Ali.

44. Everton Weekes in full cry.

45. Fazal Mahmood with (left to right) Mueen Afzal, Syed Iftikhar Ali Bokhari and Asif Sohail at the Gaddafi Stadium, Lahore on the occasion of the Test match against England in December 2000.

46. Fazal Mahmood giving finer tips on fast and swing bowling to future cricketers at the Gaddafi Stadium, Lahore on 17 November 2002.

to my end. I said, loudly, 'This is not Hutton-like.' At that juncture he could have easily put me off, but he didn't. He lost his wicket, but didn't use the long handle. After the match was over, Hutton left the ground immediately. He did not even attend the traditional cake-cutting ceremony.

During the 1962 series, I was sent to England to reinforce the depleted Pakistan team. After the first day's play at Trent Bridge, a chit was sent to the dressing room which read: 'Len Hutton'. I was not expecting him. I had thought of calling on Sir Len after the match. After all, he was my hero and much senior to me. I came out running and saw him standing outside the dressing room. 'Sir Len, you do not need to seek permission,' I protested humbly. 'No, Fazal, there is a certain decorum and discipline about entering into somebody else's dressing room,' he replied modestly. 'However, Sir Len,' I was saying, when he cut me short saying: 'Do not call me Sir Len—call me Len.' Then he said, 'Can I suggest that we have dinner together'. I was excited. It was a great honour for me.

So we met the next day. My younger brother, the late Dr Zafar Masud Khilji, was in England doing his Ph.D. in engineering, so he too joined us for dinner. The people in the restaurant were dazzled when they saw Sir Len Hutton walk in. It was a very nice dinner, and I shall remember it forever. We were enjoying a cup of coffee after our meal, when Hutton asked me, 'Fazal, it has been eight years since the Oval Test in 1954. I have been thinking about what you did with the ball and I have not yet been able to understand. Would you tell me how you bowled that particular ball which got me out twice in the Oval Test?' I was stunned. It was the greatest compliment I could have received as a player.

Hutton was gracious. He again showered me with compliments when I was playing in the fourth Test against England on the 1962 tour. During the Nottingham Test, I bowled for almost the whole day. When I was bowling the last couple of overs of the day, the whole crowd stood up and harangued Javed Burki, the captain of Pakistan team: 'You want to kill him—You want to kill him.' But, the next day I was bowling again. In an exclusive column for *The Pakistan Times*, Hutton wrote, 'Burki worked him (Fazal) so hard that had the big police officer from Lahore been a work horse, the RSPCA (Royal Society for Prevention of Cruelty to Animals) would have stepped in and demanded that he be given a rest.'

Len Hutton began his Test career against New Zealand at Lord's in 1937. He was out for a duck in the first innings and could only score one run in the second. But, Hutton was born to attain international fame in the field of cricket. In the next Test at Old Trafford, he scored exactly 100 and from that day onwards he never looked back. In the first Test against Australia at Nottingham in 1938, he scored a fine century and, with Barnet, gave England a grand opening stand of 219 runs. Len Hutton's historic innings of 364 in the fifth Test at the Oval during the same series remained a world record till 1958. That innings was not only a display of command and delightful strokes, but it also demonstrated his deep concentration, patience, and determination. When the West Indies visited England in 1939, Hutton scored a glorious innings of 196 in the first Test at Lord's. In the third Test at the Oval, he again scored an unbeaten 165. His aggregate was 480 (96.00) in the three-Test series.

It was really tragic that physical disability ended Hutton's brilliant career when he was at his peak. He retired after the triumphant tour of Australia in 1955. Being an opening batsman, he played many wonderful innings for England. In his last season as a Test cricketer, Hutton stood himself down at number five position because of ill health. For many years he was England's batting sheet anchor. He followed on the trail of Hammond, and after the decline of Washbrook and Compton, he stood virtually alone until Peter May and Colin Cowdrey arrived on the scene. However, prolonged medical treatment failed to bring about a complete remedy to his back trouble and at the age of thirty-nine, this great player retired from Test cricket.

Len Hutton was a batsman of the highest order. Throughout his career, he played his shots according to the book. He would swiftly move his feet and play an accurate and hard late-cut.

His shots played into the covers and point position were absolutely perfect. He was an orthodox batsman and was very difficult to dislodge, but a good bowler could contain him because he would not play rash strokes.

Hutton was one of the greatest opening batsman England has ever produced. He was once dropped from the England team in 1948, but he played against Australia at Leeds and scored 81 and 57. Throughout his career, he played cricket with skill and courage. Before Hutton, most of the English batsmen were back-foot players, but he introduced a new technique and played on the front foot. His approach had an amazing effect on cricket in England. He remained the bulwark of England's batting, and not even the burden of captaincy could tarnish his batting skills. He was a complete batsman who played magnificent cricket. He would choose his strokes carefully. He never played any innings he had not planned. In the Lord's Test of 1953, Hutton played a most splendid innings of 145. His innings was faultless. Defence with safety was his main weapon, and the manner in which he played cover-drives, cuts and leg-glances revealed his superb technique. The cover-drive was his favourite shot. While in the middle, he only thought of cricket and the crowd could never divert his concentration. In the third Test against the West Indies at Georgetown in the 1953–54 series, when the crowd hurled bottles, and officials of the British Guyana cricket association tried to persuade him to leave the ground for his players' safety, Hutton refused because he wanted to play. During this five-Test series Hutton's, aggregate was 677 (96.71). He scored 169 in the third Test at Georgetown, and 205 in the fifth Test at Kingston. These were his last three-figure scores in Test cricket.

Sir Len Hutton was the first professional captain of England. He proved that a professional cricketer could ably lead a team. He knew the finer points of the game and was modest. He was a big success as a captain, with faultless field placing and intelligent bowling changes. He first led England against India in the Leeds Test of 1952, and won the first three Tests in a row. His aggregate in the four Tests of the series was 399 (79.80), including 150 at Lord's and 104 at Manchester. Under his skilful captaincy England won the Ashes in 1953, after twenty-two years. He defeated Australia twice in successive rubbers, which was a great personal triumph for Hutton. He captained England in twenty-three Tests, and won eleven and lost four. As a captain, Hutton never lost a rubber. He was a good close fielder and also a useful leg-break bowler.

In the 1954–55 series against Australia, England's defeat in the first Test at Brisbane could not shake his confidence and determination. He was calm and composed. After the defeat he cancelled all the team engagements and parties, dispersed the arrogance, if there was any in the minds of the English players, and inculcated high discipline and concentration amongst them. The result was that England beat Australia convincingly in the next three Tests, while the fifth Test was a draw.

In 1955, the MCC amended their rules to accommodate Sir Len Hutton, the first playing professional member of the club. He was knighted in 1956—an honour he richly deserved.

After England's defeat in the Oval Test in 1954, Hutton issued a statement: 'The defeat shall do no harm in any way to England's cricket, but it shall go a long way in the promotion of Pakistan cricket.' Indeed, Pakistan's standing as a cricketing country reached great heights after the Oval victory.

15

Mushtaq Ali:
Elegance Personified

The Entertainer

Fairly tall, well-built, and handsome, Mushtaq Ali was one of the most mercurial batsmen that I came across in my early days in first-class cricket. He became famous at a time when the Muslims of the Indian subcontinent were denied opportunities to excel. Before Partition, the Muslims were given a somewhat step-motherly treatment in India. So, when players like Mushtaq Ali emerged on the scene, they naturally fascinated everyone, particularly fellow Muslims.

Mushtaq Ali was a gifted player who would mesmerize a crowd with his artistry at the crease. When walking majestically to the crease, his stance conveyed the message to the bowlers that they would have to be extra cautious while bowling to him. He could pull the ball outside the off-stump and despatch it towards mid-wicket for a four with effortless ease. When he was set, he would delight the spectators with the flow of his fine array of strokes. His flashing shots changed the fate of the game on several occasions. As long as he was at the crease, spectators and players alike would be spellbound by the lively game.

In his early days, Mushtaq Ali was ably coached and groomed by the great batsman of his times, C.K. Nayudu. At the age of nineteen, Mushtaq made his Test debut for the All-India team against England in the second Test at Calcutta in January 1934. He was included in the team as a left arm medium-fast bowler, and got the wicket of England's captain, Jardine, in this Test. In the next Test at Madras, he got Verity out leg-before-wicket with his swift and deceptive action.

When Vizzy led the All-India team to England in the summer of 1936, Mushtaq Ali was an automatic choice. He immensely benefited from that tour which familiarized him with the English wickets and climate. He impressed all-time greats like Jack Hobbs with his elegant style of batting. His overall aggregate was 1078 runs (25.06), including four centuries, with 141 against Surrey at the Oval, 140 against Gover's XI at Scarborough, 135 versus Minor Counties at Lord's, and 112 against England in the first Test at Manchester.

In the first innings of the Manchester Test, Mushtaq Ali was run-out in a peculiar fashion. Vijay Merchant hit a hard straight drive that struck Mushtaq Ali's bat who was backing up. The ball was deflected to the fielder at short mid-on, who made no mistake and threw down the wicket.

In the second innings, India was facing a deficit of 368 runs. Both Mushtaq Ali and Vijay Merchant scored 203 runs, and established a record for the first wicket partnership against England. Mushtaq displayed a brilliant exhibition of drives, cuts, and hooks. His hundred, completed in about two hours, is probably the fastest by any Indian in a Test. In the third Test at the Oval, Mushtaq Ali undoubtedly played one of the best innings of his career. He relished the well-pitched up balls and invariably hit them across the ropes. He scored 52 in this Test. In the three Tests, Mushtaq's aggregate was 202 runs (33.66).

The discontinuation of international cricket during the Second World War was a great blow for Mushtaq Ali. However, he played in the Ranji Trophy and Bombay Pentangular. In the final of the Ranji Trophy in 1944–45, Mushtaq scored a century in each innings. When Test cricket resumed after the war, Mushtaq made a second trip to England in 1946 with the All-India team led by Nawab Iftikhar Ali Khan Pataudi. Though Mushtaq had lost some of his magic, he played two glorious innings against Glamorgan at Swansea and against South of England XI at Hastings. On both occasions, he proved to be a great batsman capable of demoralizing any bowler. His leg glance was both daring and elegant, and his innings of 93 against Glamorgan was marvellous. He batted, with great courage and was remarkably good on his feet, producing a variety of elegant strokes. At Hastings, Mushtaq batted delightfully, often jumping yards down the wicket to drive, besides executing superb cuts and the leg-glances. Mushtaq always introduced a spirit of adventure into his play.

When the West Indies visited India in 1948–49 to play a five-Test series, Mushtaq Ali played in all the Tests and scored 240 runs (40.00). His performance in the third Test at Calcutta was exceptionally good. He scored 54 in the first innings and he was at his most flamboyant in the second innings. Short-pitched balls, good-length deliveries, and balls that were pitched well up—all were hit ruthlessly. The West Indies' fast bowler, Jones, had no idea where to pitch the ball to Mushtaq Ali. After the match, Jones himself acknowledged Mushtaq's supremacy. When he was out after scoring a sparkling 106 in the second innings, he received a big ovation from the crowd on his way back to the pavilion.

Communal bias deprived this very talented batsman from achieving great heights in international cricket. Mushtaq was not selected in the Indian team in the first two Tests against the first Commonwealth team that visited India in 1949–50. However, he was included in the team for the third Test at Calcutta. His knocks of 40 and 45 in both innings did not disappoint his fans. Mushtaq played the most responsible innings of his career in the Kanpur Test. The wickets were falling at the other end, but he patiently ramained at the crease. He scored 129 out of a total of 218. In the final Test of the series at Madras, Mushtaq played a daring innings. On the fourth day of the match, India needed 229 runs for victory. Mushtaq was badly hit by a rising ball from Fitzmaurice and a finger of his right hand was fractured. He could not resume his innings on the last morning of the match. The Indian team collapsed. The score was 255 for seven. Four runs were needed for victory. Mushtaq could not resist the temptation. His colleagues helped him with his pads and gloves. He walked to the wicket with his usual grace. The crowd was electrified to see him. Mushtaq played a couple of balls with absolute calm. Then he stepped forward, and with one hand drove a delivery from Smith to the boundary. What a shot that was! The crowd went wild with joy.

When India visited England in 1952, the selectors unfairly left out Mushtaq on the pretext of his poor performances at home. His omission proved a blunder as he had rich experience of English conditions. Mushtaq Ali was also not included in the Indian team when Pakistan visited India in 1952–53. However, he appeared for the Central Zone against Pakistan and played a sterling innings of 73. His wristy strokes were a delight to watch. Some of his shots were so powerful that the fielders hesitated to stop them. Imtiaz Ahmad injured his finger when he tried to stop a full-blooded drive from him. He had his finger in plaster and had to rest for a week. After the series against Pakistan, the Indian team toured the West Indies, but again Mushtaq was not selected.

Mushtaq Ali was a fine cricketer. He played some fine knocks in Bombay's famous Quadrangular and Pentangular tournaments. Had there been modern day television in those days, recordings of Mushtaq Ali's batting could have been used to coach one-day batsmen of the present era. He scored 135 and 157 against the Europeans in 1937 and 1938, and a brilliant 110 against the Rest in 1940. Under his captaincy, the Muslims defeated the Hindus in 1944.

I did not have many opportunities to play against this great cricketer. However, we both faced each other in a Zonal Tournament in 1945 at Bombay's Brabourne stadium. Mushtaq played for the South Zone while I appeared for the North Zone. I was thrilled when I got him out in the match and felt on top of the world. It was a big boost for me as a young bowler when Mushtaq Ali said, 'Well bowled,' and walked back to the pavilion.

Mushtaq Ali was fond of fast bowling. He would race down the wicket to play the genuine fast bowlers. My friend Keith Miller called him 'the Errol Flynn of cricket'. They had an interesting encounter when the Australian Services XI visited

India in 1945. In the match played at Delhi's Feroze Shah Kotla ground, Mushtaq Ali opened the innings to Keith Miller's bowling. The stadium was jam-packed. Keith began to run from his bowling mark while Mushtaq Ali started coming out of his crease to meet the ball half way down the wicket. Keith thought that something was wrong with Mushtaq Ali. He stopped, but saw that Mushtaq Ali was signalling him to come on. Keith was amused, and Mushtaq Ali went on to score a brilliant century (108) in this match.

Mushtaq played entertaining cricket. The crowds loved him. When he went in to bat, the news would go round the city like wildfire and within a few minutes, the crowd would swell into thousands, leaving the ground when Mushtaq got out. At least ten to fifteen thousand people would come to watch him batting, even in a local match. He would play leg-glance with absolute ease. However, on most occasions he got out playing his favourite shot. Boldness and aggression were the main features of his batting. His batting style was very similar to Keith Miller's and Denis Compton's. He had swift footwork that would give him enough time to play his shots. With his extraordinary footwork, he was always well placed to hit every ball. That didn't mean that he would not hit a wild shot. On the contrary, he would jump out of his crease with perfect footwork, making the good length ball into a half volley.

Mushtaq Ali was a master of the bat in his own right. Neville Cardus once wrote about him that, 'His cricket at times was touched with genius and imagination.' Mushtaq Ali came to Pakistan to play a charity match in aid of the Prime Minister's Flood Relief Fund. The match was played at Karachi in September 1955. He played for the PM's XI and scored 52 in the first innings. There were unconfirmed reports that Mushtaq had privately shown his desire to settle in Pakistan provided a reasonable job was given to him.

Mushtaq Ali also played the Lala Amarnath benefit match in Bombay after the end of five-Test series between India and Pakistan in 1960–61. In this match, he scored 73 runs. That was my last meeting with the great batsman. The MCC gave this great cricketer honorary life membership on 5 July 1960.

Mushtaq now lives in Indore in India. He is still an asset to Indian cricket. My friends who have seen him in recent days have told me that he still sits, thinks, and tries to infuse into Indian players that old spirit, the fighting spirit—'Never say die'. A long and happy life to Syed Mushtaq Ali.

16

Lala Amarnath: An Indian Legend
'Even my wife could have held this catch'

Cricket in pre-Partition days was a game mostly for the high-born and the rich. But, eventually the game attracted a large number of people from the middle-classes who played the game with commitment and attained international fame. Among them was Lala Amarnath who started playing cricket in his hometown, Lahore, and later dominated Indian cricket for a long time.

From the very beginning, Lala took the game seriously. He would play not for money but for the love of the game. He worked in the railways workshop in Lahore, on a salary of half a rupee a day. That money was probably enough for him to live reasonably well in those days.

Lala Amarnath played for the Crescent Cricket Club while I played for the Mamdot Cricket Club, both of which were famous clubs of Lahore. In pre-Partition days, these two clubs would play the final of almost every prestigious tournament in northern India. While playing club cricket, Lala Amarnath realized that he was a very good all-rounder, and soon his cricketing abilities earned him a place in the Maharaja of Patiala's team as a professional.

Lala was quite senior to me, but we knew each other well. Both Mamdot and Crescent had their nets in the famous Minto Park, but I became closely associated with Lala Amarnath in 1944 when we faced each other at Patiala in a Ranji Trophy match. I am proud that my first wicket in first-class cricket was that of Lala Amarnath, who by then was an established All-India Test player. He had played against England in the home and away series of 1933–34 and 1936. That match was my first-class debut. Amarnath tried to drive my fourth delivery, but the ball turned sharply, took his outside edge, and went into the safe hands of Dr Jahangir Khan, another All-India Test player. My team-mates gathered around me, and I was jubilant after claiming the wicket of Lala Amarnath, the great Test cricketer.

Later, Amarnath captained North Zone in a zonal tournament which replaced the Pentangular. This tournament eventually became a basis for the selection of the All-India team to tour Australia in 1947. My selection in the team was certain, but I stood down as my country, Pakistan, had emerged on the world map. When the Indian team was about to leave for Australia, Lala approached me through a telegram insisting that I not miss the tour. He was very affectionate towards me.

Amarnath is rightfully considered a 'pure romantic, the Byron of Indian Cricket', a competitive cricketer. He was an all-rounder of world class. He could bowl in-swingers, which were his most effective weapon. Many times he also opened the bowling attack. He had an easy and alert run-up. His batting was exceptionally good, although he was a little weak on the hook shot. He scored 109 runs for Southern Punjab against the MCC in 1933–34, in a brilliant display of batting. In 1936, he scored 130 and 107 for India against Essex at Brentwood. His innings of 163 against Australian Services XI at New Delhi in 1946 was a true demonstration of his class as a batsman. His cuts and drives were a real delight for the spectators. In 1946–47, he scored 262 for India-in-England against the Rest of India, in Calcutta. Amarnath was a reliable close-in fielder. He could also be used as a makeshift wicketkeeper.

Amarnath toured England again in 1946. Though he was not successful with the bat, he impressed people with his accurate bowling. He always kept the batsmen guessing. During the match against Somerset, he tied down their attacking batsman, Harold Gimblett. Amarnath always cherished his encounter with Gimblett. 'I hardly allowed Gimblett to play his strokes. During the course of play, in sheer disappointment, he asked me if I could bowl a half-volley. Oh yes, I told him, I bowled one in

1940,' Lala recounts. In the first Test at Lord's, Amarnath scored 50 and took 5 for 118 in the first innings. In the second Test at Old Trafford, his match analysis was 8 for 167 in 81 overs.

Amarnath was a bold and aggressive captain. When Merchant could not take the trip to Australia because of a fitness problem, Lala Amarnath was asked to lead the Indian team on their first tour of Australia in 1947–48. Though he performed moderately with the bat in the Tests, his batting in the side matches was brilliant. His aggregate was 1162 runs (58.10), including five centuries and a score of 228 not out against Victoria. For the latter score, Lala Amarnath came to bat when Mankad, Hazare, and Rangneker were back in the pavilion without a run being scored. Bill Johnson destroyed the Indian batting line-up. However, with great courage and determination, Amarnath rescued his team from total collapse and set the example for the remaining batsmen with his outstanding performance. He was also the leading wicket-taker in the series on the Indian side. Amarnath's captaincy in the Australian tour was excellent. His policy was to provide opportunities for every player during the matches without disturbing the balance of the team. Though he had to face criticism at home, yet he led his team well, and by his personal example tried to inspire his players to perform.

Amarnath established himself as a shrewd captain on the Australian tour and proved that he was no ordinary captain. In the third Test, Amarnath rightly judged the worsening condition of the wicket, and declared India's first innings 103 runs behind Australia. He wanted to run through the Kangaroos on a bad wicket. This was a superb tactical move, but unfortunately he was up against Sir Don Bradman, who anticipated the move and disrupted Amarnath's strategy by sending tail-enders first.

When the West Indies visited India in 1948–49, Amarnath was retained as captain of the Indian team as Merchant was still unfit. During the series, Lala surprised many by his excellent wicketkeeping when Sen, the regular wicketkeeper, was injured in the beginning of the West Indies' first innings. Amarnath took five catches in the match. During a three-day match at his favourite ground in Patiala, Lala scored a brilliant, unbeaten double century (223).

When the Pakistan team visited India in 1952, Amarnath was the captain of the Indian team. We lost the first Test match at New Delhi, but convincingly won the second Test at Lucknow. During the second innings of the Lucknow Test, we were very close to victory with only Lala Amarnath offering stiff resistance. In fact, he was India's last hope. When he reached the crease to start his innings, Mahmood Hussain was bowling. In pure Lahori style to which Lala was fully accustomed, I shouted from my slip position in slang Punjabi, 'Moode, aidha cir parr dae', meaning, 'Mahmood, knock him down with a bouncer.' Lala survived Mahmood's bouncers, and then I took the ball from Mahmood, saying, 'Give me the ball, I will knock him down.' Lala was my captain before Partition. I had played under his captaincy and respected him. But, at Lucknow, we were playing against each other and naturally we had to apply psychological tactics against each other. Moreover, Lala was friendly with most of our players and this kind of banter was normal between us.

I placed Zulfiqar Ahmad at square-leg, asking him to get ready for the catch which would land straight into his hands, and then hurled a bouncer. Lala trying to fend it away offered a simple catch to Zulfiqar, which he dropped. Instead of cursing himself, Zulfiqar yelled at me, 'I was not ready and you delivered the ball.' We were all amused at his innocence. Lala, too, enjoyed the moment and observed to Zulfiqar, 'Even my wife could have held this catch.' Lala went on to play an admirable innings on the jute-matting surface, and remained not out with 61.

Lala Amarnath was a wonderful stroke player, totally different from the others. When I batted for a long innings in the Calcutta Test of the 1952 series and saved the match, Lala praised my resistance and announced, 'Fazal was the saviour of the match.' It is odd that both in India and Pakistan the cricket bodies do not do justice to experienced senior players. Lala Amarnath, too, became a victim of this injustice when he was not included in the Indian team that visited England in 1952.

The BCCI made an amazing statement that Lala was not included in the team because his performance at home was not satisfactory. This was ridiculous. Amarnath had vast experience and knowledge of English conditions. India lost three Tests, and I am certain that Lala's presence in the team could have made a difference.

Lala retired from Test cricket in 1954 but his passion for the game did not end, and he continued playing first-class cricket in India. He got 7 for 30 for Patiala against Services in 1956–57. This was his best bowling figures in first-class cricket. Again, in 1958–59, he did remarkably well for the Railways against Patiala at Bombay, 7-7-0-4. He came to Pakistan as the manager of the Indian cricket team in 1955, and was a dynamic figure both off and on the field, in tactics and in his handling of the team. He knew what his team was up against, and also that Pakistan's morale was very high as we had just come back from the Oval after beating England. He understood his team's anxieties. Lala's presence was good for his team, because he knew how to keep the spirits up.

The matches played at Dhaka, Bahawalpur, Lahore, and Peshawar were all drawn. Pakistan had a fair chance of winning the Karachi Test where the wicket was very fast. We played with three bowlers, Khan Muhammad, Mahmood Hussain, and myself. However, the Karachi match was also drawn, mainly because of Lala's planning and strategy.

I still remember his words which tied me to a 'gentleman's contract' with him. During the closing moments of the final day's play of the Karachi Test, while I was sitting with Lala and talking about the proceedings of the match, Kardar and Alimuddin were at the crease. I told Lala that Pakistan could win the match. 'I can draw the match even sitting in the dressing room,' Lala said firmly. I insisted that he tell me what plan he had in mind for drawing the game. So, we made a 'gentleman's contract', meaning that whatever he would tell me, I would not pass on to anyone. 'Tomorrow morning we will allow Kardar to score freely till lunchtime. After the lunch interval, we will give him some more runs so that he can forget about the result of the match and look forward to his century. When Kardar is in his 70s, we will contain him with an attacking field. Thus, for the sake of his century, he will continue batting and waste precious time. Ultimately, there will be very little time left for your bowlers to exploit our batting.' The depth in Lala's reasoning really amazed me. There is certainly a lesson for present day cricketers. Indeed, retired cricketers are precious assets for their respective countries.

Next morning, what happened was exactly as Lala had planned. I was morally bound by the 'gentleman's contract'. However, without telling Kardar about Lala's plan, I earnestly requested him to declare the innings, but he would not listen to me and continued batting till he was out seven short of his century. By then, very little time was left for our bowlers to get the Indian batsmen out. I still wonder how things went exactly according to Lala's plan. The Lala Amarnath I knew was a shrewd schemer and planner. He would manoeuvre his team sitting in the pavilion. The 'gentleman's contract' with Lala showed the special understanding between us.

In April 1960, Lala Amarnath led an Indian Starlets team to Pakistan. He put up an all-round performance in the Multan match where he scored 59 runs and took 4 wickets for 85. Then, in the Karachi match, he played a fine innings of 80.

When I led the Pakistan team to India in 1960–61, the first person who met me at Bombay's Brabourne stadium was Lala Amarnath. He seemed delighted to see me. We greeted each other and talked of the good old days. Lala was in trouble, and I silently listened to the sad story of such a great and well-known cricketer struggling in India. The same night, our team was invited to a dinner hosted by the Indian film industry. Lala Amarnath was very well received and was a respected figure. Personalities like Om Parkash, Raj Kapoor, Pran, and Dev Anand, and some leading ladies of Indian filmdom, were present. While talking to Raj Kapoor, I told him, 'Amarnath is not well-off. I feel sorry for him.' Raj was taken aback. He pulled out his chequebook and wrote a cheque of Rs 100,000, which was a lot of money in those days, for a Lala Amarnath benefit match.

Thus, after the series, a Lala Amarnath benefit match was played between Pakistan and the Bombay C.C. President's XI at the Brabourne stadium, Bombay. Lala's old friend, the great Syed Mushtaq Ali, also played in the match. The crowd thronged the stadium on all three days in a demonstration of their love for Lala Amarnath. Later, Amarnath's sons became outstanding cricketers, particularly Mohinder Amarnath, who emerged as a batsman of world class. As far as technique was concerned, Lala was the best Indian batsman of his time.

Lala Amarnath visited Lahore in 1978. He was asked to give his views on the game for the radio commentary because he understood cricket so well. When he came to Pakistan, he introduced his two sons, Surinder and Mohinder, to me and asked them in his typical Punjabi, *'Papay daha goodaoun nou hath lagao'*—meaning, touch Fazal's knees. Like obedient sons, they both touched my knees as a token of respect.

During our conversations in Lahore, we both agreed that the Indian team was handicapped because players like him, Hazare, Gupte, and Merchant were not included. Lala told me that present day players had money and facilities, but hard work, dedication, and fair play were missing. I again met Lala in Jaipur in 1987 when I had gone there to witness the Pakistan-India Test match. Lala met me with touching warmth, affection, and concern.

Amarnath was a brilliant cricketer who raised India to world stature in international cricket. He is the first Indian to have scored a century (118) in a Test debut. He achieved this in the first Test against England at Bombay in December 1933. India had already lost two second innings wickets for 21 runs when Lala Amarnath went to bat. He attacked the bowling and rallied his team with an inspired display of batting. He hit 21 boundaries in this innings. When Amarnath completed his century, some women gave him their jewellery as gifts. A millionaire gave him £ 800 and another presented him with a car.

Lala remained a very vital figure in Indian cricket even after his retirement from Test cricket. He was a good captain. There was flair in his captaincy. He commanded the respect of his players. On the Australian tour of 1947, he did not refuse Bradman who persuaded him to allow wickets to be covered during the Test series, although that was not the practice in those days.

Lala was open and candid. He was the most outspoken player of his time. During the England tour of 1936, Amarnath resisted the high-handed methods of the team manager, Major Britton-Jones, especially when he intervened in the batting order of the players. During the match against the Minor Counties, Lala was first asked to pad-up, and then was told to wait. Lala was hurt. He exchanged hot words with Vizzy, the captain of the team. Both Vizzy (Maharajkumar of Vizianagaram) and Jones held a meeting and decided to send Amarnath back for disciplinary reasons. Both Sir Don Bradman and Hammonds mention the incident in their books published nearly ten years later. They stood with Amarnath, and paid tribute to him not only as a cricketer but also as a gentleman.

After his retirement from Test cricket, Lala Amarnath served Indian cricket as a selector, and finally, as chairman of the selection committee.

I was in the middle of writing this book when Lala died at his home in New Delhi. His death is a great loss to the game of cricket in general, and to India in particular. Lala, as I knew him, was a good friend.

17

Denis Compton:
Cavalier Cricketer

'Luck is going my way'

The ever-smiling and fascinating cricketer, Denis Compton, was the hero of thousands everywhere. His jovial company was always very welcome. I first saw Denis Compton in 1944, during a match at the Feroze Shah Kotla ground in New Delhi, where he played for the Delhi Rovers against Mamdot Cricket Club, Lahore, in the final of the Roshanara Cricket tournament. I was a young man then and knew very little about him. In those days, it was normal practice among local clubs to include the best available cricketers in their team to win prestigious tournaments. Since Denis Compton was posted in New Delhi as a British army officer during the Second World War, the Delhi Rovers approached him with an offer, one rupee for each run that he scored up to 50, and after that, two rupees for every run. Denis had been away from international cricket for a couple of years, but he willingly accepted the offer. Like a hungry lion, he played a marvellous innings and scored a double century. We lost the final, but for me it was a wonderful experience—playing against a brilliant and unorthodox batsman.

During his stay in India, Denis Compton played for different teams. He scored 1306 runs in nine matches including 7 hundreds. Playing for Holkar in the Ranji Trophy final against Bombay in 1944–45, Denis scored an unbeaten 249. During this innings, he had a 209-run partnership for the third wicket with Syed Mushtaq Ali. Compton also represented the Europeans in the Bombay Pentangular matches in which, in 1946, he scored 91 and 124 in two innings.

In 1953, when I was leading the Pakistan Eaglets team in England, Denis Compton and I did not face each other on the cricket ground. However, I encountered him at Lord's in the 1954 series. I was bowling against the most cavalier batsman of the world at the time. At the Feroze Shah Kotla ground in 1944, it was different because I was a teenager. My approach was different then and so was my attitude. But, at Lord's I was a changed cricketer, having established myself as a recognized opening bowler in international cricket.

Test cricket is entirely different to all other forms of cricket. It is a test of endurance, stamina, understanding, and attitude. It is a Test match because you are testing the capability of a player.

In the Lord's Test, we played first and were bowled out for 87 runs. It was a very poor score. My feeling was that I could bowl England out within 100 runs. We got Len Hutton out for a duck. Compton walked up to the crease at the fall of Simpson's wicket. He took his guard, and looked around the field. I knew that a batsman who can't hook, looks hesitantly towards fine-leg. He looks more than once and tries to establish that he is a fine hooker, although he is not. But, Denis Compton was in a different class. He did not apply any negative tactics and remained very much within the framework of discipline and decency. Compton's great innings for England revealed his grace and his spirit of indomitable courage.

At Lord's, I was aware of his glamour and dominance as a world-class batsman. While walking towards my bowling mark, I looked at the Pakistani flag fluttering on top of the pavilion building and prayed to Allah to help me get him out early. The heavens were on my side that day. Compton couldn't stay long. He was beaten twice. On the third delivery, he came out of his crease and tried to play me on the off-side, had a good shy at the ball, and was clean bowled.

Although I didn't get close to Denis Compton, we had seen and known each other's temperament and calibre. It was only after the next Test match at Nottingham that we came to know each other better. Pakistan batted first and made a very modest score. Denis Compton was now a different batsman from what I had seen at Lord's. He was very difficult to contain. He scored 278 runs, his best in Test cricket. When he was on 20, he misread my leg-cutter which moved off the wicket. He came forward in an attempt to play a cover-drive, and was beaten by the ball which took his edge. But, Imtiaz Ahmad dropped the catch as well as missed a stumping chance. 'No,' I shouted in sheer disappointment, and Denis Compton, frowning at me, said, 'Luck is going my way.' I stared at him, but only saw his smiling face. Although he got further chances at 120 and 171, his style of batting that day was mesmerizing. He would come out of the crease and hit hard with great skill. At 120, in an attempt to hit me over my head, Compton hit a skier. Both Ghazali and Aslam Khokhar ran for the catch, but collided with each other and the ball dropped yards away from them.

Compton was at his best at Nottingham. While tackling accurate bowling he used his feet and played his strokes with absolute ease and command. He sent the ball to all parts of the ground in a flurry of strokes. His second hundred was very quick. He took just a few minutes more than an hour. As far as I can recall, he would hit the ball towards Wazir Muhammad and call to the batsman on the non-striking end 'Run two, Wazir there!' And, he would make his runs comfortably.

I had pulled a leg muscle which forced me to shorten my run-up. I wrapped a plaster round my leg, and bowled 47 overs. Compton knew of my injury, so whenever I succeeded in checking his flowing strokes, he would be vocal in his praise for my bowling. He also encouraged me many a time while I was batting in the second innings.

Compton played another masterful innings in the third Test at Manchester, but, unfortunately, missed his well-deserved century by only seven runs. The Manchester Test was washed out. After the match, the former England Test cricketer, Alf Gover, was coming to London. There was room in his car, so I requested Gover if he could give me a lift up to London as I wanted to consult Dr Tucker. Denis Compton and Godfrey Evans were also going to London in the same car. During the journey, they kept on talking about county cricket. When we reached the outskirts of London, I asked Denis Compton, 'Denis, what do you think about Pakistan cricket?' He looked at me with his ever-smiling face and asked Alf Gover, 'Don't you think it's time for a drink?' Gover parked his car at a road restaurant, and my question was sidetracked. Again, in the restaurant, the conversation turned to their domestic cricket. I posed my question this time to Evans. At that point, Denis Compton replied in his usual carefree style, 'Fazal, you are getting into Test cricket as a newborn cricketing nation. You are a young side. If you take some time to mature, you can be as good a side as any county in England.' Naturally, I was hurt. Having played against Len Hutton, Denis Compton, and Peter May in the previous Tests, I knew their calibre. I firmly believed they were not that difficult a side to bowl out. And recalling Keith Miller's words at Colombo that you have got to bowl them out, I said, 'Denis, our next match is at the Oval and I think that we shall have a good shot at you.' 'No,' he said smilingly, 'You can't do it. As I said, you are a good county side. All the same, you have the potential, but England is a far better side.'

We had played against good players in England in 1953. In our match with the West Indies Test team, we had overpowered them. I said, 'Let's see what happens at the Oval.' I got Compton out in both the innings of the Oval Test. In the second innings, Denis snicked the ball behind the stumps into the safe hands of Imtiaz Ahmad. Standing out of his crease, he waited for the umpire's decision, and Imtiaz threw the ball into the wickets, so he was also stumped, out. Denis stood there and looked at umpire Lee, and started walking. Lee said, 'Denis, you should have walked in the first place.' 'I was wondering whether I was caught behind or stumped-out,' replied Denis. 'No, you were caught behind first before you were stumped,' retorted Lee.

Compton started his first class career as a slow left-arm bowler. Playing for Middlesex against Sussex, he batted at number eleven. However, he performed well and started moving up, ending the season with well over 1000 runs. In his debut Test against New Zealand in 1937, Compton made 65 runs in the only innings. He hit his first century (102) at Trent Bridge against Australia in 1938. By the time South Africa visited England in 1947, Compton had become a mature batsman. In five Tests, he piled on 753 runs (94.12). His aggregate included four centuries—208 at Lord's, 163 at Nottingham, 115 at Manchester, and 113 at the Oval. When Australia toured England in 1948, Compton scored 562 (62.44), including 184 at Trent Bridge and 145 at Manchester.

Compton was an unorthodox batsman. He would always take a chance to hit the ball wide off fielders. When he was well set, he would come down the wicket even against the fast bowlers. He scored exactly 300 against North-Eastern Transvaal, at Benoni, when England visited South Africa in 1948–49. That was the fastest triple century scored, and took only 181 minutes.

Denis was a cheerful character, and I remember that after our victory at the Oval, he brought twelve bottles of champagne for us. He was jubilant about Pakistan's victory and celebrated it with the Pakistan team.

Denis Compton was a very accommodating player. He would help incoming batsmen to adjust at the crease, even if they were from the opposing team. He would just walk up and put them at ease.

There is no doubt that Denis Compton, the Brylcream Man, was a marvellous character in international cricket. He was such a complete cricketer. The Second World War had taken five of his best cricketing years because no international cricket was played during that period. Yet, he sought his greatest enjoyment in the game, which was important to him. He entertained his countrymen who wanted to forget the miseries of the war, and lived his life to the fullest.

Compton's initial movement back and across, combined with a wonderful eye, quick reaction, back-lift towards third-man position, and plenty of guts were what made him such an accomplished hooker of the ball. It also meant that he was never unduly worried by great pace. Throughout his career, he delighted the crowd with his excellent footwork. However, knee trouble in the later stages of his career reduced the nimble movements of this great batsman. In 1950, his knee was operated upon, but the same problem cropped up again in later years. In November 1955, Compton had to undergo an even more serious operation when his kneecap was removed. But, he was a determined cricketer and did not allow this to end his career although this injury did keep him out of Test cricket for quite some time. He missed the first four Test matches against Australia at home in 1956, but he played in the Oval Test. When he appeared from the dressing room to start his innings, the crowd gave him a standing ovation. After all, he was the darling of the crowd. His old friend and foe, Keith Miller, was bowling. Like a true professional, he bowled him one of the fastest balls of the day. Compton was batting after a gap of almost ten months. It took him more than half an hour to score his first run. But, once settled, he played his leg-sweeps, late-cuts, and peerless cover-drives with absolute ease and scored 94 runs.

Compton was a courageous batsman and always played a team game. He was hit by a bouncer by the Australian fast bowler Ray Lindwall in the 1948 Manchester Test and required a number of stitches. It was the type of injury which would have put off many players from facing pace bowling. But, not the determined Denis. He returned to the crease with the score at 119 for five, and was undefeated at the close with 145 to his credit. He never bothered to wear a thigh pad, even when Miller, Lindwall, and Johnston were hurling their fastest deliveries. His 184 in the first Test at Nottingham was the most heroic innings ever played. England was struggling in the second innings, 344 runs behind. But, Compton demonstrated remarkable self-restraint against the fire of Keith Miller. His magnificent innings only ended when, while hooking a vicious bouncer from Keith, he fell on his wicket.

Some think of footwork only in terms of going down the wicket, but this is not true. Correct footwork is one of the foundations of batting, and is just as essential inside the crease. In this context, when Denis Compton played back, he would give himself maximum room by going right back on to the stumps, to the extent that on occasions he tread on his own wicket. The sweep shot was his favourite stroke and he always played it with authority. The ball would cross the ropes in seconds.

Denis was one of the biggest box-office draws. He was a source of delight to the spectators all over the world who would throng the stadiums to watch him play. He always batted with ease and enjoyed each and every moment. His cricket always looked fresh. Nature was generous to Compton. He was bestowed with natural gifts. With his loose limbs and broad shoulders, he became known to millions as the 'Lord of cricket'.

Denis Compton's exuberant health, his indomitable spirit, and his sense of humour enabled him to face difficult times with a sense of humour. In 1954, when his aeroplane belly landed at Karachi airport while he was on his way to Australia, he relaxed at the bar as if nothing had happened, and downed a dozen pegs of whisky. His knee problem was caused by football, as Denis was also a very good football player. He was a dangerous winger and scorer of goals. In the Oval Test against India in 1946, he ran Merchant out by kicking the ball from mid-on straight into the stumps.

Compton had an amazing ability to hit any ball anywhere, irrespective of whether the bowler was a spinner or a speedster. When he was set, he was not only difficult to dismiss, but his wide and frequently unconventional range of strokes, combined with his ability to improvise, made him difficult to contain. One expects a bad ball to be hit over the ropes by a class performer, but Compton had the ability to treat even the good deliveries in the same fashion. It was impossible to place a proper field against an in-form Compton, and eleven fielders looked too small a side to field. In his innings at Trent Bridge, we found ourselves in the same position. He was at his brilliant best and could do whatever he liked.

Denis was a jovial man. I recall an interesting incident which occurred in the Trent Bridge Test. When Wazir dropped Compton, other fielders started laughing at him. It amused Compton to see that instead of cursing the fielder who had dropped the catch, these players were laughing. He could not resist, and asked Imtiaz Ahmad: 'Every time some one drops a catch, the rest of you start laughing. Why do you laugh?' 'We laugh because next it could be any one of us who might drop a catch,' Imtiaz responded. He enjoyed the joke, but it was true. The set thinking of our fielders then was why hold catches when we could get them out in other ways.

It would be unfair to ignore one particular aspect of Compton's brilliant cricketing career. He was a good bowler also. He would bowl occasionally and often break long partnerships with his leg-break bowling. Had he concentrated a little more on his bowling, he could have been a fine all-rounder.

18

Sir Frank Worrell: Rhythm and Style

'Oh, Faz—they can't get me out!'

I first met this great batsman in 1949 when the Commonwealth team played an unofficial Test against the Pakistan team in the Bagh-i-Jinnah ground at Lahore. We shook hands and exchanged greetings. Frank Worrell had made his name in international cricket while I was just getting into competitive cricket at the international level.

In this match Frank Worrell only scored 16 runs. There is an interesting story behind his poor performance. An evening before the start of the match, Frank and his team-mate Holt, stayed till late night at a city bar. The liaison officer of the Commonwealth team, Sultan F. Hussain, a renowned sports journalist, told me that, with great difficulty, he managed to drop them to their hotel. Next day, Holt made 162 runs. He kept on yelling throughout his innings, 'Oh! Man, I can't see the ball.' But, he would make a wild hit and the ball would go over the fence. But, Frank was so tired that he could hardly stand at the wicket.

In 1953, the Pakistan Eaglets were on tour in England and I was then an established Test bowler. We played a match at Ebbw Vale in Wales against a full strength West Indies team in which all the three W's—Weekes, Walcott, and Worrell played. The West Indies could just draw the match. In reply to our score of 283 for 3, they could only score 128 for 8. Worrell (43) was the highest scorer. I got 4 wickets. Every good ball bowled by me was lauded. We had a better understanding of each other after that match.

Worrell was only nineteen years old when he became the youngest triple-centurion of all time in February 1944. Playing for Barbados against Trinidad, he scored an unbeaten 308 at Bridgetown. In this innings he shared an unbroken fourth-wicket stand of 502 with Goddard. Again, in 1945–46, Worrell became the only batsman in first-class cricket to take part in two partnerships exceeding 500 runs. It was at Port-of-Spain, against the same Trinidad team, that he and Walcott made an unbroken stand of 574 runs for the fourth wicket.

Worrell started his brilliant Test career against England in the second Test at Port-of-Spain in 1948 where he missed a well-deserved century by only three runs. But, in the third Test of the series at Georgetown, he got his first Test century by scoring 131 not out. His innings was a display of exquisite drives and pulls, and contributed significantly to the West Indies' victory in the Test. The same year, he signed a professional contract with the Central Lancashire League (CLL), and played for Radcliffe. It was a good break for young Worrell as CLL was a cricket academy where a young, talented player was bound to improve. A young cricketer gains tremendous experience and maturity from playing in league cricket. This grooms him not only as a player but also as a man. There is much to learn about human relations from the kind, friendly, and warm people of the north of England.

The series against England in 1950 was a personal triumph for Worrell. His brilliant performance brought him into the limelight when he topped the Test batting average, scoring 539 runs at 89.83. It would not be wrong to say that he touched the heights of fame on that tour. His all-round performance in the third Test at Trent Bridge, where he scored 261, was ample proof of his outstanding qualities. It was such a dazzling innings that there was talk of Hutton's then Test record being in danger. Worrell also opened the bowling in the match, and took 3 for 40. At the Oval, he again delighted the crowd with a brilliant innings of 138 runs. The consistency in his performance on the tour earned him a place among Wisden's five cricketers of the year.

The West Indies toured Australia in 1951–52. In the third Test at Adelaide, Worrell established himself as a bowler by bowling unchanged throughout the Australian innings of 82, and grabbed 6 for 38. He scored a superb 108 in the fourth Test at Melbourne. A lifting delivery from Keith hit him on the arm, and he was in considerable pain during his innings. But, he showed admirable determination and courage, and during the later stage of his innings, he practically played one-handed and scored 337 (33.70) while taking 17 wickets (19.35). When India toured the West Indies in 1951–52, he scored a delightful 237 in the third Test at Jamaica. In 1953–54, he scored another brilliant knock of 164 in the fourth Test at Port-of-Spain against England.

Sir Frank Worrell was slim, lithely built, and elegant. He was a marvellous, right-handed batsman who could play every orthodox stroke. His stance at the wicket was perfectly balanced, dominating, and majestic. One could easily single him out by the supple beauty of his strokes. He had quick judgement and footwork, batted with style and exquisite timing. He would lift his bat from shoulder to shoulder. Normally, he batted in the middle order but could play at any number. In the 1957 series in England, the West Indies openers were not doing well against the sustained accuracy of the English fast bowlers, so Worrell opened the innings in the last two Tests. Though he himself had scored very few runs in the first two Tests, yet he opened the innings in the third Test, and batted through the innings.

I was in England playing league cricket with East Lancashire and met Worrell before the start of the third Test against England at Nottingham in 1957. Naturally, we talked about cricket. He seemed perturbed as he had scored very few runs in the previous two Tests. 'Franky, not striking form?' I asked him straightaway. He glanced at me. I can still recall the brightness which shone in his confident-looking eyes. 'Oh [Fazal], they can't get me out in this Test,' he said with quiet determination, and repeated his words. He knew what he was saying, and he meant it.

England played first and declared at the score of 619 for 6. Frank Worrell opened the innings for the West Indies and started playing his natural strokes in a cavalier fashion. At tea, while he was walking back to the pavilion, Frank saw me, standing near the ropes on the boundary line and shouted, 'Hey Faz, you see they can't get me out.' A record number of over 60,000 spectators witnessed Worrell scoring a brilliant century. He was determined to score a double century, but fell short of partners at the other end and ended up scoring 191. His excellent batting was an exhibition of powerful hooks and sizzling drives. This was an incredible innings played under pressure. England had piled up as many as 619 runs, and the West Indies needed 470 runs to avoid a follow-on. But Worrell rose to the occasion and played a determined innings. I recall his words, 'Faz, they can't get me out.' It was Worrell who time and again proved to be the mainstay of the West Indies, both in batting and bowling, during the 1957 tour of England.

Worrell was made captain for the first time on the Australian tour in 1960–61. He was the first coloured West Indies captain, and his was the most popular side ever to visit that part of the world. He destroyed the myth that a cricketer of colour was not fit to lead the West Indies team. As a captain, Worrell's influence over the players was commanding. They respected him. His greatest contribution was that he ended the rivalries between players of various islands and knit them into a team. He was calm and cool, and never lost his nerves. It was under his captaincy that the West Indies were involved in two of the most breathtaking finishes in Test history—at Brisbane in 1961 and at Lord's in 1963. He seldom lost his grip on the state of the match and players performed well under him. This was clearly demonstrated in the first ever tied Test match in cricket history at Brisbane in 1961, when Australia needed only 27 runs for victory in about thirty minutes, with a couple of wickets intact. Worrell maintained his calm, and commanded his bowlers and fielders in such a manner that even in the most exciting moments of the match they played firm and positive cricket. He insisted on playing attractive and sensible cricket. Worrell was admired by cricket lovers for the spirit in which he played the series. He made cricket an exciting game to watch. When the West Indies left Australia in 1961, more than half a million people gathered in the streets of Melbourne to bid farewell to Worrell and his team as he led the team through the streets in open cars. It was a highly emotional farewell for the West Indies team who had lost the series.

Frank was a true sportsman and never objected to any verdict given by the umpire. In the Melbourne Test of February 1961, umpires Hoy and Egar, after consultation, gave a controversial decision in favour of Australia at a crucial point, but Frank accepted the decision without demur in the true spirit of good cricket and fair play. He was a man of great cricketing qualities who infused discipline in his team and gave clear instructions to the players to walk if they were given out. He did not hesitate to even reprimand Garfield Sobers who showed dissent at an umpire's decision in a Test during the series. After that, everyone just walked as soon as the umpire's finger went up.

Frank was not an individual player but was a team man. In the first Test at Bridgetown during the 1959–60 series against England, when his captain, Alexander, declared the innings at a point when the West Indies' batsmen were finding it difficult to score against England's steady bowling and defensive fielding, Worrell was only a hit away from his double hundred. He accepted his captain's decision smilingly, and did not flinch.

Frank was very hard to dismiss, and to set a field to him when he had settled at the crease was simply impossible. He hardly ever played a crude or misplaced stroke. He was not aggressive in batting, but artistic, with style and elegance. He would tell the bowler that he was in no hurry. He was seldom seen playing across the line, which is why he rarely played the hook shot.

Worrell was a shrewd medium-pacer with an easy, relaxed action who could give anxious moments to any batsman. Many a time he opened the attack either with Gilchrist or Gomez. His bowling in the fourth Test at Leeds against England in 1957 was simply superb, picking up 7 wickets for 70 runs.

When Pakistan visited the West Indies in 1958, Frank Worrell was away for higher studies and could not play against us. Thus, I missed encountering this great cricketer.

In the beginning of 1962, an Indian team visited the West Indies. Worrell scored 332 (88.00) in five Tests. His highest score was an unbeaten 98 in the fifth Test at Kingston.

Worrell was a true nationalist. He was a man of strong convictions. I vividly remember the second Test match at Lord's in 1963, where the last moments of the fifth day's play were thrilling. Both England and the West Indies could have won the match. Colin Cowdrey came in to bat in the last over with a broken right arm wrapped in plaster. The last pair for England was at the crease. They needed six runs to win the match in more than half an hour's play. The West Indies needed only one wicket, and was in a good position to win the match. They were already one up in the five-Test series. Frank didn't attack, and the match was drawn. The next two Tests were also drawn. We met each other after the series, and I asked Frank, 'How did that happen? You could have won the match.' What Sir Frank Worrell told me was a true reflection of his nationalism. Frank was concerned about the economics of the tour. He was confident that he could beat England any time, but by playing a draw he had kept the hopes of the English crowd alive, and they thronged the grounds in the remaining Tests. The tour was a great financial success for the West Indies cricket, but this would not have been possible if they had won the match at Lord's. 'Faz, my country needs foreign exchange,' Sir Frank Worrell told me. How many people would think in terms of national interest in this way? Worrell would not make any kind of move which would deter the progress of his country, by words—or deeds. This is not the cricket that we see in many parts of the world today.

In the Lord's Test of the 1963 series, when Wes Hall started his last over, which could have won or lost the Test, Worrell went to him with some advice. 'Make sure you don't give it to them by bowling no-balls.' Worrell was the calmest man at Lord's that day.

Worrell was generous. When Indian captain, Nari Contractor, was in hospital because of a Griffith delivery during a side-match at Bridgetown in the 1962 series, Worrell was one of the donors of blood which saved his life.

It was not generally known that Worrell was also a superstitious man. During the 1951 tour of Australia, playing against South Australia, he was bowled first ball by Geoff Noblet. Determined to make a fresh start in the second innings, he changed his clothes and got a new pair of trousers, hoping that by discarding his old clothes he would change his luck. But, he was again out on the very first ball. As he came in, crestfallen, Walcott, the next batsman, said with a laugh: 'Why do I have to face a hat-trick every time I follow you?'

Frank announced his retirement after the England tour of 1963. The following year, Her Majesty the Queen knighted this complete cricketer, philosopher, and captain.

Worrell was soft-spoken and sedate. In a few words he would convey volumes. Throughout his life, Frank never lost his sense of humour or his sense of dignity. He lost no friends, made no enemies, and won much respect. Frank was a great cricketer, a great captain, and an exemplary ambassador for the West Indies cricket. He was an educated man and a man with a future. He studied economics and sociology at the Manchester University. He was elected a Senator in the Jamaican parliament. Had he lived longer he would surely have made an even greater contribution to the West Indies. Tragically, he died of leukaemia in 1967 at the very young age of forty-two. A memorial service was held in the Westminster Abbey and the flag at the Radcliffe town hall was at half-mast on the day of his death. Such was the esteem in which he was held by Radcliffe that, in 1964, a street near the cricket ground was named Worrell Close.

After his death, the Frank Worrell Trophy was created for permanent competition between the West Indies and Australia.

19

Keith Ross Miller:
Extraordinary Class

'You can't go out off the field'

Keith Miller was born in Sunshine, Melbourne at a time when Sir Keith Smith and Sir Ross Smith were creating history with the first flight from England to Australia. His parents named him after these two famous airmen—Keith and Ross. Years later, Miller's own exploits in the air as a pilot earned for him the reputation of being a dashing fellow. Keith Miller had an endearing and refreshing friendliness, and an unassumed spontaneity which won the hearts of his fellow cricketers and fans alike.

I saw Keith Miller the first time when he came to Lahore in 1946 with the Australian Services XI. The match was played against the Northern Indian Cricket Association. Keith Miller was known for his physique, health, and stature. He was a model of concentration and application.

I came in close contact with Keith Miller again when we played together for the Commonwealth XI in a match against the MCC at Colombo in February 1952. I was selected in the Commonwealth XI because only two months before I had routed the MCC at Karachi and earned a memorable victory for Pakistan. In fact, this was the victory which helped Pakistan in getting full membership of the ICC. Keith Miller must have heard about me for when I arrived in my Colombo hotel, I found dozens of chits in my key-box asking me to contact Keith immediately on arrival. Since it was past midnight, we met the next morning in the tennis court of the hotel, where he greeted me with great enthusiasm. 'Hey, where have you been hiding

yourself? I was looking for you. We have got to beat the MCC'—
'I will try,' I said, modestly. 'No question of trying, you have
got to beat them,' a confident Keith Miller said firmly.

The next day, Keith Miller scored 106 runs. Neil Harvey got 74
and Imtiaz Ahmad scored 42 runs. Our total was 517 runs. Then
it was the MCC's turn. Keith and I opened the bowling attack.
The pitch was fast. Miller was the big personality of the match.
After scoring a century, he was all set to give the Englishmen a
difficult time with the ball. He proved that he could be regarded
as the leading all-rounder of the world. The entire MCC team
was bundled out for 103 runs in the first innings, and was made
to follow-on. I had taken four wickets. At the end of the innings,
when we were going back to the pavilion, I heard a loud voice
behind me call out, 'Fazal, you can't go off the field.' I looked
back and saw Keith coming towards me. I wondered what he
meant, but then be said, 'You have bowled well and taken
wickets. Everyone will pay you compliments in the dressing
room. Naturally, you will feel elated and become complacent
and lose your concentration.' Keith Miller came near me, held
my shoulders, and repeated his words emphatically. He was a
genius who knew how to handle an upcoming bowler. He was
determined to beat the MCC. We both sat on the ground outside
the pavilion, and discussed the strategy to be applied against the
MCC in the second innings. 'Fazal, give them a 100-odd runs in
the second innings and finish the match.'

As the team came out, we joined the boys and walked to the
wicket. Miller got the first wicket, and Tom Graveney came out
to bat at number three. Keith Miller asked me to bowl from the
other end, and said, 'Fazal, don't get him out. Give him 20-odd
runs. This guy has to play against us next season and I want to
find out his weak points.' I had easily dismissed Graveney in
the first innings for a duck and was determined to repeat it in
the second innings also. At first I was perplexed but then
I understood the intent and admired his foresight. I was
impressed by the great all-rounder's understanding of the game.
I repeated his words, 'Twenty-odd runs, granted.' However,
Tom Graveney was the top scorer in the second innings. Vinoo

Mankad got him out when he was two short of a well-deserved 50. After the fall of Tom's wicket, Keith took the ball from the other end, saying, 'Right, let's call it a day', and the whole team was out for 155 runs. That was typical of Keith Miller. He would win matches according to his whim.

Keith was a fantastic right-handed batsman. His batting technique was from shoulder to shoulder-lift and finish, i.e. he would lift the bat up to his shoulder and finish up to the shoulder. He was quick-footed. Whenever Ramadhin threw the ball up, he would advance to meet him on the half-volley. In 1953, when I was in England with the Pakistan Eaglets, the Australian team was on tour. Since Keith Miller was there, I wanted to meet this wonderful and charming man. One evening I found him sitting in a bar in a London hotel, surrounded by dozens of fans. There were women too. Keith saw me coming, stood up on the table holding a glass of whisky, and said to his fans, 'Hey, listen every body! Here comes a blue-eyed handsome guy, I am envious of him. He is going to tour England next year. I am envious of him because you are going to forget me for him. I can very safely say that England will have to struggle against him and that he shall pose a big challenge to the English batsmen.' I was embarrassed. Keith was an immensely generous person. He himself was a very handsome man. He had been blessed with everything that a man could want. There are very few people like him.

Keith Miller began bowling in 1945 when he visited England with the Australian Services XI. Keith eventually became a great bowler who would put in every last ounce of energy into his bowling. He could bowl long spells and could move the ball either way at varying pace. His long hair would drop over his eyes and he would flick it back with a jerk of his head which would get the women's hearts beating wildly. When bowling with Ray Lindwall, Keith formed the best and most consistent bowling attack in Australian cricket history. They appeared together in almost fifty Test matches. The secret of his success was determination, application, and concentration.

Keith was an honest and straightforward man who never minced his words. He was one of the finest men one could wish to meet and he loved cricket. Sir Frank Worrell wrote this about Keith Miller in his book, *Cricket Punch*:

> Many of his actions were meant to be nothing more than an effort to keep the game alive. He was once playing against us when the match had fallen into the doldrums. The spectators were almost asleep, and so were the players. Miller walked up to me and said, "I shall wake these b------s up. I am going on to bowl and the third, fourth and fifth balls of my over will be bouncers." He was true to his words. The ball simply whistled over my head, but I had taken evasive action in time, knowing fully well that Keith would not double-cross even his worst enemy. The crowd sprang to life. From all round the ground came the boos and jeers. And Keith Miller smiled. He had done what he said he would do.

During the 1954 series against England, when I arrived at the Oval cricket ground, I got a telegram from Keith Miller saying, 'You should damn well beat England. Best of luck!' During the match, yet another telegram from Keith Miller said: 'Keep it up!' It was reminiscent of Keith Miller during the course of the match against the MCC at Colombo in 1952. The last telegram from him said: 'Congratulations, you have done it!' These gave me a lot of moral support and added to my determination. I was reminded of his words in Colombo: 'Fazal, you can't leave the ground because you will lose your concentration.' 'You can do it', was what he said when I was playing against the MCC at Colombo. Most people never thought we could beat England. But, I knew in my heart that we were capable of doing it.

Keith Miller admired Pakistan. He always stood by Pakistan and became popular with Pakistani crowds when he came to play in the Relief Fund match at Karachi in 1955. Playing for the Governor General's XI, Keith regaled the large crowd with a galaxy of huge sixes, straight hits and cross-fire. He scored 132 and 50 in the two innings.

Keith Miller was indisputably one of the greatest all-rounders of all times. In the 1953 Test series with England, Keith Miller emulated the earlier achievement of Wilfred Rhodes with 2000 runs and 100 wickets in Test cricket. It was his all-round performance in the West Indies that made Australia the first team to win a series in the Caribbean in 1955. He scored 439 (73.16) runs with three hundreds in five Test matches, and took 20 wickets (32.00). He hit 147 in the first Test at Kingston and 137 in the fourth Test at Bridgetown. At Kingston, in the fifth Test, Keith proved that he was the best all-rounder of the world. He scored 109 and got 8 wickets in the match.

Keith was a cricketer who could change the fate of the match at will. The Lord's Test of the 1956 series is remembered as Keith Miller's match. He walked into the field rubbing his hands and said: 'Hey, boys! Let's win this match!' And, he did. He took 10 for 152 in the match which was a great feat for a thirty-six year-old bowler. Australia won the match by 185 runs. He was the leading Australian wicket-taker in the series (21 at 22.23).

After the 1956 Ashes series, the Australian team stopped for one Test at Karachi. Keith Miller was also in the team. On reaching Karachi, he greeted me with his familiar smile. We talked of the good old days spent together in Colombo and in England. A few days before the arrival of the Australian team, I was sitting in Lahore's Shezan hotel with the late Mian Salahuddin and some other friends discussing the performance of the Australian team in England. I told my friends that Australia would have to struggle for runs in Karachi and predicted that I would get them out for a 100-odd runs. My friends branded it as 'big talk'.

I told Keith Miller about my conversation with my friends in Lahore. He burst into laughter and said: 'Yes, we have been forewarned in England by your friend Denis Compton to tackle you carefully. I know that you can win.'

There is an interesting story about this Karachi Test that I got from Munir Hussain (the famous radio and TV commentator) who was the liaison officer with the Australian team. In the first innings of the Test, Keith Miller was the number four batsman. He put on his pads and told Munir he was going to sleep. He was to be woken up only when his turn came. Munir woke him up asking Keith to go in to bat. He got up rubbing his eyes and asked: 'Is McDonald batting'? 'He is back in the pavilion,' came Munir's reply. 'What about Harvey?' 'He is also out.' 'Who got the wickets?' Keith asked. 'Fazal', replied Munir. 'Oh, he is on the run again. Well, do not disturb my bed because I will be back soon,' Keith Miller told Munir.

After the Karachi Test of 1956, both Keith and I were entertained by the late Nawab of Junagarh, Dilawar Khanji, at his residence. There was also a routine farewell dinner from the BCCP. I was the vice-captain of the team but I had not been given a seat on the head table. Keith Miller, who was wandering near that table, asked where my seat was. Then an extra seat was brought in for me. Recently, I sent Keith a Christmas card and he replied: 'Fazal, I am simply delighted, I am honoured!'

The great Keith Miller is my friend. He never forgot me. When the Pakistan team was touring England in 1962, and it lost its first three Tests under the captaincy of Javed Burki, I was requested by the then BCCP president to fly to London to rescue the team. Keith Miller, who was covering the series for the *Daily Mail*, wrote in his piece: 'England is on trial, Fazal arrives.' This alerted the English players, and he was proved correct. My first spell in the Nottingham Test was quite economical. I got a wicket also. The match was drawn. During the match, Keith asked me, 'Why did you not come in the very first place?' After the match, Keith angrily asked the manager of the team why had I not been picked for the tour in the first place. Naturally, the manager had no answer.

Keith Miller had a sense of humour and he spiced his conversation with sparkling wit. He never lost an opportunity to laugh at the mistakes of rival batsmen. In a Test match, when a yorker hit one of the English batsman's toe and narrowly missed his stumps, Keith appealed. The batsman said, 'It hit my toe.' Keith Miller could not resist the following reply: 'Toe, my foot! The ball is to be hit with the bat not with the toe.'

Keith Miller also visited Pakistan with the Australian team in 1979. He was invited by the Pakistan Television Corporation for expert comments on the game. During the Faisalabad Test, there was a slight drizzle which did not affect the wicket at all but Javed Miandad did not play till lunch. The Australians were not satisfied and they wanted to resume play. Keith Miller was also upset. He came to me and said, 'Fazal, tell them there is nothing wrong with the wicket. It is absolutely alright. It can last for eight days.'

There is an interesting incident that reflects Keith's attitude to the game. He had been celebrating the birth of his fourth son and arrived late for a Sheffield Shield match against South Australia. The players were leaving the dressing room. He told his team-mates, 'I will only bowl a couple of overs, to get the grog out of my system and then Alan Davidson can take over.' Ninety minutes later, the team was back in the pavilion. South Australia had been knocked over for 27 runs and Keith Miller had taken 7 for 12. What a feat and exhibition of determination, concentration, and application.

Keith Miller had outstanding success as captain with New South Wales but, strangely enough, he was never asked to lead his country. However, in the absence of his injured captain, Ian Johnson, he led his team to victory in the Kingston Test against the West Indies in 1955.

Keith Miller loved the crowds and they loved him. In a Sheffield Shield match against Victoria, he allowed the rival team to play through steady rain on the first day. Johnson, the captain of Victoria, could hardly have refused a request for an adjournment, but Keith stayed on because he wanted to provide some cricket for the over ten thousand spectators who had gathered to watch the match.

Keith Miller first became prominent during the tour of England in 1945. He hit two centuries at Lord's. In the third Test, he took 6 for 86. In the last match, playing for the Dominions XI led by Learie Constantine, against England, Miller scored a brilliant 186 at Lord's. He reminded the public of the days of G. Jessop by sending the ball sailing over the Lord's pavilion and into the Tavern.

Keith made his Test debut against New Zealand at Wellington in 1945–46. In the 1946–47 Test series against England in Australia, Miller was at his best. At Brisbane he scored 79 and took 7 for 60 in the first innings, indisputably a great performance. In the fourth Test of the series at Adelaide, he scored his first Test century (141). When Australia visited England in 1948, Miller's performance was excellent. He finished second to Don Bradman in the batting average. He scored 384 (76.80) and took 16 wickets (20.87). In the first Test at Nottingham, he clean-bowled Hutton and Compton, the two most dependable batsmen, in both innings. His bowling helped Australia to victory by 8 wickets. Besides this, he took an amazing catch in the slips to dismiss Hardstaff for a duck. He swooped down and scooped the ball up from ankle height, then lost his balance, fell backward, and ended on his head, a rare acrobatic feat and a unique catch.

When England toured Australia in 1950–51, Keith picked up 4 wickets for 37, and then scored an unbeaten century (145) in the Sydney Test. He headed the batting with 350 (43.75). He also took 17 wickets (17.70). The following year, Keith scored 362 (40.27) and grabbed 20 wickets (19.90) against the West Indies. He scored 129 in the second Test at Sydney.

During the 1954–55 series against England, Keith Miller was the most menacing bowler with the new ball. His opening assaults at Brisbane, Melbourne, and Adelaide were positively hair-raising.

Keith's three great innings of 147 at Kingston, 137 at Bridgetown, and 109 again at Kingston in the 1955 series against the West Indies show what a great cricketer he was. In the first Test at Kingston, he also took five wickets. During his first-class career, Keith Miller scored 7 double centuries. His highest was 281 against Leicestershire at Leicester in 1956.

Keith was an honest and straightforward man who never minced his words. He is one of those few cricketers I admire immensely. Throughout his career, he played with dignity. He would charm the crowds with his powerful strokes. He would put such force behind his strokes that no fielder would put his hand to the ball. As a bowler, he was a most mercurial character.

He would throw a straight bouncer with great ferocity and venom. The batsmen found it very difficult to hook or avoid this ball.

Keith was a loveable cricketer. For nearly fifteen years, this dynamic player was a lively force in Australian cricket. He was an excellent batsman but his batting suffered because of the burden of too much bowling. He was one of those rare players who could change the course of a match, as a batsman, bowler, or fielder, in a few minutes. Dull cricket would at once become lively when Keith Miller arrived at the wicket. He would soon dominate the scene with his glorious, sparkling strokes all round the ground.

I learnt a lot from Keith Miller. As a friend he motivated me. I have received many compliments from various people, but the one that Keith Miller paid me still makes me proud. While comparing me with Jim Laker, who took ten wickets in a Test innings, Keith wrote in a British paper, and I quote, 'If Laker was marvellous, Fazal was the master.'

20

Nazar Muhammad:
Indomitable Courage
'You take care of yourself and I will do my bit'

Runs alone should not be the criterion to measure a batsman's quality. There was a majestic beauty in Nazar's batting and fielding which was unique. Though he has since passed away, memories of his supremacy in batting and fielding have not faded. Born in a modest family of Lahore, Nazar was educated at the Islamia High School, Bhatti Gate. During his school days, Nazar joined the Mamdot cricket club which was one of the leading clubs in India. After school, he joined Islamia College, Railway Road. He was such a good batsman even then that he got a chance to play at other cricket centres like Bahawalpur, Rawalpindi, Karachi, Delhi, Bombay, and Patiala (India).

I became acquainted with Nazar Muhammad in the famous Minto Park where he had come to watch a match in a local tournament. We met and soon became friends. The road behind the Badshahi Mosque, just adjacent to the walled city, used to be deserted in those days. There was hardly any traffic on it. This road became our turf wicket. We would practice here, and it would make no difference to us whether we were playing on turf or a matting wicket. We would adjust ourselves straightaway.

Nazar started his first-class cricket for Northern India Cricket Association (NICA) in the Ranji Trophy in 1940–41 against NWFP at Peshawar. Then, in the Pentangular of 1943, he scored a brilliant innings of 61 against the Parsees. He played another sparkling innings of 154 against the Rest in the same tournament.

Nazar was a brave batsman who was not intimidated by bowlers. I will narrate two very interesting incidents which reflect his steadfastness. He represented North Zone against the Australian Services XI in the Bagh-i-Jinnah ground, Lahore, in 1946. Keith Miller, the most dangerous fast bowler of his time, was also playing in the match. He was a terror for batsmen. Nazar opened the innings and faced the fiery Keith gallantly. Keith and Nazar had an interesting duel. The first ball from Keith was a bouncer which was beautifully hooked for a couple of runs. When Keith hurled a second bouncer, Nazar hit it for a six. The ball struck the Lahore Gymkhana pavilion clock in the middle and the glass broke into pieces. Another bouncer was also hit beyond the ropes. Keith was bewildered. 'Oh, bloody good hooker,' he shouted at Nazar Muhammad. Though Nazar scored only 23 runs in two innings, yet Keith did not throw a bouncer at him again.

In an inter-varsity match before Partition at the Dring stadium, Bahawalpur, Nazar was hit on his forehead by a bouncer from Phadkar. He was brought back to the pavilion for first aid but was determined to resume his innings. Ultimately, we decided to allow him because he was adamant. 'You so and so, you have been hit by a bouncer on your forehead from that ordinary bowler, Phadkar,' he cursed himself. After the fall of the next wicket, he went in and faced another ball from Phadkar. It was a bouncer which he despatched over the ropes. Another bouncer he hooked for a six, and later he was heard outside the ground telling Phadkar, 'Fast bowler—my foot.'

Nazar and I played a lot of cricket together. We represented the Rest against the All-India team that toured England in December 1946. The match was played at the Feroze Shah Kotla ground in Delhi. That was a big match for both of us, almost like a Test match. We travelled from Lahore to Delhi in the Punjab Mail. During the journey, I asked Nazar, 'How are we going to fare against the All-India team?' Back came his reply, without hesitation and full of confidence, 'Never mind who is who, you take care of yourself and I will do my bit.' So it was. I bowled the Indian team out for 109, Nazar scored 110 and the All-India team lost by 6 wickets.

After Partition, Nazar Muhammad played cricket with one ambition only and that was to get Test status for Pakistan. The MCC team visited Pakistan in the winter of 1951 to gauge the standard of the Pakistan team. In the first representative match at Sialkot, Nazar scored a brilliant innings of 140. This was an innings to watch. He treated all the MCC bowlers, especially Statham, Ridgway, and Shackleton, with contempt.

Soon after the MCC tour, Pakistan was given Test status and we went to India in 1952 to play a five-Test series. Nazar Muhammad became the first Pakistani batsman to play the first ball in official Test cricket, and scored the first century for his country. I still remember that we were both sitting together after the painful defeat in the first Test at Delhi, dejected and silent. I broke the silence and asked, 'Nazar, how do you think we are going to fare in the second Test at Lucknow?' Back came his reply, very similar to what he had said when we were to represent the Rest, 'Now they will not be able to get me out,' he said. I looked at him. His face was a portrait of confidence and determination. Before the start of the first day's play, I asked Nazar, 'What do you think of the match?' 'You look after your department and I will control mine,' was his prompt reply. The match started, and Nazar, went on to play one of the best innings of his very short Test career. Our top order batsmen failed to lend him any support with the exception of Maqsood Ahmad who scored 40-odd runs. At times Nazar had to keep both ends up. However, Zulfiqar with 34 and I with 29, helped him complete his century. He was very jubilant for not only had he completed his century but he had also joined the select band of batsmen to bat through the innings. His unobtrusive innings was a remarkable example of restraint, defence, and concentration. It was a great achievement. When I congratulated him, he smilingly said, 'Tomorrow my photograph will appear in the newspaper.' I interrupted him jokingly and said, 'Not yours alone, there will be one more.' And, there was one more because I had run through the Indian innings and bagged 6 wickets that day.

In the good old days batsmen like Nazar Muhammad would always receive the incoming batsman half way to the wicket and apprise the batsman of the playing conditions. In the Lucknow Test, when I joined Nazar at the crease, I told him that Nyalchand, the Indian spinner, would be difficult for me. 'Never mind. You take a single and I will take care of Nyalchand,' Nazar replied. And, he ensured that I did not have to face Nyalchand. This was Nazar Muhammad, my friend and a true team man, for whom his country always came first.

Nazar was one of the finest gully fielders where he held several brilliant catches. We had an understanding that whenever I was to bowl an inswinger to intimidate the batsman—when starting from my bowling mark, I would touch my shirt collar. Nazar would understand and be alert for a catch. The manner in which he got Kishenchand, the leading Indian batsman, in the Lucknow Test was marvellous. He also brilliantly held Gaekwad's catch. The two remarkable catches of Gopinath and Umrigar in the Madras Test of the 1952 series were unbelievable. These were real 'gems' which would be remembered for a long time to come and were worthy of a Hammond or a Chipperfield. Many a class fielder would not have even attempted the catch which cut short Umrigar's innings. Nazar's great work in the field inspired our players.

Nazar was an amateur cricketer and played only for the love of the game. Nazar and I would ride together on one bicycle to go and play a cricket match, and get just five rupees after the match. Yet, we would be happy and would later enjoy a cinema show.

Nazar was a batsman of the highest order. He would play all kinds of strokes with equal ease. However, he was very strong on the leg side. In the short space of time that he gave to first-class and Test cricket, he made his mark both in batting and in fielding. He was my best friend. We played together in the Mamdot cricket club and in the college team. I remember that in the nets at Minto Park, there would be healthy duels between us. He would place a one-rupee coin on the off-stump and challenge me to knock the stump and take the coin.

Very few people knew that Nazar was a very skilled singer. He had a fantastic voice. During the Indian tour of 1952, a big dinner party was arranged in Bombay. The seventy guests gathered consisted mostly of people from the film industry. After dinner, the famous Indian playback singer, Talat Mahmood, sang for two hours. When he took a break, Nazar was asked to sing a few lines, which he did by singing, *Piya bin na aaye chaine*, meaning, 'I feel uneasy without my beloved'. Talat was so impressed that he would not sing after that. Nazar also composed a very famous song, *Aa ja balam aai baharain*, meaning, 'Come my love, the spring has arrived'. His elder brother, Feroze Nazami, was a famous music director of the subcontinent.

After the Indo-Pak Test series, Nazar Muhammad had an accident which ended his career forever. He slipped and fell from a building that broke his right hand. It changed the course of his brilliant future and world cricket lost a wonderful batsman. This misfortune snatched from him the opportunity to reach the greatest heights in international cricket.

I was in England with the Pakistan Eaglets team when I got the news that Nazar had met with an accident. When I came back, I called on him and learnt that instead of being taken to a proper doctor, he was taken to some kind of a local wrestler. Nazar had not fractured his arm but had just dislocated it. His arm had come out of its socket. The wrestler at first stretched his arm, then tried to push it back into the socket, and finally tied it with a hockey stick to keep it straight. I took Nazar to Dr Col. Shaukat, even though he was reluctant to go to a doctor. Col Shaukat said that there was a growth in the socket which was restricting the free movement of his arm. In 1954, Nazar decided to go to England. Muhammad Hussain, a close relative, arranged this trip. Dr Tucker, who was one of the leading doctors in England, treated him. He was very expensive, but he treated Nazar for free, and even brought food from his home for him. Dr Tucker operated on him twice, but the damage had been done by the wrestler. The growth in the socket would not allow the bones to be fixed in their original setting.

Nazar hailed from a family which had very meagre resources but who had integrity and a sincerity of purpose. After his return from England, Nazar had to face many hardships. He had to support his family but had no job. The irony of fate is that the people who were then governing the game of cricket hardly knew its meaning. As a result, Nazar was rejected. He did not want his son, Mudassar Nazar, to play cricket. But, Mudassar had the potential. I remember that when I insisted that Nazar allow Mudassar to play cricket, he was in tears. 'I will not allow any of my sons to play cricket,' he said. 'Mudassar is like my son and I too have a right over him,' I argued with him. So, after much convincing, he agreed. Later, Mudassar helped create a unique record in the history of Test cricket, making Nazar and himself the only father and son combination to bat through a Test innings. Mudassar did this against India in Lahore in the 1982–83 series.

With the assistance of Syed Fida Hassan, chief secretary of West Pakistan and once the president of the BCCP, Nazar found a job. His remuneration was not more than Rs 150 per month. After that, naturally, he would not talk about cricket. However, Nazar was a strong man. He endured the ups and downs of cricket and worked very hard to look after his family. He was quite contented and happy. He kept his chin up and played that innings of his life with quiet determination, even in adverse circumstances. The great Nazar Muhammad died on 12 July 1996 in Lahore. May Allah rest his soul in peace.

21

Neil Harvey:
Second to Bradman

'Oh, I forgot!'

Whenever I think of the Colombo Test against the MCC in February 1952, in which Imtiaz Ahmad and I were representing the Commonwealth XI I am reminded of an Australian who could have been another Bradman—Neil Harvey. There is no doubt that he was one of the most outstanding batsman produced by Australia after the legendary Sir Don Bradman.

During the Colombo Test, while bowling to Tom Graveny, I asked Keith Miller for a good fielder at short leg. Tom was a little weak on the leg side. His stance was such that if one were to bowl to him on the leg stick, a leg-cutter, he would go across the wicket and the ball would invariably go uppishly in the region of short-leg or fine-leg. On Keith's suggestion, Harvey was placed at short-leg. My third or fourth delivery was accurate to the last detail. It pitched on to the leg stump, and Tom snicked it into the safe hands of Harvey, who held the catch, put the ball in his pocket, and started rubbing his hands as if nothing had happened. This was my first introduction to this great batsman. Neil Harvey also displayed guts in his batting and scored 80 runs in the Colombo match.

Harvey was a marvellous fielder. He was the best fielder of his time. I have not seen any cricketer in my whole career who could throw the ball from a fielding position, equally fast with his left as with his right hand. At cover-point, Harvey would easily save fielders at extra-cover and point as well. A batsman would seldom sprint for a run when the ball was in Harvey's possession. I saw Neil Harvey again in England in 1953 when I was leading the Pakistan Eaglets. The Australian team was also there, battling for the Ashes series with England. I was keen on watching the English batsmen since I was to tour England again with the Pakistan team the following year. So, in between our matches, I managed to watch the Lord's Test match between the two great teams of the world. In fact, it was a clash of the titans. Harvey was batting on 72 runs when I entered the Grand Stand. Alec Bedser, that great exponent of the leg-cutter and the in-swinger, was bowling. I watched Alec Bedser very closely, as I was interested in seeing how he bowled to a left-handed batsman. Both the batsman and bowler were greats in their own spheres. Bedser bowled an in-swinger to Harvey from the middle of the crease, followed by another one. Then he bowled a leg-cutter, inducing Harvey to play through the covers. Harvey tried to drive the ball, left a gap between bat and pad, and was bowled. The great batsman was bowled off a conventional error. I was excited as it taught me how to dismiss a left-handed batsman. The left-hander is always prone to leaving a gap while playing through the covers. Even today, most left-handed batsmen are vulnerable to that kind of a delivery—trying to drive an incoming ball. An intelligent bowler can easily exploit this weakness, and some do. In fact, I took the wickets of Neil Harvey and Garfield Sobers six times out of ten on just that kind of a delivery.

Harvey first came to Pakistan in 1956 with the Australian team to play the one-off Test match in Karachi. Though the Australians had lost the Ashes series to England, yet cricket pundits were predicting a humiliating defeat for Pakistan, especially because the Australian team had a galaxy of stars of international fame. But, we convincingly beat them by nine wickets. When Harvey came in to bat after the fall of Burke in the first innings, the entire scene of the Lord's Test passed before my eyes. In both innings of the match, I dismissed Harvey on deliveries identical to those by which Bedser had dismissed him in the Lord's Test of 1953.

In 1959–60, the Australians visited Pakistan fully prepared. Neil Harvey was also in the team and we faced each other in the Dhaka Test in November 1959. I realized that Harvey had completely overcome his susceptibility to the incoming ball to which he had normally succumbed, because every time I tried to exploit this weakness, he would control and restrict his bat, and give a twinkling smile to show that he knew what it was about. He was a difficult batsman to dislodge that day. He hammered the bowlers and executed all the strokes in the book with confidence and grace, and got into the 90s. The new ball was due. I took it and showed it to the crowd. It is quite natural for a batsman who is in his 90s to try and complete his century very quickly. Harvey seemed to be in a hurry. He was anxious to complete his well-deserved century. I knew that I had only one ball to get him out. Once he got his 100, he would hammer me. So, I bowled a very measured and strictly controlled out-swinger, inviting him to play through the covers, which he did. The ball came into him and he was bowled. It was similar to the ball he was bowled out to at Karachi in 1956. Every detail of my plan had come through. Neil Harvey, like the great batsman he was, stood at his crease absolutely flabbergasted. He put his bat down, took off his gloves, and muttered, 'Oh, I forgot. I forgot.' His words not only acknowledged the skill of his opponent but also showed his greatness. This was his way in sharp contrast to other batsmen who would just walk off the field and not acknowledge the bowler. Neil Harvey was at his best in the Dhaka Test match and was batting with absolute ease. I still shudder to think of what would have happened if he had survived that particular ball. Technically speaking, he was the most correct batsman I have played against. He would use his bat to advance towards the ball. His innings at Dhaka will long be remembered.

In the final Test of the series in Karachi, Harvey played another good innings. Every time I bowled the kind of ball that surprised him in Dhaka, he would not play into the covers. It was a very interesting duel, but I realized that I had to use different tactics to get him out. When his score reached 54, I bowled him a kind of slinger, imparting reverse-spin, which came in like an off-break. He thought the ball would come in, but it went away. He snicked, and it went to the safe hands of Imtiaz. Harvey was gracious once again, looked at me, and remarked, 'Too good for me!'

Neil Harvey was born in a family where cricket was an integral part of their daily life as his father was a club cricketer. He made his Test debut in Melbourne against India in 1947–48, scoring 153. He scored a glorious century (112) on his first appearance against England in the fourth Test at Leeds in July 1948, and found himself famous overnight. The confidence with which he played at once revealed that here was a left-handed stroke-player of great quality. The circumstances under which he played this grand innings make it still more memorable. Australia had lost Morris, Hasset, and Bradman for 6, 13, and 33 runs respectively. His memorable partnership with Keith Miller, who scored a brilliant 58, retrieved Australia's deplorable position at a critical time. This Test also revealed Harvey to be a brilliant fielder. Bradman has described Harvey's return to the wickets as glorious. His catches were equally marvellous. The way he caught out Washbrook at long-leg, only a foot from the boundary, in the second innings off Johnson, would be remembered for a long time.

Harvey was particularly successful against South Africa. In the 1949–50 series, he hit four centuries in the Tests—178 at Cape Town, 151 at Durban, 116 at Port Elizabeth, and 100 at Johannesburg. When the Springboeks visited Australia in 1952–53, Harvey made 834 runs in the Tests, again hitting four centuries—109 at Brisbane, 190 at Sydney, 116 at Adelaide, and 205 at Melbourne. South Africa had a special place in his heart. Harvey, in fact, married a South African girl. In 1953, Harvey became the third Australian batsman to reach the 2000 aggregate in England after Sir Don Bradman and McCabe. He made 2040 (65.80).

The Caribbean tour of 1955 was a personal triumph for Harvey. He was at his best, and in five Tests he scored 650 runs (108.33). These included three magnificent hundreds—133 in the first Test at Kingston, 133 in the second Test at Port-of-Spain, and a fine 204 in the fifth Test at Kingston. His innings of 162 in the first Test against England at Brisbane in 1954–55 was an innings of a great batsman. His straight-drives and on-drives were superb. He scored 354 runs (44.25) in five Tests against England in the series. Harvey would surely always remember his innings against India at Bombay in 1956, when the spectators garlanded him after he completed his century.

Though Neil Harvey was short and stocky, he looked wonderful. His footwork was perfect and his technique won him plaudits even from his critics. There was fluency and elegance in his strokes. He would reach the crease and soon become the master of the situation. He enjoyed batting, particularly against fast bowlers, but this did not mean that he was weak against spin bowling. He was a batsman who could play on any kind of wicket. He was a perfect exponent of stroke-play and would play any shot, including the cover-drive and the hook. He was very strong on the on-side and could face the fast bowlers, particularly their bouncers, with great ease. He has played many good innings in times of crisis.

Harvey never led his team in any series. Even when Ian Craig and Richie Benaud, who were both junior to him, were given preference over him, he played under them like a great team-mate and always gave one hundred per cent of himself. In the second Test match against England at Lord's in the 1961 Ashes series, Harvey was asked to lead Australia in the absence of the regular captain, Richie Benaud, who dropped out because of a shoulder injury. He led his team ably and won the match, and proved that given a chance, he could be a good captain also. However, his own batting was affected as he could manage only 31 runs in both innings, falling victim to Trueman.

Left-handed batsmen have natural advantages as well as disadvantages. They also have an edge over the bowler, but can be vulnerable against a leg-cutter. The advantage that they enjoy is that there are very few bowlers who can bowl leg-cutters. It is the leg-cutter that works on a wicket where there is a bowler's rough which the bowler can then exploit to his advantage. One can count on one's finger tips the number of bowlers who could bowl leg-cutters or fast leg-breaks. Bowling with the wrist is different to bowling with the fingers or with the seam. And, that is probably the reason why left-handed batsmen are vulnerable to leg-cutters or fast leg-breaks. However, extraordinary batsmen, like Harvey, move their feet in such a manner that it is very difficult for any bowler to dislodge them.

22

Everton de Courcy Weekes: Killer Instinct

The merciless hitter of the ball

Everton Weekes was the most punishing batsman I ever saw, and very difficult to keep down. Few batsmen could surpass him in power, brilliance, and the majestic manner in which he played throughout his career. He started playing cricket at the age of twelve for the St. Leonard School side. His batting ability caught the eye of Edward Hoad, the former West Indies Test batsman, who coached him, and, at eighteen, Weekes made his first-class debut for Barbados.

Weekes demonstrated his brilliance in batting in the fourth Test at Jamaica against England in 1948, where he played a stunning innings of 141. He emerged from the match as one of the most ruthless hitters of the ball. He established a new record by scoring five centuries in successive Test innings. He made 141 against England in the fourth Test at Kingston in 1947–48. The West Indies then toured India in 1948–49, where Weekes scored four centuries in a row—128 at Delhi, 194 at Bombay, and 162 and 101 at Calcutta. Weekes equalled the world record of Alan Melville and Jack Fingleton by scoring 162, his fourth successive Test century, in the third Test at Calcutta. In the second innings of the same Test, he scored 101, his fifth consecutive Test century, which is a world record. He missed his sixth consecutive century by only 10 runs when he was run-out for 90 at Madras.

When Weekes toured England in 1950, he proved that he was a true world class batsman. He became the first batsman after the great Don Bradman to make such an impression on his first English tour as a ruthless compiler of big scores. His total aggregate was 2310 runs, wich he scored with the help of a 300, four 200s, and three 100s. He scored 232 against Surrey, an unbeaten 304 against Cambridge University, 279 against Nottinghamshire, 246 not out against Hampshire, and 200 not out against Leicestershire. He then went on to score a delightful 129 in the third Test at Trent Bridge, and equalled the 1933 record of George Headley, the former West Indies Test cricketer, of seven 100s on an England tour. However, he missed surpassing Headley's aggregate by only 11 runs. Owing to his incredible performance, *Wisden* included him among the five best cricketers of the year.

During the Australian tour of 1951, Weekes failed to score a century but made up by scoring three centuries in the home series against India in 1953. His 207 runs in the first Test at Trinidad, a glorious innings of 161 at Port-of-Spain, and a brilliant 109 at Jamaica were proof of his class as a leading batsman of the day. Again in the home series against England in 1954, Weekes scored 206 in the Trinidad Test. At Jamaica, he missed his century by only 10 runs. When Australia visited the West Indies in 1955, Weekes scored a brilliant century at Port-of-Spain.

When Weekes toured England in 1957, he managed to score only 1096 runs compared with 2310 in 1950. This was because of a sinus problem that he had developed in late 1956. He also had a broken finger. He still managed to play a great innings of 90 at Lord's.

Weekes was short but of compact build. His batting style was absolutely perfect. He would not plan his innings like Len Hutton but play his strokes spontaneously. He would arrive at the crease and delight the crowd with his electrifying drives, hooks, and cuts all round the wicket. His eyesight was exceptionally good which provided him enough time to play his strokes. His defence was correct and sound. The square-cut was his favourite stroke which he would play with remarkable power. Weekes was very strong on the back foot. He always wanted to dominate the bowlers. It was seldom that he allowed bowlers to tie him down for long. Indeed, Weekes was a master batsman who tamed the most fearsome bowlers of his time. Everton Weekes came to Pakistan with the West Indies team to play an unofficial Test match at Lahore in November 1948. Before the start of play, he inspected the wicket with Walcott. I remember that he knocked on the wicket, and said: 'Hundred!' Walcott followed, and said the same. I heard that and thought that if they were going to get a hundred each they might pile up more than 500 runs. Their remarks showed the confidence that these great cricketers had.

Weekes was immensely quick on his feet. He possessed all the strokes in the book, and could play on both sides of the wicket. We had many encounters in Test matches and faced each other in the West Indies when Pakistan toured for a five-Test series in 1958. In the first Test at Barbados, Weekes played like an old master and scored a marvellous innings of 197. He was dominant, brilliant, and unstoppable. I used all my tricks, but he defied them all. However, in the third Test at Kingston, I managed to get him out when he was again set for a big score.

Weekes announced his retirement during the Pakistan tour to the West Indies in 1958, but two years later he was recalled by the West Indies cricket board in the home series against England, and he played two Tests.

Everton Weekes was also a good wicketkeeper. He kept wickets against the Pakistan Eaglets at Ebbw Vale. I had scored a century in that match, and Weekes had praised every shot that I played during my innings.

I had a fairly interesting encounter with this great batsman when I was playing league cricket for East Lancashire in 1959. We had a match against Bacup, and Everton Weekes was their professional cricketer. Over ten thousand people were in the ground to watch that game. They had all paid for their tickets. It was billed to be a decisive battle between the best bowler and best batsman in the league. It was raining when we arrived, so we sat in the pavilion waiting for the rain to stop. But, the rain continued and we prayed that there should be a respite so that the spectators could watch some cricket. The rain finally stopped after the tea interval. The Bacup captain and Everton Weekes approached my captain, and I was also asked to join in. It was decided that both sides would play forty-five minutes each because thousands of people could not be disappointed. The match started with an understanding that whosoever scored more in the stipulated time would win. It was like a one-day match. East Lancashire batted first, and scored 80-odd runs.

Everton Weekes opened the innings, but at number two. I started the bowling and took two wickets in my first over. From the other end, Weekes hammered the bowling and scored 18 runs. The match became more interesting when I took another two wickets in my fourth over. Weekes, at the other end, was rampant. He was scoring at will. Finally, Weekes came to my end and was to face me in the last over of the day, needing six runs to win in an eight-ball over. He played my first delivery into the cover position which was smartly fielded. With six runs needed to win, Weekes faced my second ball and took two runs. On the third ball, he was dropped in the slips. There was a lot of tension. Amid yells and shouting, he took another two off my fifth ball. I managed to contain him in my sixth and seventh deliveries. Finally, it came to the last ball, with Bacup requiring one to tie and two to win. Everton Weekes pushed the last ball on to the on-side and ran between the wickets. I picked up the ball from mid-on but realized that the batsman was in my way. So, I just held the ball in my hand. The batsmen completed one run.

The match ended in a tie. The crowd got their money's worth and they demanded that Weekes and I walk hand in hand around the ground. We did, while the crowd stood on either side, clapping and chanting. When we reached the gate, an envelope was given to each of us. 'Hey, Fazal, there are shillings in it. Let's walk across the road and have a drink,' Weekes said smilingly. That match is even now talked of in league cricket.

Weekes was the greatest batsman ever produced by the West Indies. He loved cricket, and he enjoyed it.

23

Imtiaz Ahmad: Pillar of Pakistan Cricket

The darling of Lahorites

'Get at the bowler before he gets you,' is one of the commandments in the cricketer's Bible. Imtiaz always followed this dictum when he was at the crease to bat. His dominating poise at the wicket conveyed to the bowler that although wickets had fallen, the innings would start afresh. When he came in to bat, the fielders would invariably spread out. The spectators knew that the bowlers were likely to be treated ruthlessly. Yet, he would often lose his wicket because of his daring and because he would try to play his strokes before he had settled in.

Imtiaz was born into a cricketing family of Lahore. His father was also a wicketkeeper-batsman, who played club cricket. From his early days, Imtiaz showed signs of greatness. His father was very proud of him. He would invariably introduce Imtiaz with pride. 'You know he is my son,' he would say. He wanted his son to be recognized in international cricket.

I first met Imtiaz at Minto Park where the Mamdot and Ravi Gymkhana cricket clubs would conduct their net practice. He was a member of the latter club. In the rainy season, when Minto Park would turn into a huge pond, we would practice on the road adjacent to the historic Badshahi Mosque. When Imtiaz joined Islamia College, we became team-mates and played a lot of cricket together in inter-varsity tournaments, the Ranji Trophy, and Test matches. He was a good cricketer during his college days. When he was seventeen, Imtiaz hit the headlines by scoring 138 against the Australian Services XI at Lahore in 1945.

A very interesting incident reflects his determination and concentration as a batsman. Before Partition, the Punjab University cricket team played an inter-varsity match with Benaras University, at Benaras. The university was celebrating its golden jubilee. I was leading the Punjab University side. We boarded a third class compartment of the train from Lahore, and after a thirty-six hour journey, reached Benaras and were accommodated in the university hostel. The food which was served to us consisted of small *kachories* which did not satisfy Imtiaz's appetite. So, he made a deal with the hostel superintendent that he would score as many runs as the number of *kachories* he would eat. He finished 118 of those, and next morning his innings was exactly 118, and we won the match.

Imtiaz received international recognition in November 1948 when Pakistan played its first unofficial Test against the West Indies team in Lahore's Bagh-i-Jinnah cricket ground. The West Indies had a galaxy of stars on their side, such as Everton Weekes, Clyde Walcott, George Headley, Christiani, and Stollmeyer. Imtiaz, undaunted by the big names, scored 76 in the first innings and a magnificent century in the second. He thus became the first Pakistani batsman to score a century on his debut in an unofficial Test. He played every bowler ruthlessly, particularly Gomez and Goddard.

The Commonwealth team played a two-day match at Karachi in December 1949 against the Pakistan Universities XI. Imtiaz played a captain's innings in that match and scored an unbeaten 165. The Commonwealth cricketers acknowledged his achievement as the best batting performance of a Pakistani cricketer against them.

Imtiaz can be ranked amongst great contemporary cricketers like Compton, Miller, or Mushtaq Ali. He was equal to them in his talent and genius, and played some world-class innings. During the Indian tour of 1952, he scored an unbeaten 213 against Central Zone at Nagpur in an exhilarating display of batting. On the England tour in 1954, he scored a brilliant century in the last match of the tour against Tom Pearce's XI. It was a farewell match, and Imtiaz delighted the crowd with his magnificent stroke-play in scoring 105. However, the greatest innings of his life was played at Bombay in 1950, playing for the Prime Minister's XI against the Commonwealth team, in which he scored 300 runs. His innings was a mix of aggression and style in which he displayed complete and masterful brilliance of stroke-play. This is the highest innings played in first-class cricket by a wicketkeeper.

Though Imtiaz was a little bashful, he was a good team-mate. But, while playing he would not be humble or modest. When I was bowling in Kingston, where Sobers scored 365 runs, I remember Imtiaz telling me: 'Come faster.'

Imtiaz was an essential part of the Pakistan team. He was an automatic choice. Without him the Pakistan team was never complete. He missed only one of the first forty-two Tests played by our country. His batting performance has been regarded as one of the most remarkable in the annals of cricket. Imtiaz's position in the batting order was constantly changing, but he preferred to open the innings. For the sake of the team, Imtiaz would volunteer to play at any position. He was a tower of strength for Pakistan in all the forty-one Tests he played for his country. He possessed great fighting skills. His powerful hooks and sweeps, especially against the best fast bowlers, were a treat to watch. In *Pace Like Fire,* the famous West Indies' fast bowler, Wes Hall writes:

Pakistan played its first match of the 1958 West Indies tour against Barbados. Imtiaz, one of the finest hookers I have ever seen, must have laughed all the way to the wicket. Every time I flung down a short ball he would lean back and really hammer me to the boundary. Normally I can sleep anywhere and even an alarm clock perched six inches away from my ear fails to rouse me. The boys kid me that I am the only man ever to sleep through an earth tremor and wake up wondering why the picture had fallen off the wall. But this night it was different. All I could see was Imtiaz, standing there with a bat four times the size of him, swotting every ball I tossed down like he would swot a disagreeable fly.

Imtiaz became the first wicketkeeper in Test cricket to score a double century. He did this at Lahore in the second Test against New Zealand in October 1955. It was a difficult innings, played under adverse circumstances. Pakistan was struggling at 111 when Imtiaz went in and played a solid and flawless innings. He hammered every loose delivery and helped Pakistan win the match.

Imtiaz was an attacking batsman with wonderful timing. His batting against genuine fast bowlers was always superb. He could despatch the most lethal bouncers past the ropes with absolute ease. In the first Test against the West Indies in Barbados in 1958, Pakistan had been forced to follow-on and were struggling to score 473 runs to avoid an innings defeat. Though Hanif played the longest innings in Test history and scored a triple century, yet it was Imtiaz whose punishing knock in the one-day cricket fashion demoralized the West Indies pace attack. He was particularly ruthless against Gilchrist who was then the fastest bowler in the game. His hooks and pulls against him were perfect and precise. Though he was unlucky to miss his century by nine runs, yet he laid a sound foundation for the Pakistan innings. Again, in the third Test at Kingston in the same series, Imtiaz once again played a dashing innings and scored 122. He had a very interesting duel with Gilchrist, who was hurling a bouncer-barrage against Imtiaz only to see the ball crossing the ropes.

The Pakistan team toured India in 1960-61 to play a five-Test match series. Our players, particularly Imtiaz, were the target of bad umpiring throughout the tour. I remember one day before the start of the fourth Test at Madras, the players came to my room and complained, 'Skipper, when the ball hits our pads or we miss a ball outside the off-stump, the umpire invariably raises his finger.' As captain of the team and as a player, I had my own reservations about the umpiring. However, I convinced them to maintain discipline in their batting and not to let the ball hit their pads or to play outside the off-stump. Suddenly, Imtiaz announced, 'I will open the innings.' So, next day, he opened with Hanif Muhammad. Together, they put on more than 150 runs in a first-wicket partnership. Imtiaz played a well-disciplined innings. The way he hammered the Indian bowlers made them look like an ordinary side. When Desai bowled him, he had already scored 135 runs.

Imtiaz played his last Test against England at the Oval in 1962. In the first innings, he scored 49 runs and then hit a great 98 in the second innings. This was the venue where the great Sir Donald Bradman was out for a duck in his last innings. So, in lighter vein, Imtiaz could boast that in his last innings he had scored 98 more than Bradman did on the same ground.

Imtiaz was a natural stroke-player. Even the best bowlers could not keep him tied down for long. He would pull to square-leg from outside the off-stump without any qualms, and was equally good against spin bowling. He would sweep a good-length ball to leg or cut it past point. He would not bother to see the hands of the bowler to distinguish the off-break from the leg-break but would see the spin in the air and adjust his footwork accordingly. His batting style endeared him to the Lahore crowd. The spectators would shout for a boundary or a hit over the ropes, and he would come down the wicket and oblige. In the Lahore Test against the West Indies in 1959, when opener Ijaz Ahmad was injured after being hit by a bouncer from Wes Hall, there was pin drop silence in the Bagh-i-Jinnah ground. Imtiaz was batting at the other end. In the next over, he took a single and came to Hall's end. Hall hurled two bouncers which Imtiaz despatched with such velocity that before the fielders could even move from their positions, the ball had cleared the ropes. The crowd was electrified and loved him.

Imtiaz was a wicketkeeper of the highest standard. He rarely missed anything behind the wickets and stumped everyone who left the 'stable'. He had watched me both in the nets and during matches, and he knew all the tricks that I had. So, when he kept wickets, he would position himself accordingly. For me, he was the most difficult batsman to dislodge in our domestic cricket.

He held 33 catches off my bowling, and encouraged me each time. In fact, it was Imtiaz who took all the seven catches off my bowling in the historic Oval Test match in 1954. It was our combination that brought about that glorious victory for Pakistan. On the same tour of England, Imtiaz played in 28 of the 30 first-class matches, with a tally of 86 victims from behind the stumps. This was a remarkable performance and a record for a visiting team.

Imtiaz led the Pakistan team against Australia in the second Test at Lahore in 1959. I was the regular captain of the team but had to pull out because of a stiff knee. Pakistan lost, and although Imtiaz could have easily drawn the Test, he would not do anything which was not fair. For him, victory and defeat were secondary. The game mattered more. Australia won the match with just ten minutes to spare.

Imtiaz was a strict disciplinarian. I recall an incident when during a side-match on the Indian tour (1960–61) in which he was leading the team, a senior batsman of the team misbehaved. The manager of the team refused to take any action. That was the only occasion when I saw him lose his temper. Two weeks later, he opened for Pakistan at Delhi along with the same player with whom till then he was not on speaking terms. This player had become vulnerable to Desai, the Indian medium-pacer. Imtiaz faced Desai for seventy minutes and ensured that this batsman did not have to face even one delivery from Desai.

Imtiaz was the last among the pioneers of Pakistan cricket. He left the international arena in 1962. Throughout his Test career, he maintained that the country came first. He did not object when a very junior player was made the captain of the Pakistan team. After the woeful defeat in England under Javed Burki, Imtiaz announced his retirement from international cricket. However, he was approached by the BCCP in 1964 to come back and scout for young talent for the team that was to go on the Australian tour the same year. Imtiaz organized a camp in Karachi and worked hard to build up a balanced team. He was in top form in the nets and was sure of his selection in the team. But, sadly enough, only a week before the departure of the team to Australia, Imtiaz was discreetly told by the BCCP, 'Thank you very much, but you have done your job.' With tears in his eyes, he went to rejoin his duties in the Pakistan Air

Force. Later, he was again approached by the BCCP to lead the national team against the Commonwealth XI and Ceylon. He did not refuse the offer, because for him the country always came first.

He can take pride in the fact that he played for his country as an amateur. In the late fifties, even when he was already a Test player, he would travel by bus or a tonga from his residence inside the walled city to the distant Bagh-i-Jinnah cricket ground and Gaddafi Stadium. I doubt if Pakistan will ever again produce a modest and gentleman cricketer like Imtiaz.

24

Hanif Muhammad:
Master of Concentration
'Gentlemen, I am playing without my Bradman'

The short and boyish looking Hanif Muhammad was one of the most gifted batsman to dominate the cricket world in the late 1950s and 1960s. He was third among the five Muhammad brothers who influenced Pakistan cricket in its early years. His father was a good club-cricketer, and his mother was a regional badminton and table tennis champion. Since his childhood he appeared destined to become a great batsman. His mother had encouraged all the brothers to play cricket. Like many in the subcontinent, he learned by playing with his brothers under the street lights in Junagadh. At the time of Partition Hanif's family migrated to Pakistan and settled in Karachi. He continued his schooling at the Sindh Madrassah where he was ably trained and coached by Master Aziz, a veteran cricketer. Hanif soon became known for his extraordinary batting talents. In an inter-school cricket tournament he scored 305. His unblemished skill won him a place in the Pakistan Eaglets touring England in 1951 where he also got training at the Alf Govers Coaching School.

Hanif developed so quickly that he had established himself as an opening batsman of the highest class before the age of nineteen. It was evident that he was destined to rank among the world's leading batsmen. At seventeen, he was selected to play in the unofficial Test against the MCC at Karachi. He opened the innings in the match, and scored 64 in the second innings, courageously defying the bowling of Statham, Shackleton, and Carr for almost four hours. His intense concentration and classical technique surprised the visitors. He also kept wicket and dismissed three batsmen (2 ct, 1 st) in that game.

Hanif was chosen as a wicketkeeper-batsman to tour India in 1952–53. In the opening match against North Zone at Amritsar, he scored 121 and an unbeaten 109. He also made a brilliant 203 against the Bombay Cricket Association and 135 against South Zone at Hyderabad. Hanif made his Test debut in the first Test at New Delhi where he played a memorable innings. Vinno Mankad, with his deceptive spin bowling, was almost unplayable on a turning wicket. Hanif was the only batsman who mastered his bowling and scored 51. He became the first Pakistani batsman to score a 50 in a Test match. In the third Test at Bombay, Hanif demonstrated his unique temperament by staying at the wicket for close to six hours. He was unlucky to miss his century by 4 runs. In the final Test at Calcutta, Hanif scored his third 50 of the tour. He scored 287 runs (35.87) in the five-Test series. His total aggregate of the tour in all games was 917 runs (at 65.50).

The tour of England in 1954 proved a personal triumph for Hanif. He scored a total of 1623 runs in the first-class games, and 181 runs in the Tests. In the first Test at Lord's, when Pakistan was struggling in the first innings, Hanif spent almost three and quarter hours to score 20 runs. This innings was to leave a different impression of Hanif on cricket followers in England. In a sense, this was unfair, for under different conditions, as at Trent Bridge, he could be an exciting batsman to watch. In the second innings, he stayed two and a half hours for his 39. He batted with remarkable fluency, and delighted the crowd with some glorious hooks and on-drives. He sent Bedser three times over the ropes in one over. There are very few batsmen who have hit Bedser like this in a Test match.

Hanif scored his first Test century (142) in the second Test against India at Bahawalpur in 1954–55. This was scored in more than eight hours. Other than this innings, he did not quite live up to his reputation during the series. In the five-Test series, he scored 273 runs at an average of 34.12. later, when New Zealand visited Pakistan in 1955–56, Hanif scored 103 in the Dhaka Test.

In the 1950s, Pakistan's batting undoubtedly depended very largely on Hanif, and he very successfully saved many matches for his country. Though he was young, yet he exhibited a temperament equal to that of the most experienced players in the game. Nothing disturbed him and little could tempt him. He knew just what to do and when to do it. In later years, the performances of Boycott and Gavaskar reminded me of Hanif.

His most brilliant and match-saving innings was his 337 against the West Indies at Bridgetown in 1958. He stayed 16 hours and 39 minutes at the crease to get those runs. Staying at the wicket for such a long period, and that too under a burning sun, was not a joke. It was the true test of a batsman and the making of a master. The West Indies crowd was hostile to him during the first two days of his batting, but turned friendly on the third day. They then started instructing him on how to tackle Gilchrist and the others. One spectator sitting on top of a tree would forewarn Hanif whether the next ball would be bouncer or a yorker.

Pakistan was bowled out for 106 runs conceding 473 runs as a first innings lead. When they went in for a second time, it was Imtiaz Ahmad who demoralized the West Indies quickies with his blistering innings of 91. This made the situation some what better, but the danger of defeat had still not been averted. At this juncture, Hanif took command of the situation and played the longest innings on record in Test cricket. During the course of his innings, Hanif achieved the unique distinction of featuring in century stands for the first four wickets—152 with Imtiaz Ahmad, 112 for the second wicket with Alimuddin, 154 for the third wicket with Saeed Ahmad, and 121 for the fourth wicket with his elder brother, Wazir Muhammad. This still stands as a world record. He fulfilled the impossible task of saving Pakistan from defeat. After this innings, his name became synonymous with concentration and determination. He came to be known as the 'Little Master'. In the five-Test series, Hanif made 628 at an average of 69.77.

Hanif has another memorable innings to his credit. In the semi-finals of the Quaid-i-Azam trophy in 1958–59, playing for

Karachi against Bahawalpur at Karachi, Hanif surpassed Sir Don Bradman's then record of 452 and made 499. He got these runs in just eleven hours before running himself out in the second last over when going for his 500th run. His record was surpassed by Brian Lara in 1994.

When the West Indies played a three-Test series against Pakistan in 1958–59, Hanif scored a century (103) in the first Test at Karachi. In the second innings of the match, he injured his finger playing a Wes Hall delivery. The injury appeared to be minor, but before the start of the second Test at Dhaka, he reported unfit. A night before the start of the match, I declared in the team meeting, 'Gentlemen, I am playing the Test without my Bradman.' Everyone was taken aback. It was a severe blow to the morale of the team. Everyone was aware of the importance of Hanif's presence in the side. Nevertheless, he was unfit and Pakistan played without him for the first time. Luckily, Pakistan went on to win the Dhaka Test.

When Australia visited Pakistan in 1959–60, Hanif scored an unbeaten 101 in the third Test at Karachi. His total aggregate in the three-Test series was 304 runs. In fact, it was a match saving century.

Pakistan toured India in 1960–61. Hanif was a prolific scorer in this five-Test series. He scored 410 runs at 51.25. His aggregate included a fine 160 in the first Test at Bombay. Nobody was expecting Hanif to play in that match because he had a serious toe injury, but he withstood the pain and played a courageous knock for his team.

Hanif became the first Pakistani batsman to score a century in each innings of a Test, which he did against England in 1961–62. He achieved this distinction by scoring 112 and 104 in the second Test at Dhaka. In the three-Test match series, he made 407 runs (67.83).

Hanif captained Pakistan for the first time against Australia in 1964 at Karachi. In the same season, he led the team in the only Test at Melbourne, making 104 and 93 runs to avert a possible defeat. He could have scored a hundred in each innings, but Jarman, the Australian keeper, made a wrong appeal in sheer excitement, and the umpire, too, moved by the nature of the appeal, raised his finger. He also kept wickets throughout the match, taking 5 catches in both innings. Hanif scored 100 not out at Christchurch against New Zealand in 1964–65, and shared a 217 runs record for the sixth wicket against the same country at Lahore in 1965. In this match, he scored an unbeaten 203.

Hanif played a match-saving innings against England in the first Test at Lord's in 1967. This innings is still considered by most critics as one of the best played at the cricket headquarters since the Second World War. Pakistan was struggling against England's total of 369 at 25 for 2 on the second afternoon of the match. Hanif came in and defied John Snow, Ken Higgs, and Illingworth for more than nine hours. He went on to score an unbeaten 187. After this innings, he was named as one of the five best players of the year by *Wisden*.

Though there were certain periods when Hanif would struggle for runs, yet his career record puts him among world-class batsmen of all times. Throughout his Test career, spanning over seventeen years, Hanif remained a source of inspiration for young cricketers. He was an asset to Pakistan and was such an indispensable member of the team that he missed only two of the first fifty-seven Tests played by Pakistan.

During his career, Hanif opened the innings variously with Nazar Muhammad, Alimuddin, Imtiaz Ahmad, Ijaz Butt, and Muhammad Ilyas. He was never bothered by crowd response, he would concentrate on his batting, and wait to hit the bad ball. He was a batsman who would not bother about wickets falling at the other end but would guard his wicket and, on occasions, hold up both the ends. On several occasions his defiant innings saved Pakistan from defeat. At the crease, his stance was casual, but balanced. Hanif's style of batting was elegant. He would twirl his bat in his hand. His defence was solid and he possessed a wide variety of strokes which he executed with perfect technique. He was a batsman who used his feet exceedingly well and was solid when coming behind the ball. However, he had difficulty in playing the hook and the pull shots. On the West Indies tour in 1957–58, C. Walcott advised him not to play the hook shot on hard and fast wickets. Hanif was an orthodox batsman, totally indifferent to criticism. He would play his innings according to the book and seldom play a wild shot. He never seemed to be in a hurry. He was equally good against all types of bowling. Though he was a defensive batsman, yet he played some innings to please the spectators. On the Indian tour of 1960–61, Hanif scored 222 runs against the Combined Universities at Poona. He scored his centuries between the pre-lunch and post-lunch sessions.

Hanif captained Pakistan in eleven Tests from 1964 to 1967. He won two and lost the same number of matches. Under his captaincy, Pakistan won the home series against New Zealand in 1964–65.

Hanif was a quick fielder. It was he who smartly ran-out McConnon in the famous Oval Test in 1954. Later in his career, he fielded in the slips. When the pressure was not too great, he also bowled a mixture of medium-pace and off-breaks. Hanif could bowl with both arms. It is quite interesting that his only Test wicket, that of Indian opening batsman Punjabi, was claimed with a left-arm delivery. During the Pakistan match against Somerset in 1954, Hanif caused considerable amusement among the crowd by bowling left-arm—in the last over before lunch. He had sent down four with his right arm and the last two with his left. He got Smith's wicket in that over.

Hanif also has the distinction of carrying his bat on two different occasions in first-class cricket. In 1953–54, playing for Bahawalpur against Sindh, he remained unbeaten with 147 in a total of 252. On the England tour in 1954, he batted against Essex at Southend with an unbeaten 142 in a total of 241.

His last appearance in a Test, against New Zealand at Karachi in 1969–70, marked the first appearance of his youngest brother, Sadiq Muhammad. It was only the third time in Test cricket history that three brothers played in the same Test.

There were some internal politics in his final exit. Hanif was forced to retire from Test cricket at a time when he could have played a few more years for Pakistan. Had he not been forced to retire, he could have become the first Asian batsman to complete 4000 runs in Test cricket. He retired with 3915 runs.

Hanif is a beacon of light for future Pakistani cricketers. Today, when I sometimes see Pakistan's collapse in a Test match, I strongly feel that we need a batsman of Hanif's calibre who could hold up one end. Hanif has been chief selector and an expert commentator on radio and television during recent Test matches. He has also been included in cricket's Hall of Fame. It is a big honour and recognition for Hanif who occupies a special place in Pakistani cricket.

25

David Sheppard: Epitome of Fair Play and Sportsmanship

The preacher who played cricket

In the beginning of his career, David Sheppard was an ordinary batsman, but hard work and mental tenacity took him to the top. He was a right-handed batsman with a repertoire of many graceful strokes. I first met him at Trent Bridge in 1954. He was leading England in the match as Len Hutton, the regular captain, was indisposed. I wondered at that time what was so special in this young cricketer to have been asked to lead England ahead of Dennis Compton, Alec Bedser, and a few other senior and seasoned cricketers.

David Sheppard was not Len Hutton as a captain or as a batsman, but what happened was that England easily won the match by an innings and 129 runs. Sheppard opened the innings with Simpson. His stance was perfect, and when he batted he looked to me a fairly good batsman. There was a forthrightness both in his batting and leadership. Though he scored only 37 runs in the match, yet his partnership with Simpson established a sound foundation for England's innings.

During the third Test at Old Trafford in 1954, I was bowling to Sheppard from the return crease. I bowled one delivery slightly outside the leg-stump with two fielders at short-leg and leg-slip. Sheppard moved his feet so as not to allow the ball to go in the leg-slip, but there was reverse spin on the ball which took his off stump. I was elated.

Sheppard was an amateur in the true sense of the word and a different kind of player. He was a slow left-handed bowler at number eleven in his school days, but as he played more he gave up bowling and established himself as one of England's leading batsmen. His batting style was a bit defective in the beginning, but Sir Len Hutton helped him to change it for the better. His defence became stronger and he started playing on and leg-side strokes. He enjoyed playing cricket and whenever he got a chance to play in a Test, he did his best for his team.

Sheppard made his debut against the West Indies at the Oval in 1950. He then went on the Australian tour with the MCC in 1950–51, but his performance was disappointing. There had been interruptions in his career. Often it seemed that he would retire from international cricket, but somehow he continued playing, though not very regularly. After successfully leading England in two Tests against Pakistan in 1954, Sheppard was not included in the England team to tour Australia in 1954–55. After that, he gave up regular cricket and joined the church. He was, however, recalled to play in the Manchester Test against Australia in 1956. Many were surprised at the selection as he had only played four innings for his county Sussex during the season. His two previous appearances were two years earlier when he captained England against Pakistan in 1954. Like a true sportsman, Sheppard accepted the offer, played in the Test, scored a fine century (113), and proved to the selectors that he was still a good batsman.

Sheppard was among the very few who could infuse a different spirit into the general approach to cricket. He delighted the crowd with his stylish, upright, and forceful stroke-play, and liked to play through the covers the very first delivery he received. His batting was aggressive and his favourite shots were played in the area from mid-off to mid-wicket. He would also cut and pull with absolute ease.

Sheppard was tall and well-built. He was the kind of batsman who could bat at any position, in any situation. If the team collapsed, it would not perturb him because he would not be intimidated by the superiority of the bowlers. He would just go and bat as if nothing had happened around him and score runs. He would snatch any opportunity to attack. The English team was in trouble in the fourth Test at Leeds against the West Indies in the 1957 series. Sheppard went to play in the middle-order and started his innings with four consecutive boundaries. He scored 68 runs and stood firm in the crisis.

Coincidentally, during the Pakistan tour of England in 1962, Sheppard too was not included in the first three Tests. So, we both played for our respective teams in the fourth Test at Nottingham. When he came in to bat I noticed a visible change in his style. He was struggling for runs, which was unusual for him. I knew Sheppard was easy-going, not temperamental, and a professional in the sense that he had command over his stroke-play. But, as he gradually settled during his innings, he started to play his strokes freely. On the Australian tour in 1962–63, Sheppard made 1074 runs (38.35). He hit 113 in the third Test at Melbourne and contributed to England's only victory in the series.

Sheppard was a fielder of the highest class. He preferred to field near the bat where he rarely missed a catch. The batsman would not risk taking a sharp single if the ball went to Sheppard.

Sheppard's dealings with people, even with cricketers to whom he was indifferent, was absolutely fair. He was handsome and confident. Not only did he please and bring a smile to the spectators, his association with the people outside the ground was also wonderful. As a natural stroke-player, Sheppard would go for the ball and hit even the first ball of the innings with confidence, sometimes for a four.

He was against apartheid. He refused to associate with the whites of South Africa since they did not give equal rights to the blacks. In 1959, when South Africa was touring England and the English selectors invited him to play in the Nottingham Test, he declined the offer, not wanting to associate with the touring team. I recall that the crowd, which was normally thirty to thirty-five thousand during Test matches, came down to five thousand. Even today, Sheppard is a great exponent of fair play.

Sheppard was a true ambassador for England. In 1961, Sheppard represented his county, Sussex, in a committee constituted by the MCC to examine the state of first-class cricket, and to suggest changes in its structure.

Sheppard was posted as preacher in many parts of England. I never had any religious discussions with him. We only talked cricket. When you play Test cricket, you do share a private moment with players, and sometimes you get close to each other or sit together at a dinner table. But, sadly, I did not get an opportunity to get close to Sheppard. I wish I had. However, we both share memories of the Oval ground. Sheppard scored his first Test century (119) against India in the fourth Test at the Oval in 1952, and I am still known as the Oval hero in Pakistan. The decade of the 1960s saw a change in my life, and I became more religious. I wrote a book entitled *Urge to Faith,* and sent a copy to David Sheppard for I knew he understood the subject of my book, which was the promotion of human welfare. He wrote me a letter appreciating my work, and quoted *Cry of the Common Man* by Longfellow. Here are some of the verses:

My Darling! why art Thou under a veil?
The Light is veiled, strange, Thy shadow is also veiled.
I long to see Thee knowing that I cannot see.
Yet, Thy shadow should be visible.
Look: Mankind await the sight of Thy shadow.
This waiting has lasted for centuries.
When will this waiting end?

Sheppard was ordained to the ministry of the Church of England in 1956. He became the first ordained minister who was called to represent England in Test cricket. Last I heard, David Sheppard was the Bishop of Liverpool.

26

Richie Benaud: Leader Par Excellence

True ambassador of cricket

After losing the Ashes series against England in 1956, the Australian cricket team arrived in Karachi to play one Test match in October. The team included Colin McDonald, the great opening batsman; Keith Miller, the greatest all-rounder of all times; Neil Harvey, the prolific left-handed batsman; and Ray Lindwall, the most fearsome of fast bowlers. The people of Karachi were looking forward to the game and were expecting great feats from them. However, they did not realize then that a great cricketer, administrator, and captain was emerging from amongst these stalwarts—the tall and handsome Richie Benaud.

Richie was then in the process of establishing himself amongst the top players of the cricketing world. During the Karachi Test, I observed that he had set very high goals. Later, I learnt that before coming to Pakistan, he contacted Denis Compton in England to get all kinds of information about Pakistani cricketers. The message he got from Denis was in exactly these words: 'Beware, Fazal is there.' So, Richie Benaud did a lot of forward thinking and arrived in Pakistan, fully prepared. He played extremely well in the Karachi Test. In the first innings, I dismissed him easily, but he was a different batsman altogether in the second innings. He delayed our victory to the fourth day, something we could have easily achieved on the third day had I run through his resistance. Though Richie could not prevent Pakistan's victory, he made his presence felt by playing a defiant innings of 56. He played a courageous innings when the other stars of the Australian team were struggling against our pace attack. Richie's bowling was also good. Although he did not have much success in that match, he bowled well to get the prize wicket of Imtiaz Ahmad. All the while, during the game, Benaud's sharp mind kept registering the strength and weakness of individual Pakistani cricketers.

The next encounter with Richie took place when he led the Australian team to Pakistan in 1959–60. Benaud had nurtured and groomed his team to play cricket on any kind of a pitch— turning, fast, slow, or rough. Their batting was mature, their fielding was extraordinary, and the mastermind behind the scene was Richie Benaud. In the first Test at Dhaka, he displayed his keen cricketing sense and sound leadership qualities by some clever field placing and skilful handling of the team. Soon, he made us realize that the Australians were a totally different team from the one we had faced in 1956. Although I took five wickets in this Test, yet Australia had an edge over Pakistan and beat us at Dhaka.

I missed the second Test at Lahore because of a knee injury. This match was won in the last few overs, again by Australia. However, I played the third Test at Karachi. During that Test, both teams were told that the president of the United States of America, General Eisenhower, would visit the National Stadium to witness the Test match between Australia and Pakistan. The secretary of the BCCP, Muhammad Hussain, and I were sitting together in the stadium when the information was given to us over the telephone. We decided that General Eisenhower should be greeted in a president-like fashion. We contacted the first secretary of the Pakistan embassy in Washington over the phone and requested him to have a bottle-green jacket made by the president's tailor and to despatch it to Karachi by the first available flight. This was done. A Pakistan team monogram was placed on the pocket of the jacket. When President Eisenhower came to the stadium, and both teams were presented to him, I said to him, 'Mr President, may I have your jacket please.' He was amused by my request but gave me his jacket. I then presented him the blazer which had been especially flown in from Washington. Eisenhower wore the blazer and exclaimed with joy, 'Field Marshal, it fits me. Oh, how jolly well it fits me!' (Field Marshal Muhammad Ayub Khan was then the president of Pakistan and had accompanied Gen. Eisenhower to the match.) Richie Benaud and the Australian team manager addressed him in a light mood, saying, 'Mr President, you have joined the other camp.' His reply was, 'Of course, I am wearing their colours.' President Eisenhower watched the match attired in the green blazer.

Richie Benaud made his Test debut in the fifth Test against the West Indies at Sydney in January 1951. He took the wicket of Valentine, the best spinner of the day. Richie was a fine all-rounder, stepping into Keith Miller's shoes when the latter retired from Test cricket after a splendid career, in 1956. In South Africa, in 1957–58, Benaud finally established himself as an all-rounder of the highest order. He scored 329 runs in five Tests, with two centuries, averaging 54.83, and took thirty wickets averaging 21.93. His aggressive batting made him a great favourite with the crowds. Benaud's all-round performance was a major factor in the Australian success. His splendid century (122) at Johannesburg was scored under tremendous pressure. Five Australian batsmen were back in the pavilion and they were struggling to avoid a follow-on. But, he played a brave innings. His overall aggregate of the tour was 817. He worked very hard on his bowling and took 106 wickets which surpassed the previous record of 104 by Barnes.

Richie Benaud was appointed captain in the home series against England in 1958–59. There were fears that the burden of captaincy would affect his form. But, he proved this wrong with his outstanding performance. His magic bowling played a major role in Australia's triumph in four Tests.

Richie was a determined cricketer who never lost hope. His smiling face always spoke of his inner calm and concentration. I remember a match when Benaud changed the whole game by his determination to play for a result. In the fourth Test match of the 1961 Ashes series at Old Trafford, England needed 256 runs to win the match in about four hours time. Victory looked certain when the second wicket fell at 150. The determined

FROM DUSK TO DAWN

Benaud started concentrating on the new batsmen with his
shrewd spin bowling. He single-handedly ran through
England's batting, and the last eight batsmen could only score
51 runs. He took 6 for 70 by bowling into the bowler's rough.

Richie had a very pleasant personality. During the series with
Pakistan in 1959, on his arrival he promised to play positive
cricket, and he didn't deviate from that promise. Even during
difficult times in the match, he remained cheerful and bold. He
never questioned any umpire's decision and would never
willfully waste time in field-changing or tactical conferences.
Richie was always courteous and whenever a request was made
to him concerning the game in the run of play, he would agree
with a smiling face. Richie was one of the friendliest men on a
cricket field and would talk fair and square both off and on the
field. We thoroughly enjoyed playing cricket against each other.
There was not a fraction of misunderstanding anywhere even in
our after-dinner speeches.

It is very difficult to differentiate between Benaud as a bowler,
a batsman, and a captain. To me, he was best as a captain, better
as a bowler, and good as a batsman. Benaud was a great leader.
He had the potential and the capability, and was brave, never
hesitating to ask the rival captain to play first after winning the
toss. He never deliberately played for a draw and his
declarations were always sporting. As a captain, he commanded
the respect of his team-mates and his seniors. He knew how to
keep them happy. He was always one of them, but was also a
strict disciplinarian. When he led the Australian team on the
England tour in 1961, he had given clear instructions to his
players to maintain a sporting spirit. They were not to object to
any decision by an umpire. It was his shrewd and inspiring
captaincy that won the series against Pakistan in 1959. Under his
captaincy, the Kangaroos won the Ashes in the summer of 1961
and defeated the West Indies in the home series the same year.

Benaud was a delight to watch when he was in an attacking
mood. He played some great innings. On the England tour of
1953, he hit eleven sixes and nine fours in his innings of 135
against T.N. Pearce's XI. When he disappointed as a batsman he

made up with terrific bowling. Benaud's batting in the fifth Test against the West Indies at Kingston in 1955 where he completed his century in only seventy-eight minutes was brilliant. In five Tests, he scored 246 (41.00) and took 18 wickets (27.00).

His marvellous innings against the West Indies in the tied Brisbane Test (1961) would be remembered for long. Australia was struggling hard to save itself from defeat at 92 for 6 when he joined Allen Davidson and gave a 134 run stand for the seventh wicket. His powerful and beautiful drives were always a joy to watch. He brought his team very close to a hard fought victory but the last over of Wes Hall turned the tables on Australia when he got three of their batsmen out.

Benaud knew the art of leg-spin and googly and could bowl top spin very effectively. In the three Test series against India in 1956 he proved himself to be a world class bowler. His 11 wickets for 105 against India in the third Test at Calcutta were the highest quality leg-break googly bowling. Later, at the end of his career he developed the 'flipper' which tormented even the best batsmen. On the twin tour of India and Pakistan in 1959–60, Benaud took 47 wickets (20.19) in eight Tests. In his first series as captain, he got 31 wickets (18.83) against England. Benaud has a unique record in Test cricket in that he took three wickets without giving any run against India in the first Test at New Delhi in 1959. On the hard Australian wickets, he was more dangerous with his clever change of pace and teasing flight.

Richie Benaud was superb at public relations and was always ready to please others. His comments when he was around the mike were incisive, short and to the point. He was specific and did not beat about the bush or make irresponsible comments. Benaud was also a very fine speaker but would only narrate facts, not unsubstantiated rumours. The last time I met him was in 1978 in England. The finest compliment that came from him for me was 'Fazal, was the best bowler in the world in his times, a great exponent of the leg-cutter and the in-cutter.'

Richie loved to talk about the three Test matches against Pakistan—one played at Karachi in 1956, which the Australians lost, the second at Dhaka which they won in 1959, and the third Test at Lahore which Pakistan could have drawn but which it finally lost because Imtiaz Ahmad, the captain of the home team, did not employ any negative tactics and continued playing positive cricket.

Richie was a tremendous cricketer. He would not allow things to get boring and was astonishingly versatile. He was admired by the lovers of cricket for the spirit in which he played the series against the West Indies in Australia in 1960–61.

Richie Benaud knew the art of mixing with people. He was cricket's gift to the press. He is a household name as a cricket journalist and broadcaster. Even today, when I watch television and switch over to a sports channel, it is always pleasant to see his smiling face on the screen and talking about cricket. He has the ability to use this medium of publicity to great advantage. He continues to contribute a great deal to the promotion of cricket.

27

Sir Garfield Sobers: All-round Genius

Played cricket like a cavalier

One of the most versatile cricketers that I came across in my Test career was from Barbados who would go on the rampage from the very first ball that he received. He was a gifted player who, with his outstanding performances, dominated cricket in the West Indies and in the cricketing world for nearly two decades. This was Sir Garfield Sobers.

Sobers started playing cricket at the Bay Street School in the parish of St. Michael when he was ten years old. He was a keen player of soccer, golf, and basketball in his early days. He was destined to become one of the greatest cricketers in Test match history. In his Test debut, at Sabina Park, Kingston, against England in 1954, he caught the attention of critics by claiming 4 wickets for 75 runs. He had luckily been included in the side in place of the regular spinner, Valentine, who had reported unfit before the start of the match.

In his early days, Sobers was more successful with the ball than the bat. It may appear amazing that this fine batsman came to bat at number nine on his Test debut. Sobers concentrated on his batting after the Kingston Test, and during the Australian tour of the West Indies in 1955, he went in at number six in the second Test at Port-of-Spain and faced the assault of the great Keith Miller and Ray Lindwall, playing a brave innings of 47. Sobers emerged as a mature batsman during the West Indies tour of England in 1957. In the five Tests there, he scored 320 (32.00) and took five wickets (70.10). His innings, against Nottinghamshire at Trent Bridge boosted his confidence.

However, Sobers touched the zenith of fame in the home series against Pakistan in 1958. He scored 828 runs (137.33) in five Tests. In the third Test at Kingston, Sobers achieved recognition by establishing a new world record in batting by surpassing the great innings of the Sir Len Hutton. On a perfect pitch, Sobers played his strokes freely throughout his innings. Our bowling was sadly handicapped. Fast bowler Mahmood Hussain had pulled a thigh muscle. He could not complete his over and bowled only five balls in the West Indies' first innings. Kardar was bowling with a broken finger. Our most effective spinner, Nasim ul Ghani had fractured a thumb quite early in the West Indies' innings.

Khan Muhammad and I, along with the other bowlers, fought against all odds. Our team-mates encouraged us. We tried hard to get Sobers out before he surpassed Hanif Muhammad's 337 runs, but he continued hammering our bowlers indiscriminately. The crowd at Kingston was ecstatic. It would not accept any appeal from a bowler against Garfield Sobers. Naturally, he was a little anxious and did not want to make a mistake at that juncture. However, the tension ended when an on-drive from him went past the fielder. The entire crowd ran into the field and danced. They even carried Sobers on their shoulders. Indeed, Sobers had played a great innings.

We ran back to the pavilion and watched the action on the ground from there. The entire cricketing world was listening to the run of events at Kingston, Jamaica—Sobers breaking the record of that great exponent of fair play, Sir Len Hutton. Suddenly, the telephone rang and caught our attention. It was a call from some people in England who asked me, 'How come you allowed that man to break Sir Len Hutton's record?' I had no reply.

It was undoubtedly Sobers' day and he took full advantage of the home crowd and played a record-breaking innings. Interestingly, it was his first innings of three figures in Test cricket. Sobers had not scored a 100 in his first sixteen Tests. But, once he had done it, he never looked back and went on to achieve all the glories that cricket could offer. This gave him the confidence he needed to become a world-class batsman.

Sobers attained further glory in the fourth Test of the same series at Georgetown, where he scored a century in each innings—125 and 109 runs. After Pakistan's visit, the West Indies toured India in 1959 where he scored centuries in the first three Tests. He scored 557 runs, averaging 92.83. However, Sobers did not get many runs on the Pakistan tour in 1959, where his total aggregate was 160 runs.

Sobers was undoubtedly the greatest all-rounder of all time. He was the natural product of the West Indies' cricket environment. Nature had gifted this tall Barbadian with every thing that made him a great cricketer. Perhaps, very few people know that Sobers was born with six fingers each on both hands. Later, the extra fingers were surgically removed. In 1959, he survived a car accident in which his very good friend, Collie Smith, died.

Sobers was essentially a larger than life cricketer. The harder the struggle, the more determined and versatile he would be. His defence was resolute. He scored even in the presence of the indomitable three Ws. Sobers would appear from the dressing room in a graceful and relaxed manner, and move with long strides to the crease. He was a highly combative cricketer and played some brave innings for the West Indies. On his first tour of England in 1957, when many seniors performed poorly, Sobers batted with immense concentration and determination. In the Lord's Test of 1966, when the West Indies were tottering at 95 for 5 in the second innings, Sobers (163 not out) lifted his team from the brink of defeat to set a new West Indies Test record of 274 for the sixth wicket with Holford (105 not out).

At his best, Sobers would score freely. The crowd loved him and he seldom disappointed his fans. He was a naturally attacking batsman but could play defensively if the situation so demanded. Sobers' century (132) in the tied Brisbane Test match (1961) would be remembered forever. His innings was a beautiful example of full, flowing strokes, mostly with the top hand.

In the beginning of 1962, the Indian team visited the West Indies. Sobers' all-round performance was instrumental in the West Indies winning the series by a big margin. He scored 153 in the second Test at Kingston and 104 in the fifth Test at the same venue. On each occasion, he took five wickets as well.

Sobers was the most prolific left-handed batsman of his time. If Neil Harvey is known to be the second Bradman, Sobers broke the record of Sir Len Hutton.

Sobers was a very fine stroke-player. He would hook majestically. His athletic build made him a hard hitter who could hit the ball with speed and strength. This tall left-hander was a cricketer of some outstanding qualities who overshadowed everyone else from the West Indies. He had a perfect text-book style. He was equally good on his front and back foot and his defence was as good as his attack. He would always go for the ball. Sobers always played according to the situation. If his team was in trouble, he would build his innings steadily. He would wait until things improved and then launch his attack. He was a bit vulnerable against the movement of the ball, both in the air and off the ground. However, he would play dangerously to an incoming ball.

Sobers was appointed the West Indies captain in the home series against Australia in 1965. The West Indies won the series 2–1. He scored 352 (39.11) and took 12 wickets (41.00). The late Frank Worrell very ably guided young Sobers in cricket. As a captain, Sobers was sporting. He would not hesitate to declare the innings for the sake of a result. He always showed an instinctive tactical sense which never let him down. He captained in thirty-nine Tests, and proved himself a worthy successor to Sir Frank Worrell.

Sobers scored 722 runs against England on the 1966 tour. His average was 103.14. In the first Test at Manchester, he scored 161 and was the central figure in his team's success in that Test. In the second Test at Lord's, he scored an unbeaten 163. In the fourth Test at Leeds, he led his team to victory with a superb all-round performance. His contribution was outstanding, scoring 174 runs and taking 8 wickets for 80 runs.

In 1971–72, Sobers was selected to represent the Rest of the World against Australia. The tour was arranged hurriedly when the official visit of South Africa was cancelled following continued international pressure against apartheid. Sobers played a magnificent and unforgettable innings of 254 against the formidable attack of Dennis Lillee and Jeff Thomson. His innings was a blend of elegant stroke-play, power, and aggression. Sir Donald Bradman described his innings thus: 'I believe Gary's innings was probably the best ever seen in Australia. The people who saw Sobers, have enjoyed one of the historic events of cricket. They were privileged to have such an experience.'

Apart from his batting, Sobers' bowling could get him a place in any Test side. As a bowler, he was three-in-one—a genuine opening bowler with an occasional fast ball, an orthodox slow left-arm bowler, and a skilful exponent of spin which he learnt from George Tribe. Sobers had great stamina and endurance. Even after playing a long innings, he could be asked to bowl for three to four hours at a stretch. There are very few bowlers in cricket history who could bowl like him. In the sixties, Sobers developed the left-arm wrist-spin, breaking the ball sharply and concealing his googly well. However, out of deference for his captain, the late Sir Frank Worrell, he trained to become a Test-class fast-medium bowler because that was what the team needed. On many occasions he seamed the new ball, either with Hall or Griffith, and could bowl the chinaman and googly as well as the left-arm orthodox spinner.

Sobers was a magnificent fielder in the slips and held some spectacular catches. He could also field close to the batsman, and was brilliant on the leg-side where he held many splendid catches on Lance Gibbs' bowling.

Before the West Indies' tour of England in 1973, Sobers had a knee operation. There was speculation if he would make the tour, but he did although he only played in the Tests. His performance was instrumental in the West Indies' winning the series of 2–1. He scored 306 (76.50) in three Tests. At Lord's, in the third Test, he played his last glorious innings, and remained unbeaten with 150. Sobers retired from Test cricket in 1974.

Sir Garfield Sobers was a congenial personality. He was ever smiling. Self-control and command of circumstances were his two dominant qualities. He once paid me a wonderful compliment when he said, 'If Fazal Mahmood could not get a wicket he would contain the batsman.'

Australia had a special place in Sobers' life. He fell in love with a pretty Australian girl whom he had first met in England. They married after a brief but passionate affair.

In 1975, Sobers was knighted at Barbados in recognition of his great services to the West Indies team and cricket.

Reflections

Part III

28

Looking Back

I played cricket in a period when there was no television. Thus, cricketers were not as recognizable as film stars. I had never seen internationally recognized players playing until I met them on the cricket field, and knew them only through newspaper accounts. England's Sir Jack Hobbs was a master batsman when I was still a toddler. I heard in England that when Surrey would win the toss at the Oval, Hobbs would often complete a hundred before lunch. When Hobbs and Sutcliffe would open the innings for England, with Hammond coming at number three, the rest of the team could go shopping. Australia's Sir Don Bradman was the one name that I heard most during my early days in first-class cricket. He was such a devastating cricketer that bowlers would think twice before bowling to him. It is well known that the infamous 'bodyline' bowling was invented only to stop his onslaught against England.

I had interesting encounters with some of the finest batsmen of the world during my Test career. England's Peter May was the best batsman in the mid and late 50s, but was quite unlike Hutton or Compton. His square-cut, which he would play with immense power, was savage. He could play straight, both off the back and front foot, with such perfection and force that the bowler had to jump in the air to save himself from the sting of that shot. Peter May was a soft spoken gentleman off the field. He was a great player.

Tom Graveney was another good English batsman. However, he was weak against the ball coming from the leg—the blind spot. Ted Dexter was a copy of Peter May, but he was usually a little unsure against the incoming ball. Colin Cowdrey was also

a great batsman. When I was on the England tour of 1954, I saw
that the most outstanding and upcoming batsman of England
was Colin Cowdrey. He played for Oxford University, the MCC,
and Kent against the Pakistan team, and was selected for the
England team to tour Australia in 1954–55. When I was asked
on television as to who would be the find of the Australian
tour, my answer was Colin. I was right, and Colin proved it on
the tour.

Bob Simpson of Australia was another good batsman. I
played a couple of matches against him in the Lancashire league.
In one match, I did not allow Bob to score in both innings. In
the first innings, he was dropped twice off my bowling.

India has produced many outstanding batsmen. I have not
played with all of them. Nawab Iftikhar Ali Khan Pataudi was a
very fine cricketer. I first saw him playing in the annual festival
match in the 1940s between the Governor's XI and the Punjab
University XI at the Bagh-i-Jinnah cricket ground, then known
as Lawrence Gardens. The old blues of the Punjab University
were included in the team to play against the stalwarts of India.
The Nawab was a master. He could steer the ball through any
field setting. During the match, he would ask us where he
should hit the ball. When Munawwar Ali Khan, our speed
merchant, was bowling, there was a gap between short-leg and
the first leg-slip. The Nawab was asked if he could glide the
ball through that gap. He took his front foot across the line of
the ball and glided it through that gap for a four. The Nawab
scored a 100 in his first appearance against Australia. The critics
called it a slow innings, forgetting that he played under difficult
conditions when his stay at the crease was very necessary.

In 1959, when I was in England playing league cricket with
East Lancashire, an upcoming Indian batsman called Abbas Ali
Baig approached me with the request that I should give him
some tips to improve his batting. I coached him for a while.
Hanif Muhammad was concerned about this and asked me why
was I coaching Baig since one day he was going to play for
India against Pakistan. I was a cricketer and did not feel that it
was wrong to give tips to a batsman, whether from India or

from any other country. Later, Baig played for India in the Manchester Test and scored a century on debut. He was very successful on English wickets. Baig played against Pakistan when we toured India in 1960–61, but he scored very few runs against us. Baig had the tendency to play the cut-shot. In fact, that was his favourite shot and I was aware of it. This shot can be played easily on English wickets where the ball comes a bit slow but on Indian wickets, where the ball would come early, he was always vulnerable. I was leading the side in India. When Baig would be at the crease, I would place two fielders in the gully and two in the third-man position. Then, I would ask the bowler to bowl outside the off-stump inviting Baig to play the cut-shot. He would play the shot, and without fail be caught at gully.

Pakistan's Saeed Ahmad was a dashing batsman. During a side-match on the West Indies tour, Dewdney's bouncer hit Saeed on the head. He was asked by his partner to go back to the pavilion for treatment, but he refused with a loud 'NO' and kept on hooking Dewdney whenever he could. Dewdney tried to outplay Saeed with a fast bouncer, and Saeed responded by hitting it so hard that it landed in the crowd at point.

I have seen fearsome fast bowlers in my cricketing career. Among the fastest were Gilchrist, Frank Tyson, Freddie Truman, and Wes Hall. Gilly (Gilchrist), however, was the fastest of them all. In my opinion, he was faster than Jeff Thomson or Shoaib Akhtar. He was brutal. Gilly had a very unique habit. He had a fairly long run-up. For his first ball, he would appear from behind the screen, run up to the bowling crease amid chants of 'Gilly' 'Gilly'. I remember that during a Test match on the West Indies tour in 1958, I was sent in by Kardar to bat at number eight. Gilly was fielding at third-man. He walked up to me and asked, 'Have you been sent in or have you come in on your own?' 'Sent,' was my reply. 'Ok, let the b— come later,' he declared, and after that he did not bounce at me.

England's Frank Tyson was a savage bowler. When I faced him in the Oval Test in 1954, he was then an upcoming player. My first encounter with Freddie Truman was very interesting.

When I was leading the Pakistan Eaglets team on their England tour in 1953, we played a match against the Royal Air Force team of which Freddie was a member. When I came in to bat he was bowling, and he came up to me and asked, 'Are you a Test cricketer?' I replied in the affirmative. 'Then, I will blow your head off,' he said in a serious tone. He encircled me with seven fielders. I used the long handle against him and soon the close-in fielders were on their way to the ropes. I managed a decent score.

In the subcontinent, the most outstanding fast bowler was undoubtedly Muhammad Nisar. He was the fastest bowler ever produced by our part of the world. He caused a sensation with his pace in the English cricket camp when he visited England in 1936. Throughout his career, he never bowled a bouncer. Whenever his captain asked him to do so against a well-set batsman, Nisar declined by saying, 'This is not my style.'

Mahmood Hussain was a slinger in the beginning. However, when he toured England with the Pakistan Eaglets team in 1952, he was trained and coached in the Alf Gover coaching school. With this, his action became over arm and his bicep would touch his ear. Everton Weekes gave him high praise during our West Indies tour in 1958. His in-swinger was a wicket-taking ball. He was a very fine bowler, with decent length and direction. Had he bowled in present day conditions, he would have come out with flying colours. Khan Muhammad was another intelligent bowler. But, frequent fitness problems and differences with Abdul Hafeez Kardar shortened his Test career.

India produced good batsmen like Mushtaq Ali and Lala Amarnath in the pre-Partition period when I, too, was playing for India. Vijay Merchant was also a fine batsman. He would carefully build his innings but at times it was felt that he played more for himself than the team. Merchant piled up runs in the Ranji Trophy and surpassed Vijay Hazare's record of 316 by scoring 359 runs in 1943–44. A shoulder injury forced his early retirement from Test cricket. Hazare had intense concentration, and rarely lofted the ball. He was the first Indian to score a century in each innings of a Test match. He achieved this feat in the fourth Test at Adelaide against Australia in 1948. Umrigar and Manjrekar were good batsmen on easy wickets. However, Umrigar was shy of genuine fast bowling. Gul Muhammad, an All-India Test cricketer, also played for Pakistan. He was a great batsman with sparkling footwork and a prolific run-getter in the Ranji Trophy, but he disappointed in Test matches. His fourth-wicket partnership (577) with Hazare is still a world record in first-class cricket.

The best known spinners of my time were Valentine and Ramadhin of the West Indies, Appleyard, Johnny Wardle, and Jim Laker of England, Richie Benaud of Australia, and Nehalchand, Subash Gupte, and Ghulam Ahmad of India. 'Those two jewels of mine—Ramadhin and Valentine,' was the famous line in our days. They were successful against batsmen from England, Australia, South Africa, and New Zealand, but our batsmen were quite capable of playing against their spin. Imtiaz Ahmad played these two spinners with great ease during the course of his great innings of 300 against the Commonwealth XI at Bombay in 1951. When Imtiaz reached 292, Vijay Merchant sent him a message at the crease that he had only one more over to complete his triple century because he intended to declare the innings. Valentine was bowling that last over. Imtiaz faced his last three balls, and hit him past the ropes on two successive deliveries to complete his triple century. Had the captain allowed him one more over, Imtiaz would have created a new batting record on that wicket, surpassing the 309 made by Hazare in the Bombay Pentangular in 1939–40. I was never a very good batsman, but I did score a ton against these two spinners in England in 1953 when the Pakistan Eaglets team played a match against the West Indies.

Among the Indian spinners, I rate Gupte as the best. He was known as 'Fergie' by his team-mates. He was one of the finest leg-break googly bowlers of all times. It was difficult to spot his googly as he would flight the ball cleverly and constantly experiment in his endeavour to find a way to deceive the batsman. One had to concentrate really hard to play him. He won the Bombay Test against us in 1952. It was only in the latter part of the 1952 tour that we discovered that whenever he wanted to bowl a googly he would tighten his grip twice at the bowling mark. This would provide the signal to our batsmen.

England's Jim Laker could spin sharply and with great accuracy. I played against Laker during our England tour of 1954, stretching my long legs and showing him the long handle. His performance against Australia (1956) at Old Trafford was unique. He took 9 for 37 and 10 for 53.

During the pre-Partition days, Habib played for the Mamdot Club. Although he had broken his right arm in an accident, he managed to get extra turn by bowling vicious off-breaks at medium-fast speed. A side which scored more than 80 runs against him was lucky. Muhammad Amin was another great leg-break googly bowler. In spite of being an average fielder, he could have walked into the Pakistan team as a spinner. Before the Pakistan tour to England in 1954, a training camp was held in Bahawalpur. At the end of the camp, two teams were organized to play a trial match. Amin's performance in that match was excellent. He took seven wickets, but in the end the son of a bureaucrat was preferred over him. Had he been in England with the Pakistan team, we might have won the four-Test match series.

Haseeb Ahsan was a good off-spinner in the Pakistan team that toured the West Indies in 1958. Even Everton Weekes had a lot of praise for him. After the West Indies tour, Haseeb played league cricket in England. He also toured India in 1960–61 where he bowled exceptionally well. Even his critics could not fault his bowling action, but on the England tour in 1962, he was dubbed as a 'chucker'. Neither the captain of the team nor the BCCP took a stand in Haseeb's favour. Their inaction ruined the career of a very fine bowler. Compared to Sri Lanka's Muralitharan, Haseeb's action was by far cleaner and more correct. He was better than Murli in the art of spin bowling. The difference was that Haseeb bowled with speed, and his fingers and spin worked more than Murli's.

Nazar Muhammad and Neil Harvey were great fielders, specially Nazar who was in a class of his own. I have yet to see anyone as good in the gully even in present day cricket. Even the brilliant Jonty Rhodes of South Africa does not compare with him.

In conclusion, I want to mention two interesting stories concerning the English umpire, Frank Chester. During a Test match in 1954, one of our fielders dropped a sitter at short-leg. It was an easy catch and anyone could have caught it. Chester could not resist remarking: 'Hey, sonny, come here,' he said to the fielder. As the fielder went up to him, he said, 'Go and sleep in your mother's lap. This is Test cricket.' The second story is about a yorker that I bowled to a batsman, whose name I do not recall, in a side-match during the 1954 tour. The ball hit him on the ankle, and he rolled on the ground in sheer agony. I went up to him, and so did Frank Chester, who asked the batsman, 'Hey, sonny, can you walk?' With much difficulty, he replied that he could. 'Then keep on walking—you are out,' and Chester raised his finger.

29

Apartheid: This Ain't Cricket

Cricket implies fair play. All those values and principles which govern the promotion of morality in human life are enshrined in the game of cricket. The traditions of cricket make the game mean more than the mere laws of cricket.

All civilized people feel concerned when there is domination of one man over another. Every one has the right to live the way they choose. No segment of a society can be allowed to impose its will on others, more so when this is done on the basis of colour and perpetrated by a people who were essentially colonizers against the natives they colonized. But, just such an abhorrent society existed in South Africa, and I was a witness to it when I stopped over in that country back in 1957. This prompted the first move in my effort to help in dismantling such an unjust system when I played an important role in the withdrawal of Test status from South Africa.

In 1957, I was travelling from Karachi to Liverpool in the SS Caledonia when war broke out between Israel and Egypt and the Suez canal was closed. The ship was diverted to the Cape of Good Hope, and after ten days of sailing, the ship docked at Durban. We, the browns, blacks, and the coloured, witnessed the restrictions imposed on coloured people in that part of the world.

Twenty of us, comprising young and old, men and women, walked towards the city. We could not hire a cab. We were denied even a drink of water in the restaurants. There was no place for us. In the parks, even in the buses, admission was restricted. Our small caravan reached a point where white people walked on one side of the road and apartment blocks were segregated as being exclusively for the whites and the coloured. While still walking, I saw a young brown girl of eight or nine. When I approached her, she started running towards her house. I ran after her and knocked at the door of the house she had entered. Someone came out, stared at me, and asked: 'Is that Fazal? Has the ship arrived?' My reply was in the affirmative. I told him that I had a group of about twenty people with me and that we were very thirsty. The person, to my good luck, was from Hyderabad (Sindh). He opened his store and we were able to quench our thirst.

I saw apartheid and experienced it. I was told of the maltreatment meted out to the coloured by the whites. Naturally, I came back to the ship with a heavy heart, grieved and hurt. My two fellow passengers, Mitchell and Col. Conville, consoled me and even expressed dissatisfaction over the South African policy of 'apartheid'.

It was a sheer stroke of luck that I replaced Tayfield, the South African player who played for the East Lancashire league as a professional. While playing for the Lancashire league, I started writing articles for the paper, *The News*. Incidentally, the South African cricket team was touring England that year. I got an opportunity to express my viewpoint over South Africa's policy of racial discrimination. I wrote articles against it under the heading 'This Ain't Cricket'. Reverend David Sheppard was extended an invitation to play against the South African team. He declined the invitation with these remarks: 'They do not associate themselves with the blacks. So I won't associate myself with them.' This created quite a stir in England. I wrote an article with the suggestion that Test status for South Africa should be withdrawn. One day, late at night, I received a call from Charles Griffith, the then secretary of the MCC and the ICC. He said: 'Another feather in your cap. Your articles were taken up and discussed in the ICC meeting and the Test status of South Africa has been withdrawn.' The Nottingham Test between England and South Africa saw much less attendance. From 35,000, the crowd went down to 5000. This was enough to show the resentment of cricket lovers towards the abhorrent policy of South Africa.

The Test status of South Africa was restored only after Nelson Mandela became the president of South Africa in 1992.

30

The Captaincy Issue in the 1950s

The captaincy of a national team is indeed a matter of pride. It is quite natural for every player to aspire to lead the national side. But, it is demoralizing and unquestionably unethical if a captain's appointment is made through political influence. When the West Indies came to Pakistan to play the one-off Test match in November 1948, Mian Muhammad Saeed was the seniormost available player to lead the home side. Till then, Gul Muhammad, an All-India Test cricketer, had not opted for Pakistan while Amir Elahi, another All-India Test cricketer, was away in Baroda. Hafeez Kardar, himself an All-India Test cricketer, was studying at Oxford in England.

Mian Saeed ably led the Pakistan team against the mighty West Indies and in March 1949, under his leadership, Pakistan toured Ceylon and won the two-Test match series 2–0. Kardar arrived in Pakistan, perhaps in the summer of 1949, when Pakistan had already played three Test matches. The Commonwealth XI was to visit Pakistan in November 1949. Kardar was invited by the BCCP to play in the Test against the Commonwealth XI but he declined the offer saying that he was ill. He was not. Perhaps, he did not want to play under Mian Saeed and wanted to lead the Pakistan team himself. Kardar's claim was that he was an All-India Test cricketer and, therefore, he deserved to lead the side. But, Mian Saeed was senior to Kardar and had played against Tennyson's team that visited Lahore in the late 1930s. Saeed had also led Northern India in the Ranji Trophy, besides which, before Kardar became an All-India Test cricketer, he played two matches under Saeed—for Northern India against the Southern Punjab at Lahore in January

1945, and then against Bombay in the semi-finals. In the latter match, Kardar scored 145 and a duck. Besides Mian Saeed, Nazar Muhammad was also senior to Kardar. When Kardar could not find any favour from the people at the helm of the BCCP affairs, he had no other option but to decline the offer to play against the Commonwealth XI. Kardar was considered a strict disciplinarian, but when it came to himself, he showed utter disrespect towards his seniors. When Pakistan lost to the Commonwealth XI, some urchins from the old city were allegedly hired to pelt stones on Mian Saeed and myself. We were whisked away by security men into the Lahore Gymkhana pavilion. Mian Saeed again led the Pakistan side in the home series against Ceylon in 1950, and we won both the matches.

Mian Saeed retired from first-class cricket after Pakistan's success over Ceylon. When the MCC came to Pakistan in 1951, Kardar was appronted the captain. Naturally, there was some resentment among the players. The reason was obvious. Kardar was not part of the Pakistan cricket team that had played Test matches against the West Indies, the Commonwealth XI, and Ceylon. He had gone to England for higher studies before Partition, and was away for almost four or five years. Moreover, both Amir Elahi and Nazar Muhammad were senior to him. Amir Elahi had made his first-class debut for Northern India against Delhi & Districts at Delhi in the Ranji Trophy in 1934–35. Nazar had made his first-class debut for Northern India against NWFP at Peshawar in the Ranji Trophy in 1940–41. Kardar, Imtiaz, and I made our first-class debuts for Northern India against Patiala in the Ranji Trophy in 1944–45 and, as such, were equals as far as seniority was concerned.

Though Kardar's appointment was resented, yet the players displayed tremendous sportsmanship. Captaincy or no captaincy, we had to win laurels for Pakistan, and in the end, no one grudged him his appointment. On their arrival in Pakistan, the MCC team captain Howard made a statement in the media that Statham, their fast bowler, would run through the Pakistan team as a 'knife runs through butter'. It was psychological warfare to unsettle our batsmen. I told Kardar not to worry, as I was myself determined to go through the MCC batsmen. I proved it in the Karachi Test by claiming 6 wickets in the first innings.

Kardar was retained as captain on Pakistan's first Indian tour in 1952. Anwar Hussain was made the vice-captain. I had been confident that I would be appointed the vice-captain of the team and, naturally, felt ignored. The senior players, too, were not happy with these decisions. They objected to his captaincy even before the team left Lahore for Amritsar. As the tour progressed, Kardar's differences with the senior players widened and Muhammad Hussain, the manager of the team, was unable to bring harmony amongst them. But, on the field, the players gave their unstinted support to Kardar. Prior to our departure for Amritsar, Kardar wanted Asghar Ali in the team but failed to convince the selectors. Upon reaching Amritsar, Kardar sent an SOS to the BCCP asking that Asghar Ali join the team. It was unnecessary as we were playing our first match of the tour and Kardar had not yet tried the other players in the team. The BCCP declined to oblige him as all the other players of the team were fit and there was no need for any replacement. When in the middle of the tour, Khan Muhammad was injured, the BCCP sent young Khalid Ibadullah as a replacement. Kardar did not reconcile with this. He openly ridiculed BCCP's decision saying that 'he has to carry another baby'. The BCCP did not take any action against him. Kardar was encouraged by their inaction and continued in this vein.

The issue of captaincy was once again raised before the announcement of Pakistan's tour to England in 1954. Mian Saeed was almost appointed captain of the team. But, Major-General Iskandar Mirza, then working in the defence ministry, intervened and Kardar was reappointed to lead the Pakistan team. I was made the vice-captain.

Before the arrival of the Indian team on the Pakistan tour in 1955, this issue came up again. The Karachi Cricket Association proposed my name and the Punjab Cricket Association seconded it. This puzzled me as I had not indicated any interest in becoming the captain. I am not sure about what actually happened, but there was speculation that an influential business family of Karachi had once again approached Iskandar Mirza, president of the BCCP, in support of Kardar. Iskandar Mirza requested Azhar Hussain, secretary of the Punjab Cricket Association, to withdraw my name, saying, 'Fazal will become the captain of the Pakistan team one day. Nobody can stop him.'

After losing the test match series to the West Indies in 1958, Kardar announced his retirement from Test cricket. The West Indies was to make a return tour to Pakistan in 1958–59. Well before the start of the tour, I asked Kardar to withdraw his decision and lead the Pakistan team in the home series. I almost convinced him. Kardar said that he was going to Calcutta to watch the third Test match between India and the West Indies, and that he would let me know his final decision after he returned. On coming back from Calcutta, he declined to oblige. Perhaps, he was reluctant to lead the Pakistan team assuming another possible defeat—the West Indies had defeated India by an innings and 336 runs, and had eventually won the series 3–0.

Kardar was then made the chief selector. The selectors had to pick a team to field against the West Indies in the home series. They announced a list of twenty-four players who were to report for the training camp at Karachi. Khan Muhammad publicly refused to accept the offer saying that 'as long as Kardar maintained his monopoly, he would not play.'

There was yet another controversy before the selection of the Pakistan team to tour India in November 1960. Perhaps, Kardar was given some indication from the highest quarters that he might lead the Pakistan team on the Indian tour. So, he went to England and had his knee operated upon. When he returned from England, his activities showed signs of a possible come back. However, this time the selectors put him on trial where he put up a miserable show and that was the end of his cricket career.

Despite all his doings, I have no ill will against Kardar. He and I were the members of Mamdot Cricket Club. We played cricket together in the Punjab University team and there was a good understanding between us. After matriculation, Kardar joined Dyal Singh College. However, I persuaded him to join Islamia College, Lahore. We graduated from the same college in the same year and our marks in the exams were also identical. We made our first-class debut (Ranji Trophy) in the same year for the same team. The misunderstanding between us surfaced when Kardar left Mamdot over a trivial issue. Nevertheless, we remained friends. Kardar went to England for higher studies. When he came back, he was not the same cricketer he used to be. His bowling style had changed. Besides this, he was an entirely changed person who now had a sense of superiority. He would just say 'hello' to his old friends and walk away. When he was made captain of the Pakistan team, I did not envy him nor did I make any fuss over it. However, after his underhand role in keeping me out from the Karachi Test, I told him in clear-cut words, 'You will only take the team into the ground but I shall lead it back with victory.' Subsequent events have amply proven that I meant what I said. Lucknow (1952), Oval (1954), Karachi (1956), and Trinidad (1958) showed that I was true to my word.

31

The Changing Face of Cricket

Gone are the days when cricket was a gentleman's game. The phrase 'this ain't cricket' is a well accepted one in the English language. It is synonymous with fair play in sports, business, and public life. Today, cricketing authorities are trying to bring back the concept of fair play into international cricket and are making codes of conduct to discipline their players.

International cricketers of the early days were amateurs who played and enjoyed cricket. They had strong national feelings and played the game in the spirit of good and competitive sportsmanship. The country always came first. There were very few professionals in our days but the relationship between them and the amateurs was always friendly and cordial. There was absolutely no ill will. Even top professionals like Sir Len Hutton maintained the best of conduct.

I regret to say that present day professionals are generally self-centred. Who cares if the team loses! There are groups within the team. All norms of cricket have been thrown to the wind. Make money in whichever way you can, even if you have to sell your soul, seems to be the motto. Match fixing has ruined the spirit of cricket.

The old spirit of amateur play has been completely forgotten and overlooked. The psychology of a present day professional is individualistic. No doubt, these professionals have calibre and good technical skills, but they are often swayed by the lure of money. More often than not, their only concern appears to be their own individual performances, to prove their ability and enhance their earnings. Once they have attained material success, they don't like to labour further. They fail to maintain consistency in their performance, but continue to ask for more lucrative terms and conditions.

Gone are the days when seniors commanded respect from their juniors. A fairly large majority of present-day cricketers appear to overlook the fact that what they are enjoying today— facilities, career, and money—are because of the love for the game fostered in the public by players of the earlier era. In those days, players, once selected in the Test side, were treated at par with each other. The seniors did command respect but the rights of others were not ignored. The seniors encouraged the youngsters and imparted knowledge to them, and the concept of foul play never crept into the field of cricket. In those days, great cricketers would perform consistently. They were full of confidence. They were models of concentration and application. W.G. Grace, Sir Jack Hobbs, Sutcliffe, Sir Don Bradman, Sir Len Hutton, Walter Hammond, Sir Frank Worrell, and Keith Miller will not be forgotten as long as this game is played.

One incident that reflects the team spirit in general, and the confidence of a player in particular, is moot here. Pakistan was playing against the West Indies in the Dhaka Test in 1959. Against India, England, and Australia, I had taken 12 or more wickets in a single Test match, and had to complete my tally of 12 wickets here as well. The West Indies batsmen were subdued. They needed about 70 or 80 runs to beat Pakistan with four wickets in hand. Sobers, and the late Collie Smith were at the crease. Mahmood Hussain and I went all out in the first over after the tea interval. Mahmood got Sobers caught at short leg by my hands. Then I clean bowled Smith. While Smith walked off the field, he made a very amusing remark. 'The thief had to be caught one day,' he muttered. With him out, I completed my tally of 12 wickets. Atkinson did not stay long. At this stage, Mahmood Hussain walked up to me, saying: 'Skipper, have you completed your quota of getting 12 wickets in a Test match?' I replied happily, 'Yes, I have.' 'So, rest of the wickets belong to me?' he asked. 'By all means, but I will only give you 20 runs to get those wickets,' I said. By then the West Indies needed 50 runs to win the match.

Mahmood bowled extremely well. When the last man, Lance Gibbs, came in, the given 20 runs had been exceeded by just one run. I looked at Mahmood Hussain. 'Skipper, give me just one more run. I promise I will not disappoint you,' he yelled from a distance. I said 'Ok, you have it.' I have yet to see a faster yorker than that which landed on Gibbs right toe, on the middle-stump. Gibbs was clean bowled and Pakistan won the match. I can happily say with pride that such was the team spirit in the good old days. Had we been playing only for personal glory, I myself would have run through the West Indies tail-enders in a couple of overs or so.

Players today have money and facilities, but seem to lack dedication, and fair play. Professionals of the old days were supposed to give their hundred per cent to the team. After scoring a century or taking five wickets in a Test match, they would not become complacent. Their entire concentration was focussed on the game of cricket. I remember that during a Test match in the West Indies, England fast bowler Frank Tyson shortened his run-up and bowled a wee bit slow. His captain, Ted Dexter, told him firmly, 'Bowl fast. You are paid for it.'

In our days, violation of discipline was considered a serious crime. No late night programmes or functions. I can very safely say that during our 1954 England tour, from 23 May to 17 August, I was always in my room before 9 p.m. It used to be clearly written in the contracts. There was no such thing as divided concentration. Today, late nights during foreign tours have become a routine matter and mobile phones have become a part of the playing kit.

Lord George Robert Canning Harris, speaking about the spirit of cricket, said:

Drink deeply of the wisdom of your forefathers. You do well to love it, for it is freer from anything sordid, anything dishonourable, than any game in the world. To play it keenly, honourably, generously, self-sacrificingly is a moral lesson in itself, and the classroom is

God's air and sunshine. Foster it, my brothers, so that it may attract all who can find the time to play it; protect it from anything that would sully it, so that it may grow in favour with all men.

It was an accepted norm in our days that a fast bowler did not bowl bouncers to the number 9-10-and Jack. Today, it is often the opposite. In a Test match on the West Indies tour in 1958, I was sent in by Kardar at number eight instead of the usual number nine. Gilchrist, who was fielding at third-man, walked up to me and inquired, 'Have you been sent in or have you come out on your own'? 'Sent', was my reply. On hearing this, he did not hurl any bouncers at me.

In club cricket, it was unheard of for an umpire to intentionally give a bad decision. The local club umpires would perform the honourable job of umpiring. Batsmen would walk if they thought they were out. There are instances when the batsmen took the correct decision by walking off the field before receiving a signal from the umpire for they knew exactly what had happened. During the Lord's Test against the West Indies, in 1957–58 Colin Cowdrey hooked Gilchrist. The bowler appealed for a catch. The umpire was not sure and hesitated in giving his decision. Colin walked off the field, saying, 'It touched my gloves.' The bowlers, too, would not make unnecessary or wrong appeals. On one occasion, back in 1925, the great Australian leg-break and googly bowler, Arthur Mailey, appealed for a leg before at the Adelaide Oval. Following his appeal, he walked back past George Hele who was officiating at the bowler's end, and said, 'Bloody cheat.'

'Who's a cheat?' demanded Hele. 'I am,' grinned Arthur, 'for appealing.'

The induction of neutral umpires in this game of fair play reflects a defeatist mentality. It seems that the umpires have lost their confidence because of criticism from the players and the media. They have to try and show that they are neutral and unbiased. However, thanks to close-circuit cameras, viewers now have an opportunity to evaluate most close decisions for themselves.

The attitude of the cricketers of the past is not found in present day cricket. Also, the crowds in those days appreciated good cricket because they loved and enjoyed the game. No one would dream of throwing empty bottles or fireworks on the field.

During the 1970s, cricket witnessed several changes. These were hostile to the spirit of cricket. What followed after, amid match fixing and betting charges, is absolutely disgusting. I am not against this form of cricket, but what I cannot digest is when a putrid shot is cheered in one-day cricket. The quality of the game has vanished. The glorious game has been reduced to 'hit and run'. It has nearly become like baseball. Indeed, the standard of fielding has vastly improved, but one-day cricket has blemished the beauty of the game. Today, one-day cricket is taking precedence over traditional Test cricket on the pretext that, in a busy world to watch a five-day match people have no time. Yes, the people who indulge in betting on one-day matches have no time to come to the cricket grounds as they can conveniently watch the proceedings on TV, sitting in their comfortable homes and offices. As far as the general masses are concerned, and these are the real fans of cricket, they still prefer to watch the game in stadiums if clean cricket is provided to them and the cost of tickets is reduced. It seems now that multinational corporations have indirectly gained control of the game.

Test cricket today is in the doldrums only because cricketers like Mushtaq Ali, Keith Miller, Sir Len Hutton, Denis Compton, Imtiaz Ahmad, Sir Frank Worrell, Everton Weekes, Richie Benaud, and many more are no longer in business. Did anybody dub them as match fixers? They were far better cricketers in character and conduct than many of the cricketers today. It has been maintained that if Test cricket fades out, it would be disastrous. Thankfully, of late, Test cricket has begun to re-emerge and has started to generate interest. In 1998, the first Asian Test championship was played between Pakistan, India, and Sri Lanka. Cricket administrators in these countries must get credit for this. The idea of holding a world test Championship is already being considered. The ICC should come forward and pursue a vigorous strategy to organize Test championships. This will liven up Test cricket. To me, Test cricket will always mean much more than limited overs cricket.

Former England captain, England's Emperor of Games, Charles Burgess Fry, once wrote: 'Cricket is the finest game ever invented for the moulding of young men.' Cricket is a decent game, but sadly most present day cricketers lack an ordinary sense of decency. Whenever I watch a cricket match on television, I strongly feel that some of the gestures made by them, especially by the bowlers when they get a batsman out, are obnoxious and uncalled for. Modesty has been thrown to the winds. In my time, when a bowler got the wicket of a batsman, he would just jump up in the air with jubilation. He would not make indecent gestures or pass rude remarks about the outgoing batsman. Even the batsman would appreciate the delivery that got him out. Also, appeals were fewer then and batsmen, very often, would walk without waiting for the umpire's decision.

When I look at the performance of the England team today, I feel sorry. Something is missing there. Their supporters must wonder if they can raise an England team comprising of the likes of Sir Len Hutton, Denis Compton, Peter May, Tom Graveney, Alec Bedser, Godfrey Evans, Jim Laker, Johnny Wardle, David Sheppard, Freddie Truman, and Brian Statham. When the trio of Sir Jack Hobbs, Sutcliffe, and Hammond were on the job, the rest of the team could go shopping, we were told. The English cricketers today need more application.

The state of cricket in the West Indies is not that good either. Gone are the days when they ruled the cricket world. They badly need players like the three W's, Sir Garfield Sobers, Rohan Kannhai, Wes Hall, Clive Lloyd, Michael Holding, Malcolm Marshal, and Viv Richards.

It is sad that the Indians have never produced quality fast bowlers. We in the Pakistani Punjab produced fast bowlers of world class and I sometimes wonder why the Indian Punjab could not do the same. If India won matches during our days, it was mainly because of Subhash Gupte, who could turn the ball even on a grass pitch. By and large, batting always remained their strength except for a short period when the spin trio of Bishen Singh Bedi, Chandrashekar, and Parsanna won matches for them.

After discarding apartheid from their society, South Africa has emerged as one of the leading teams in the world in both types of cricket. Even the sad, but bold, confession of Hansie Cronje did not dent their standards.

The Kangaroos have always maintained a balanced cricket team. When their top players joined Kerry Packer, they succeeded in re-building a good team in a very short time. This is because their domestic cricket structure is set on very sound footings.

In recent years, Sri Lanka, New Zealand, and Zimbabwe have shown tremendous potential. They have proved to the cricket world that they should not be taken lightly. Bangladesh is the babe of Test cricket. However, it needs time before it creates an impact in the Test arena.

Appendix 1

Test Careers

SIR LEONARD HUTTON

M	Inns	NO	Runs	HS	100s	50s	Avg	Ct	Wkts	Avg	BB
79	138	15	6971	364	19	33	56.67	57	3	77.33	1-2

First-Class Career (1934-60)

Runs	Inns	NO	HS	100s	Avg	Ct	Wkts	Avg
40,140	814	91	364	129	55.51	387	173	29.42

SYED MUSHTAQ ALI

M	Inns	NO	Runs	HS	Avg	100s	50s	Ct	Wkts	Avg	BB
11	20	1	612	112	32.21	2	3	7	3	67.33	1-45

First-Class Career (1932-63)

Runs	100s	Avg
12413	30	36.29

LALA AMARNATH

M	Inns	NO	Runs	HS	Avg	100s	50s	Ct	Wkts	Avg	BB	5WI
24	40	4	878	118	24.38	1	4	13	45	32.91	5-96	2

First-Class Career (1931-63)

Runs	100s	Avg	Wkts	Avg
10323	31	41.62	457	22.93

DENIS COMPTON

MInns	NO	Runs	HS	100s	50s	Avg	Ct	Wkts	Avg	5WI	BB
78131	15	5807	278	17	28	50.06	49	25	56.40	1	5-70

First-Class Career (1936-59)

Runs	Inns	NO	HS	100s	Avg	Wkts	Avg
38635	834	88	300	122	51.79	613	32.08

Denis Compton also holds the record of most runs in a single first class season, a feat he achieved in 1947.

Inns	Runs	NO	HS	100s	Avg
50	3816	8	246	18	90.85

SIR FRANK WORRELL

M	Inns	NO	Runs	100s	50s	HS	Ct	Avg	Wkts	Avg	BB	5WI
51	87	9	3860	9	22	261	43	49.48	69	38.72	7-70	2

First-Class Career (1941-64)

M	Inns	NO	Runs	100s	HS	Avg	Wkts	Avg
207	326	49	15025	39	308	54.24	349	29.03

KEITH ROSS MILLER

M	Inns	NO	Runs	HS	100s	50s	Avg	Ct
55	87	7	2958	147	7	13	36.97	38

Bowling

Runs	Wkts	Avg	5WI	10WM
3905	170	22.97	7	1

First-Class Career (1937-59)

Runs	100s	Avg	Ct	Wkts	Avg
14183	41	48.90	136	497	22.30

NAZAR MUHAMMAD

M	Inn	NO	Runs	HS	Avg	100s	50s	Ct
5	8	1	277	124	39.57	1	1	7

NEIL HARVEY

M	Inns	NO	Runs	100s	50s	HS	Avg	Ct	Wkts	Avg	BB
79	137	10	6149	21	24	205	48.41	64	3	40.00	1-8

First-Class Career (1946-62)

Runs	100s	Avg	Ct	Wkts	Avg
21699	67	50.93	229	30	36.86

EVERTON DE COURCY WEEKES

M	Inns	NO	Runs	HS	100s	50s	Avg	Ct	Wkts	Avg	BB
48	81	5	4455	207	15	19	58.61	49	1	77.00	1-8

First-Class Career (1944-64)

Runs	Avg	100s
12010	52.90	36

IMTIAZ AHMAD

M	Inns	NO	Runs	HS	Avg	100s	50s	Ct	St
41	72	1	2079	209	29.88	3	11	77	16

First-Class Career (1944-64)

Runs	100s	Avg	Ct	St
9834	22	37.97	315	77

HANIF MUHAMMAD

M	Inns	NO	Runs	HS	Avg	100s	50s	Ct	Wkts	Avg	BB
55	97	8	3915	337	43.98	12	15	40	1	95.00	1-1

First-Class Career (1951-76)

M	Runs	100s	50s	Avg	Ct	St	Wkts	Avg	BB
238	17059	55	68	52.32	177	12	53	28.58	3-4

DAVID SHEPPARD

M	Inns	NO	Runs	HS	100s	50s	Avg	Ct
22	33	2	1172	119	3	6	37.80	12

First-Class Career (1947-64)

Runs	100s	Avg
15838	45	43.51

RICHIE BENAUD

M	Inns	NO	Runs	HS	100s	50s	Avg	Ct
63	97	7	2201	122	3	9	24.45	65

Bowling

Wkts	Avg	BB	5WI	10WM
248	27.03	7-72	16	1

First-Class Career (1948-64)

Runs	100s	Avg	Wkts	Avg
11432	23	36.29	935	24.80

SIR GARFIELD SOBERS

M	Inns	NO	Runs	100s	HS	50s	Avg	Ct	Wkts	Avg	BB	5WI
93	160	21	8032	26	365	30	57.78	109	235	34.03	6-73	6

First-Class Career (1953-74)

Runs	100s	Avg	Ct	Wkts	Avg
28315	86	54.87	407	1043	27.7

Appendix 2

Art of Swing and Fast Bowling

There are three kinds of deliveries used by a bowler. The first, which keeps straight, the second, with a movement of the ball going from left to right, and the third, with ball movement from right to left. The movement of the ball has many names. The main objective of the bowler is to deceive, beat, and get the batsman out.

OUT-SWING

When the bowler glides a new ball from the leg-stump to the off-stump, it is called an out-swing. To bowl this ball, the bowler keeps the seam towards the second slip.

IN-SWING

When the bowler brings a new ball into the batsman from the off-stump to the leg-stump, it is called an in-swing. To bowl this ball, the bowler keeps the seam tilted towards second leg-slip.

SWERVE

This is a form of swing but the term usually describes the way the ball curves through the air when it is bowled by a slow-medium or slow bowler. Sometimes, the ball is made to glide so that it suddenly dips just when the batsman tries to play it with his bat. The seam can be kept such that it cuts the turf, making the ball move, either cutting in or moving away from the batsman.

DIFFERENCE BETWEEN SWERVE AND SWING

The difference between 'swing' and 'swerve' is that with swing, the ball moves at the last moment when the batsman is about to play his shot whereas the swerve movement starts from the moment the ball leaves the bowler's hand and then lands on the ground. The real movement of the ball becomes operative off the turf.

A special delivery that I used was when the ball would swerve from the moment it left my hand. It would either keep moving away or come in. During the Karachi Test in 1956, I got out Australia's opening batsman, Colin McDonald, on a ball which was pitched slightly out side the off-stump. Colin left the ball, presuming it was an out-swinger, but because of the seam the ball came into the wicket and he was bowled. In the same Test, Australian captain Ian Johnson was also a victim to this ball.

BOUNCER

There are fast bowlers who try to beat the batsman with sheer speed. Their main weapon is a bouncer, threatening to injure the batsman. For them, a yorker is a good ball to bowl. One has to draw extra strength to bowl a vicious bouncer. The ball is bowled slightly short of length with the seam hitting the turf. A good bouncer is that which, in case the batsman misses, would hit his forehead. A good bouncer was bowled by me to Garfield Sobers. It was beyond his expectations, and he was caught at short-leg. In my time, Tyson (England), Gilchrist (West Indies), Ray Lindwall and Keith Miller (Australia) were true fast bowlers, and they bowled vicious bouncers at the batsmen. Gilchrist was so quick that he would bowl slightly short of length and the ball would go over the head of the batsman.

SWING IN THE AIR

The formula of swinging the ball in the air is that the ball is held in such a manner that air glides on top of the ball, whereas the other side of the ball is also affected by the air. The ball travels straight till such time that the pressure of the air builds around it. The ball can be made to swing either side, that is in-swing or out-swing, depending on the side the seam is held.

If the surface of a new ball hits the ground, the ball tends to just skid away with the result that the shine on the ball does not last long. Ultimately, this type of a delivery is not good tactics since it deprives the bowler at the other end from making full use of the shine. The bowler can, with practice, control the movement of the ball in the air by using his fingers.

The bowler should be familiar with the art of swing, while maintaining line and length. He should also have an idea about the weather and environment. Bowlers should learn a few essentials of physical dynamics because these impact controlling the dip of the ball.

USE OF THE CREASE

The crease can be divided into three sections: (a) close to the stumps (b) middle of the crease, and (c) the return crease. A ball delivered from each of these sections has different technical implications, i.e. leg-cutter, in-cutter, leg-break, off-break, in-swing, out-swing, swerve, bouncer, and slinger. With these variations, a bowler can attempt to deceive the batsman.

Some bowlers can formulate many variations with the ball: (a) leg-cutter or fast leg-break (in the old days it was called a leg-cross), (b) in-cutter—fast off-break or fast off-cross.

The bowling of the seam bowler is differentiated from that of the wrist spinner: the wrist spinner plays to deceive with a leg-break, a googly with a leg-break action, or a top spin.

In a zonal tournament match at Bombay's Brabourne stadium in 1947, I was bowling to Mushtaq Ali on a perfect and placid wicket. Patel was the umpire. He was so inspired by my bowling that he forgot his other responsibilities. I was bowling from close to the stumps. He asked me to bowl the same ball from the middle of the crease and then from the return crease. This mesmerized the batsman. Many batsmen would be caught at cover-point while they played the shot in the mid-wicket region.

In 1953, when I led the second Pakistan Eaglets team to England, two days before the conclusion of our coaching at the Alf Gover School, I asked Gover to teach me how to bowl an in-swinger. He showed me how to grip the ball in a particular fashion and bowl from the return crease, which I did. The ball moved in the air and came in. I asked him what if one were to bowl the same delivery from close to the stumps. He replied that it was impossible. But, I did it. He looked at me and said, 'I can't make out for sure.' 'Never mind what I did to the in-swing, now tell me how to bowl the out-swinger,' I requested Gover. He told me to bowl from close to the wicket and the ball would move up, which I did with the perfect length, direction, and the movement of an out-swing. After bowling three balls I asked Gover if an out-swing could be delivered from the return crease. 'Impossible,' he said loudly. The next ball was an out-swing from the return crease. Gover sat down, and holding his head asked me what metal was I made of.

ROTATION

This is the grip where all fingers and the thumb would work equally hard to impart rotation to the ball. The ball can rotate at a speed of 25 to 30 miles per hour. A slightly responsive wicket can give an extra edge to spin bowling, especially that above medium pace. If the ball travels at a speed of 70 to 80 miles per hour, then with added rotation, it has a potential speed in the air of 100 to 115 miles per hour. With my rotation on the ball, the 'buzz' of the rotation could be heard by fielders standing at mid-on, mid-off, or the slips. In case the wicket is not responsive, the bowler's rough can always be helpful. This delivery is also known as a finger-cutter.

In a side-match at Bahawalpur against the MCC in January 1962, I bowled a leg-cutter to Ken Barrington with a lot of rotation on the ball. He took that as an in-coming ball and moved his legs accordingly. The ball moved from the leg-stump to the off-stump, and he was clean bowled. Barrington paid me a compliment, 'You are the bloody greatest.'

Australia's George Tribe was a great exponent of the chinaman and googly. C.G. Pepper (Australia) rotated the ball with the full palm of his hand and bowled flippers. Ian Johnson, the Australian captain on the Pakistan tour of 1956, rotated the ball with a reverse spin and the speed of the ball was quite slow. In the Karachi Test, Khan Muhammad had completed his shot and the ball from Johnson moved on to his stumps. This ball was known as a 'hanging ball'.

There were freak bowlers who gave an extra dimension to the art of bowling. Iverson bowled an off-break with a leg-break action. He played in only five Tests. He won two Tests for Australia and retired when his grip and reverse rotation of the ball had been exposed.

ATMOSPHERE

Weather conditions help the bowler a great deal. The ingredients which make the atmosphere helpful are (a) dew, (b) cloud cover, and (c) breeze. This reminds me of the Calcutta Test match against India in 1960–61. A small cloud covered the sun which made the atmosphere heavy. The ball started moving in the air. Polly Umrigar was bowled round his legs. It was an out-swinger, beating his pads when he left the ball alone.

If the conditions are not conducive and favourable to any kind of bowling, the bowler has to have (a) control over length and direction, (b) the ability to use the crease (c), variation in pace, (d) variation in arm direction—overhead and slinger, (e) and variation in flight, with the ball rotating in either direction.

To sum up, the bowler has to contain the batsman. It is then a test of determination, perseverance, patience, accuracy, and stamina.

BREEZE

It is well known that bowlers take advantage of the breeze. Bowling with the breeze and mustering its help is common, but bowling against the breeze is a real art. Using the fingers, the ball can be made to move far more in a breeze than in normal conditions.

PREREQUISITES

To be a good bowler, one must (a) have a good physique; (b) be reasonably tall; (c) have a chest at 33 inches, with expansion at a minimum of three to four inches; (d) have an endurance of at least 450 to 500 on the scale; (e) have determination; (f) be fit, both mentally and physically; (g) have brains, not brawn, and (h) accuracy to the last degree.

In order to achieve mastery over any facet of life, one has to work very hard—right from childhood. People who achieved greatness had qualities which helped them to rise to great heights. Some followed in the footsteps of their elders who, too, had achieved distinction in life. As a matter of fact, such people started from where their elders left off and capitalized on a natural advantage.

My daily workload was a twenty to twenty-five miles walk or run. I captained the Punjab Hiking and Mountaineering Club, participated in the monthly twenty-five miles hikes and competitive walks. Climbing mountains and trees added strength to my fingers. My spare time after studies was spent in gymnasiums. But, for me sports and games did not have priority over education.

Righ from my school days, I was quite conscious of my line and length as a bowler. My father, Professor Ghulam Hussain, helped me a lot to attain accuracy. He would place small glasses on the ground and then give me a cricket ball, saying, 'Hit and break it.' My mother was not happy with this practice of breaking glasses. But my father would pacify her by saying, 'What do you know of the records he is going to break one day with this exercise?'

In the college cricket nets, he would place a coin on the ground, and would say, 'Hit it and take it.' Then he would place the same coin on the off-stump of Nazar Muhammad, asking him to defend his wicket, and I was required to hit the wicket to win that coin.

The accuracy of my bowling at the Oval in 1954 was due to the fact that I had found a spot on the good length. I would hit the spot and Denis Compton would come and mend it with his bat. Between the overs, the earth on that spot shifted. I then told Compton, 'Now you cannot put the earth back.'

LEG-CUTTER

The leg-cutter/fast leg-break is a ball that comes from the blind spot to a right-hand batsman. Similarly, an in-cutter or fast off-break to a left-hand batsman would be dangerous for him. Leg-cutter is a faster ball than the normal three-finger cutter or the leg-break. So is the case with the in-cutter and the off-break/in-cutter

A good new ball seam-bowler is one who swings the ball in such a manner that only the seam hits the surface and then the bat. The ball comes back only when the seam hits the surface. Thus, the shine on either side of the ball stays intact for quite a few overs.

Both fingers together are placed across the seam, with the thumb on the other side of the seam. Rotation on the ball is induced by applying the full force of the fingers and the thumb to move the ball either way. England's F.S. Barnes was the inventor of the leg-cutter. From him, the art travelled to England's Alec Bedser. I have tried very hard to teach this to some bowlers in Pakistan, but they have been unenthusiastic.

It is sad that the art of bowling the leg-cutter is dying. In spite of the fact that bowlers now have added advantages with new rules and regulations—front-foot no ball, this glorious game has been reduced to hit and run. It is becoming very similar to baseball—especially in the one-day contests.

PICTORIAL DEFINITIONS

In-swing

Seam towards the second leg-slip—middle finger close to the seam, and pressure on the middle finger, while the index finger is just supporting the middle finger. When bowled by a right-hand bowler, the ball would be absolutely straight and upright while the right arm bicep would touch the right ear. The head would be absolutely straight, looking at the point where the ball would be pitched and also watching the movement of the batsman. The ball glides in the air while pressure would be on the inside of the middle finger. The air would also glide on the side of the index finger with the result that the ball would automatically move from the off-side to the leg-stump, resulting in a late swing.

Out-swing

The seam is tilted towards the second slip. The index finger touches the seam and the middle finger supports the index finger. There would be absolutely no rotation on the ball. The ball would move straight, and as it comes near the batsman, it would move away from the leg-stump to the off side. This would be the out-swing.

Leg-cutter

A leg-cutter is bowled with the seam. A bowler can muster speed and force by holding the ball across the seam with two fingers, with the thumb below the seam, thus imparting a lot of rotation on the seam. The bowler can also use the seam by cutting the wicket or the surface only with the seam without imparting any rotation on the ball.

Bouncer

Both the index and middle fingers would be on the seam, with the thumb beneath the seam which, in turn, should be pointing towards the middle stump. With an overhead action, slightly short of length, the ball would rise upto shoulder-height of the batsman. The bowler would need to draw extra strength from his entire body to deliver this ball.

In-coming ball in leg-break action

This is the action of the leg-break. The middle finger is lifted and the pressure is on the index finger, with the result that the ball would move into the batsman. As part of my bowling strategy, I would change the line of the ball every now and then. For instance, I would bowl the leg-cutter from the return crease which was a wicket-taking ball. There was also a hidden in-swinger from the return crease, an in-swinger from the middle of the crease, and an in-swinger from close to the stumps. The

ball which induced Hutton to play forward was well concealed, and I
knew that I would get his wicket with it. I would deliver that ball with
deadly accuracy, he would come forward, try to drive, and the ball
would find the edge.

Appendix 3

Views on Fazal Mahmood by some Contemporaries

INTRODUCTION

It was always a thrill to watch Fazal Mahmood bowl. This was especially so when the wicket had a little bit of grass on it. In his prime, Fazal was a handful even on a fairly flat wicket. At the Bagh-i-Jinnah, the cricket ground of the Lahore Gymkhana club, Fazal felt particularly at home. He played club cricket, first-class cricket, and Test matches on this ground. He also had net practice there. The ground is part of a park full of gardens and private clubs. Lawrence Hall, which in Fazal's time housed the Lahore Gymkhana club, is now housing the Quaid-e-Azam Library.

Fazal had a fairly long, loping run up to the wicket. He bowled with a high-arm action and could cut the ball both ways. His classic ball was that which would swing in to the batsman and then cut away viciously. He bowled with extreme concentration and his line and length were immaculate. Having seen him bowl so often, at all levels of the game, I cannot recall his bowling a wide ball or a long hop ever. In an exhibition match at the Bagh-i-Jinnah, in the very early 1950s, I recall a particularly devastating spell by him. In the closing session of the day, when the wicket begins to be lively, he made the ball rear dangerously towards the body from just short of a length. Two batsmen were hit and had to retire hurt in successive overs.

Unfortunately, there are no good, surviving films of his very special bowling action. But, there are a few contemporaries who can describe the lethal quality of his bowling. In this section, there are six different accounts from cricketing contemporaries who saw Fazal bowl from close quarters. The first is by Colin Cowdrey, who was one of the leading batsmen in the world in the late 1950s. The third is from Richie Benaud, one of Australia's greatest Test captains and all-rounders. Benaud, after retirement, has made a special niche for himself as a commentator and journalist of the highest class. The fourth account is from Fakir Aizazuddin, who played for Pakistan, and was a sound batsman. He describes a memorable encounter between Ken Barrington and Fazal in Bahawalpur in 1961. This was at a time when Fazal was considered as being 'over the hill'. The next account is from Iftikhar Bokhari, the best opening batsman never to have played for Pakistan. He describes a session at the nets in the Bagh-i-Jinnah, with Fazal at the height of his technical abilities. The final letter is a nostalgic one from the great Keith Miller, who first came to the subcontinent after the Second World War as a war hero in 1946.

These accounts provide an insight into Fazal's cricketing personality. In the absence of films, they enable the young reader, who never saw Fazal in action, to imagine what it was to be bowled at by Fazal.

Mueen Afzal

BARCLAYS BANK PLC
Public Relations Department
54 Lombard Street, London EC3P 3AH.

I recall Fazal as one of the very best bowlers that I ever played against. If there was any help in the wicket he had the fire and accuracy and skills to make batting very difficult. He was a magnificent competitor with endless stamina. I wish him good health and every success.

Yours sincerely

Colin Cowdrey
2nd May 1968

— — — — — — — — — — — — — — — — — —

I only played against Fazal Mahmood on one occasion, that time on my Test debut against Pakistan at the Oval in 1954. It is worth noting, however, that on the single occasion on which we met, he claimed my wicket twice for 3 with leg-cutters which were far too good for a humble batsman such as myself. On a rain affected wicket, Fazal captured 6/53 and 6/46: the best analysis by a Pakistani bowler in Tests in England at that time. Pakistan thereby gained their first victory in England and squared the rubber, winning by 24 runs.

I should add that the England batsmen compounded their own defeat by trying to score the 168 runs needed for victory in their last innings in unreasonably quick time. They underestimated Fazal's skill and accuracy. The batsmen of my era rated Fazal as the best bowler of medium-paced leg-cutters that has ever lived—on the mat. In England in 1954, he proved that he could do his stuff on turf when conditions were suitable.

As I recall Fazal, he had a low almost slinging action, pin-pointing accuracy and ability to make the ball jump and kick towards the slips off the wicket. In this respect he reminded me of my earlier visions of Maurice Nichols of England and Essex.

Yours sincerely

F.H. Tyson
Director of coaching
Victorian Cricket Association
7th July, 1986

Richie and Daphne Benaud
Benaud and Associates Pty Ltd
PO Box 3680, Chestnut Grove
London SW12 8XF

It was a good thing for batsmen that in the era when the great Fazal
Mahmood played his cricket, Test series were far less frequent than in
modern times. He first came to my notice in 1954 just as we were
preparing in Australia to host the series against Len Hutton's side
which had regained the Ashes from Australia the previous summer.
Pakistan undertook their first tour of England in 1954 and it was a
resounding success, with creditable performances in the first three Tests
at Lord's, Trent Bridge and Old Trafford and then a stunning victory
over England at the Oval.

We noted carefully that Fazal, who was only a name to us, had
taken 4/54 at Lord's and, at the opposite end, Khan Muhammad had
5/61; they had bowled unchanged in the England first innings. None
for 148 followed on a belter of a pitch at Trent Bridge and moderate
success at Old Trafford, and then came the Oval and that wonderful
and historic victory for Pakistan with Fazal taking 6/53 and 6/46.

Because there was no thought of Australia playing in a full Test
series at that stage, and because videotape in its modern style didn't
exist at that time, we had no way other than with Movietone News of
finding out anything about him, but we did learn a little from the
England players when they arrived in Australia, although we had
plenty of problems with Tyson and Statham on that tour without
worrying about someone against whom we weren't playing.

As it happened, the Australian and Pakistan authorities decided
that at the end of the 1956 Australian tour of England the team would
have three week's holiday, and then would play one Test in Pakistan
at Karachi and follow that with three Tests in India; the last time India
and Australia had met had been in 1947/48 in Australia. Fazal and
Khan bowled us out for 80. My most vivid memory of that day was
that we were lucky to make that many!

Fazal at one end was bowling wonderful leg-cutters at a pace twice
as fast as I bowled, and he was cutting the ball more than I could spin
it. Khan bowled beautifully at the other end, coming in from outside
the off stump at medium-fast pace.

In the second innings of 187 I made top score with 56 and it was an
unnerving experience as I played and missed at three balls every over I
faced from Fazal. We knew then that if we ever had to face him on the
mat again, we would need to do a great deal of homework.

Then, when I captained Australia to Pakistan and India in 1959-60,
we saw Fazal for the last time and his powers were still there. He

bowled a beautiful line and length and still cut the ball viciously in taking 5/71 and 5/74 in the two matches played on the matting surface.

Fazal retired two years after the Karachi Test of that series. He was a great bowler on the mat and in some conditions in England, and a fine competitive cricketer anywhere.

Richie Benaud
8 June 1999

— —

Al-Waheed Homes
43, Rose Street, McNeil Road
Karachi Cantt. Ph: 5678000

It was a pleasant Eid surprise to hear that Fazal Mahmood is writing a book. As a legacy for the cricketing public it was long overdue, and if I remember I had suggested the idea a few years ago.

I am delighted to be asked to recount the encounter Barrington had with Fazal at Bahawalpur against the MCC in 1961. Captained by Mike Smith in the absence of Dexter, the match had been reduced to two days from three due to rain with England taking first knock.

Posted on mid-on, my attention wholly riveted on Fazal's run up and delivery. I was guilty of giving away an unnecessary single, for which I was duly reprimanded. However, in the next over the left handed Pullar was bowled playing forward having his leg bail neatly removed, the bail hitting the wicket keeper Fasihuddin on his right cheek.

Fazal then asked me who was next and being told it was Barrington, he became grim and very thoughtfully walked to his bowling mark. Barrington briskly walked in and took guard. He was brimming with confidence having just completed the Indian tour with a fantastic average proving a scourge for the Indian bowling.

Fazal's first delivery he middled playing half cock forward, as per his technique. Grinning, he asked 'Fazal have you got rocks in this?' referring to the hardness of the ball. Fazal just picked the ball, rolled up his sleeve, and walked to his mark, deep in thought. The second delivery was the same. It swung in whirring through the air like a leg spinner's delivery, pitching on the leg stump, a shade shorter than the earlier one. Barrington played the same forward defensive prod. The leg cutter whipped off the wicket with the speed of a striking snake hitting the off bail. Barrington with his foot still planted where it was, looked at the spot the ball had pitched and the direction it had taken to hit the top of the off stump. He looked again in disbelief and then ruefully shaking his head, wrenched off his gloves and walked briskly back to the pavilion. Incidentally, the bail hit the wicket keeper again on the right cheek as earlier. Uncanny accuracy.

After finishing off the innings for 120 by taking five or six wickets as Fazal led the team out he was greeted by a very sad and dejected Barrington. Holding a beer mug in his hand and shaking his large head he declared 'Fazal, whatever anyone might say, for me you are the bloody greatest.' This coming from one of the best professionals England has produced since the war was a great compliment. It was the acknowledgement of one master to another. I was privileged to have watched this battle of the giants, brief though the encounter was.

With the very best regards

Yours sincerely
Fakir S. Aizazuddin
Former first-class cricketer
3rd April 1999

— —

I distinctly remember the brief encounter I had with Fazal Mahmood in cricket. It takes me back to the end of October 1956, hardly a fortnight after his tremendous bowling feat against Australia in a Test match at Karachi.

I had returned to Pakistan in mid-October 1956, after having had an exceptionally good season with the bat with Cambridgeshire, in the Minor Counties Cricket Competition. I had the honour of winning the Wilfred Rhodes Trophy that season for having topped the batting average in the competition.

It was through a mutual friend that I was introduced to this handsome cricketer one evening at Lahore Gymkhana. Fazal Mahmood had just finished playing badminton. After a brief introduction, he gave a very searching look. 'See you at the Lahore Gymkhana Cricket nets at 3.00 p.m. tomorrow to assess your cricketing talent,' was the remark he made.

I had a disturbed and practically sleepless night. Here was I, a youngster, being tested perhaps by the finest fast medium swing bowler the game had known.

I padded up and went into the net without the present safety equipments like helmet etc. which were not in vogue then. The first ball bowled to me, with the old ball, was a loosener. It was an over pitched ball bowled on the middle stump which I drove straight, close to the stump at the bowler's end. Fazal's instant reaction was to call for the new ball, which the groundman promptly provided. Out of sheer inexperience, I had precipitated the issue. What followed was a nightmare, in cricketing terms.

The new ball bowled at me was swinging very late either way at a steady speed of about 85 mph. It was being pitched on good length between middle and off stumps. With the same bowling action, with an upright straight arm practically touching the right ear at the time of delivery, the ball would swerve in or swerve out depending on what he desired. The movement of the new ball in the air was being controlled by his wrist action. All that I could try to manage was to play a hurriedly half-cock defensive shot, not knowing which way the ball would move late in the air. I was simply playing from my instinct. As the bowling action was giving me no respite, I started concentrating on the placement of his feet at the bowling crease. In order to give me a false sense of confidence Fazal did the normal thing, bowling late out-swingers from close to the stump and late in-swingers away from the stump. After having bowled a few balls in this manner, he very conveniently reversed the process. A late out-swinger, bowled with his body away from the stump, caught the outside edge of my bat. I had played it as an in-swinger. This was the demonstration of the mastery Fazal had on swing-bowling.

Even after forty three years, I recount the little episode with mixed feelings, my utter helplessness and Fazal's complete mastery over the swing-bowling.

I am glad that this great exponent of leg-cutter is writing a book about the 'greats' of his time which is certainly a unique task. I wish him every success. Good luck to you Skipper!

Syed Iftikhar Ali Bokhari
Former First Class Cricketer
Ex-Senator and Minister of State Finance & Economic Affairs.

—— —— —— —— —— —— —— —— —— —— —— —— —— —— —— —— ——

K.R. Miller
47 Nullaburra Road,
Newport Beach NSW 2106.

My Dear Fazal,

I read the write up of me by Asif, and I wonder why you to think of me so highly. I must say you are far too generous in your praise. But under it all, I guess every living person likes kudos from time to time.

Thank you, Fazal. I must say that your bowling at Karachi against us in 1956 was the best bowling I have ever seen. 6 for 34 off 27 overs in first innings and 7 for 80 off 48 overs in 2nd innings.

Quite remarkable! Your performance was even better than Jim Laker's remarkable 19 wickets at the Old Trafford.

Yes, Fazal, you get my vote. I am sorry about my poor writing but it is due to a stroke I had a couple of years ago.

The great Australian bowler Bill O' Reilly said 'Thank heavens we played cricket when we did.' Seeing the trouble the game is in today I guess you will agree.

Fazal, I wish you well, with this book. Asif Sohail is most certainly a writer of the highest order. Good Luck to you both. If you have a copy left over I would greatly love it.

Fazal I remember you and I opening the attack against England in Colombo. Wasn't it great fun?

All the Best

Keith Miller
26.10.98

Milestones

18 February 1927	Born in Lahore.
1931	Joined Kinnaird High School, Lahore.
1936	Iqbal High School, Garhi Shahu, Lahore.
1938	Joined Islamia High School, Saddar Bazaar, Lahore.
1939	Joined Punjab Club, Lahore.
	First big match in Lahore's club-cricket. Took 6 for 8 against the King Edward Medical College, Lahore.
1940	Matriculation from Islamia High School.
	Joined Islamia College, Railway Road, Lahore.
4 November 1944	Maiden first-class match in the Ranji Trophy at Patiala. Maiden first-class wicket of Lala Amarnath.
7-9 December 1946	Played for The Rest against the All-India team in England XI at Feroze Shah Kotla ground, Delhi. Bowling Analysis: 26.4-8-52-4 and 22.2-9-47-3. (The match was of 8-balls over)
17-19 February 1947	Maiden first-class century (100 not out) for North Zone against the South Zone in the Bombay Zonal Quadrangular that replaced the famous Pentangular Tournament of Bombay. Bowling Analysis: 22.2-2-64-5 and 14-3-43-2. (The match was of 8-balls over)
21-23 February 1947	Against the West Zone at Bombay. Bowling Analysis: 32.6-7-118-5.
	(The match was of 8 balls overs)
March 1947	Selected in the All-India cricket team to tour Australia.

July 1947	Master's Degree in Economics from the Punjab University, Lahore. Paper written on 'Cottage Industry and Labour Problem'.
September 1947	Declined to join All-India team on Australian tour because opted to stay in and play for Pakistan.
19 September 1947	Joined Pakistan Police Service as Inspector.
27 November 1948	Maiden international debut against the West Indies in the unofficial Test match played at Lahore.
March 1949	Toured Ceylon (Sri Lanka) with the Pakistan team and played two Test matches against the hosts.
25 November 1949	Played against the Commonwealth XI at Lahore.
Mar-Apr 1950	Represented Pakistan in two Test matches against Ceylon when the latter made a return tour.
Nov-Dec 1951	Played a pivotal role in Pakistan's victory over the MCC in the Karachi unofficial Test match. This victory facilitated Pakistan to earn Test status. Bowling analysis in first innings: 26-14-40-6.
March 1952	Selected to play for the Commonwealth XI against Ceylon in Colombo.
Dec-Feb 1952	Toured with Pakistan cricket team on its maiden Test match series in India. Played a major part in Pakistan's victory in the second Test at Lucknow taking 12 for 112.
Jun-Aug 1953	Captained Pakistan Eaglets team on the England tour. Scored a century against the West Indies.
May 1954	Made vice-captain of the Pakistan team on its maiden test tour of England. Main architect of the historic victory in the Oval Test match, London.

Dec-Mar 1954-55	Represented Pakistan in the five-Test match home series against India.
Oct-Nov 1955	Played in the home series against New Zealand.
Dec-Mar 1955-56	Played against MCC 'A' team in the home series.
October 1956	Pakistan beat Australia in one-off Karachi Test and took 13 for 114.
Jan-Mar 1958	Toured the West Indies and played in all five Test matches. Bowled 85.1 overs in the first innings of the Third test at Kingston where Sir Garfield Sobers scored 365 not out.
February 1959	Appointed captain of Pakistan team against the touring West Indies and became the first captain of Pakistan to win a Test on debut (Karachi).
Nov-Dec 1959	Captained against Australia in the home series.
Nov-Feb 1960-61	Led Pakistan team on Indian tour to play a five-Test match series.
January 1962	Not selected in the home series against England. However, called in to lead the BCCP XI against the visitors at Bahawalpur. Bowling figures: 24-13-28-6 in the only England innings. Selected to play in the third and the final Test at Karachi.
July 1962	Not selected in the Pakistan team on England tour. After persistent protests at home, was sent to England as a stop-gap arrangement. Played in two Test matches. Fourth Test at Trent Bridge: 60-15-130-3. Fifth Test at the Oval: 49-9-192-2
August 1962	Unannounced retirement from Test cricket.
1967	Honorary membership of the MCC

Police Service

19 September 1947	Joined Pakistan Police Service as Inspector.
4 February 1953	Promoted as Deputy Superintendent of Police.
1 November 1959	Promoted as Superintendent of Police.
1962	Four-month course at National Institute of Public Administration (NIPA), Lahore.
October 1968	Six-month course in Advance Administration from International Policy Academy, Washington, USA.
1 September 1970	Established Sports Board Punjab and became its first director. Served till 31 July 1972.
6 March 1976	Promoted as Deputy Inspector-General of Police (Traffic), Punjab.
8 September 1978	Appointed as Director-General Sports Board, Punjab and served till 6 October 1981.
18 February 1987	Retired from police service.

Index